GETTING
POLITICAL

GETTING POLITICAL

Stories of a Woman Mayor

Joan Darrah
with Alice Crozier

Quill
Driver
Books

Sanger, California

Printed in the United States of America

Published by Quill Driver Books/Word Dancer Press, Inc.

1831 Industrial Way #101

Sanger, California 93657

559-876-2170 • 1-800-497-4904 • FAX 559-876-2180

QuillDriverBooks.com

Info@QuillDriverBooks.com

Quill Driver Books titles may be purchased in quantity at special discounts for educational, fund-raising, business, or promotional use. Please contact Special Markets, Quill Driver Books/Word Dancer Press, Inc. at the above address or at 1-800-497-4909.

Quill Driver Books/Word Dancer Press, Inc. project cadre:
Doris Hall, John David Marion, Cheree McCloud, Stephen Blake Mettee,
Brigitte Phillips, Linda Kay Weber.

First Printing

To order another copy of this book, please call
1-800-497-4909

Cover Photograph by Glen Williams

Library of Congress Cataloging-in-Publication Data

Library of Congress Cataloging-in-Publication Data

Darrah, Joan, 1935-
 Getting political : stories of a woman mayor / by Joan Darrah with Alice Crozier.
  p. cm.
 ISBN 1-884956-30-0 (pbk.)
 1. Darrah, Joan, 1935- 2. Mayors--California--Stockton--Biography.
3. Women mayors--California--Stockton--Biography. 4. Stockton (Calif.)--Politics and government. I. Crozier, Alice, 1934- II. Title.
 F869.S8 D37 2002
 979.4'55--dc21

2002012214

Contents

Foreword

*A*s a United States Senator and former big-city mayor myself, I believe Joan Darrah's work is a compelling read for those interested in learning about careers in government and a woman's role in this demanding, yet rewarding arena. I first met Joan during my run for California governor in 1989 and have found her to be a true friend and terrific supporter ever since.

Like so many of us, Joan Darrah began her career in politics as a novice. This mother of three children fast came to realize that being a success in public life—whether you are a man or a woman—requires working long hours in the policy trenches, learning from your mistakes, capitalizing on your successes, and carrying yourself with confidence and professionalism.

In her career in Stockton local government, Joan was a prime example of a woman who followed these tenets and got involved. She did so because she cared about her community and sought to make a difference.

As mayor of Stockton, Joan encountered countless obstacles and developed the staying power that any good public servant needs to be successful. Ultimately, hers is a story of diligence, perseverance, and patience as she thrust herself into the conservative and male-dominated politics of Stockton.

As mayor, Joan reduced crime across the board and fought to keep a concealed weapons law from being approved. She also helped to revitalize the city's downtown and waterfront areas by establishing a central park and encouraging private investment. And, Joan successfully pushed for a measure that eliminated district council elections and made each local office elected by the citizens of the entire city. This action resulted in a less divisive and paralyzed city council, one that could reach solutions in the best overall interest for the entire community.

Joan Darrah was indeed a trailblazer, but we must remember that not very long ago the thought of women as able political leaders was held by few in our nation. I can vividly remember the strange looks on people's faces when I first ran for county supervisor in San Francisco. I'll never forget those inquisitive gazes upon me and the thought that must have crossed their minds: "Why is she doing this?" Many thought there must be something wrong with me or my marriage to pursue such a goal. But the underlying reason I wanted to get involved was to be a positive force for progress in people's lives.

Without a doubt, Joan Darrah made a positive difference for the residents of Stockton. She crafted rational solutions to problems, based not on ideology, but on what would work best for the majority of its citizens. This, I believe, is the true measure of an elected official and Joan passed this test with flying colors.

I say often that while women in politics to date have chipped away at the glass ceiling, we have not yet shattered it. Simply put, we have a long road to travel before women are accepted in every office as equals to our male counterparts.

While we have certainly made strides, this progress continues today, with the thousands of women seeking to fill congressional, gubernatorial, state, and local government offices and the countless others contemplating such a step. These are the women like Joan Darrah, women who are gradually changing the face of American politics. And women are doing it—to put it in her words—not by sitting back and watching others, but by being involved and "getting political."

—Senator Dianne Feinstein

Acknowledgments

I wish to express my gratitude to my colleague on the city council, Mel Panizza, who shared his videotape library of the council meetings with me. I am also indebted to the reference department of the Cesar Chavez Library of Stockton and San Joaquin County, especially Mary Ann Brooks, Beverly Hine, and Gretchen Louden. I was assisted as well by several staff people at city hall who were always willing to gather information for me: Cathy Meissner, Peggy Jackson and Raeann Cycenas in the city clerk's office and Debbie Brink in the city manager's office. John Carlson and Sam Mah in community planning and development and Ed Chavez in the police department all shared their expertise.

The Record staff, especially Jim Gold, editor-in-chief, was very helpful, as were Thai Nguyen Strom, chief librarian, and Calixtro Romias and David Finch in the photographic department.

Local historians Tod Ruhstaller and Leslie Crow provided valuable insight and perspective.

I have benefitted from the editorial advice of Marcia Newfield, "literary midwife," who read the manuscript twice and recommended revisions. Sara Blackburn offered excellent suggestions as well. Robert R. Benedetti, professor of political science and director of the Harold Jacoby Center at the University of the Pacific in Stockton, also provided very useful advice.

Jim Hock, press secretary for Senator Dianne Feinstein, was both friendly and efficient as the liaison between Senator Feinstein and me, particularly in making arrangements for Dianne's kind "Foreword" to this book. I thank both Jim and Dianne most cordially for their time and interest in this project.

I am grateful for the constant support of my husband, Jim Darrah.

It is a great privilege to write a book about an important time in one's life. The writing process lends perspective to many dimensions of experience that were not always apparent at the time but that made it what it was.

Shortly before I left office, I met Alice Crozier, whom I had known only slightly when we were in the same dormitory at Radcliffe. She suggested that I write a book about my mayoral experience and offered to help me. We started off with my dictating my memories and ideas, but since we live on opposite coasts that proved impractical. I turned to the daunting task of going through my voluminous files and watching the videotapes of council meetings. I made notes and wrote drafts and sent them to Alice, who revised and rewrote them. This book is the collaborative effort of two women, a politician with stories to tell and a professor who wanted to tell them. Although Alice and I worked together throughout, I am finally responsible for the veracity of all statements in the text.

1

Setting the Stage

*B*y titling this book *Getting Political,* I mean to call attention to the way a woman, me, changed her life quite radically at the age of fifty-four. When I became mayor of Stockton, a city of a quarter of a million people located in the middle of California's huge Central Valley, I had never held elective office. I had not even attended many city council meetings until I declared my candidacy. I was elected "off the street," and yet I managed to learn the job fast enough and well enough to get re-elected. Virtually every section of this book shows me trying to understand and respond to the demands of elective politics and the job of being mayor when all of my previous experience had been in private-sector, nonprofit organizations. I want to emphasize that if someone like me, a product of a conservative business family, the sorority scene at University of California, Berkeley, and the world of Junior Aid and United Way, could master the confrontational ways of politicians and learn to maneuver among the competing pressure groups that throw their weight around in city governments, then many other women can do it too. I did not start off like Hillary Clinton—an activist from college onward, a graduate of Yale Law School, a corporate lawyer, and a political spouse—yet I became an effective politician and left what I hope is an impressive legacy to my city.

When it comes to getting into politics, you can start from anywhere. You bring to the table whatever combination of experience and skills you have acquired and you start out trying to make them fit the new scene. My naiveté produced some laughable results early on, especially at my inaugural party and later when I redecorated the mayor's office. I simply did not think like a politician, which meant I also had no clue about how to handle the press. I kept trying to be the genteel leader of the organization, whose job it was to get along with everyone.

My first lesson in hardball came when the city manager, the administrative head of the Stockton city government, abruptly resigned. I also got into hot water over the matter of committee chairmanships. I thought the idea was to get the council's committee work done efficiently; I never considered that non-appointment to a chairmanship could be taken as a personal insult or that the next day I would be featured in the newspaper headline as a racist, a charge against which I would spend the next several months defending myself.

Later, when I was asked if it would be OK for a group to hold a gay pride march in Stockton, I didn't foresee that anyone could ever object to a few people walking down Pacific Avenue. At the next council meeting the homophobic rhetoric was truly frightening; forty residents cursed all homosexuals and reviled me as well. I was up for reelection at the time, and I swiftly learned the art of taking political cover. As I found out, Stockton is not San Francisco. I also learned the hard way that when the issue is a disastrous drug raid and major sectors of the city's population are rightfully outraged, it is more important to listen, however long it takes and however impassioned the speakers, than to attempt to keep the lid on and maintain a superficial order. I had always been a great one for decorum, but in politics one had better learn to respond to people's passions because they—the people and their passions—are real and they do not go away.

When I ran for mayor, many of my supporters were people I had known socially and through my nonprofit work. A lot of them were affluent, conservative, and Republican. I am a committed Democrat. This was fine during my two campaigns, because the mayor is a nonpartisan office in Stockton,[1] but once I got into office, I learned what the business community, especially the developers and their associates among bankers, lawyers, and union workers, expect from city government. They expect to get what they want, and they sometimes use elaborate stratagems to achieve their ends.

For most of my two terms, I would say that a majority of members of the council were more than willing to oblige the developers. But on several crucial occasions, I was not. By this time I had become politically astute enough to know how to fight against the big boys, but even so there were costs. On one occasion, the developers wanted a loophole in the Stockton General Plan, which regulates land use, so that they could overcome its several restrictions and build where they pleased.

Another time, some of the most powerful men in town were determined to bring a huge gambling casino to Stockton. On this occasion, the newspaper attacked me so vociferously for my opposition to the casino that public attention was drawn to the issue and the sponsors forfeited the chance to slip the ordinance quietly through committee. That was a battle royal, and I won't spoil the fun by explaining here how it turned out.

Another battle occurred between Stockton city hall and the Federal Emergency Management Agency (FEMA). Four of us went to Washington and enlisted the help of California's two marvelous senators, Dianne Feinstein and Barbara Boxer. After two false starts—first we begged FEMA, then we threatened them—we got the hang of how Washington works and got what we wanted.

Although I like to boast about reducing crime, which did happen during my tenure and which also produces great press during campaigns, what I am most proud of is bringing to fruition the ambitious plan for redesigning Stockton's waterfront. This took considerable political skill on my part because it was such a huge and complicated process and involved so many different people and interests. It happened in the second half of my second term. By that time, council personnel had changed and I had become much more deft at managing the political process. I had been to a conference on city planning in San Antonio from which I returned with a mission. I got my staff and council turned on, got a large task force together, hired consultants, did a lot of community outreach and involvement, got the plan funded and approved and, late in my second term, broke ground for the Weber Point Events Center. Before I left office, the council and I set up the mechanism for the continuation of the waterfront plan under my successor. All of this took a combination of my old skills, the things I knew when I took office, and an ever-increasing political awareness of what it takes to get things done.

I was limited to two terms in the mayor's office, and I did not aspire to run for the California legislature because I liked and supported the two men who already represented my district. I did, however, consider running for the U.S. Congress and that is the last story I tell in this book. It was amazing and I must say quite flattering to be urged by many people to run for that office. Luckily, I also spoke to an astute political insider, a friend of my son-in-law's from high school. By this time, I was pretty savvy myself and that made her comments all the more sobering. I believe the reader will enjoy learning, as I did, how a real pro sizes up the possible success of a national political candidacy.

Mine is very much a woman's story. It begins when my three children are small and my outside activities are focused on a woman's organization, Junior Aid (like Junior League elsewhere). I move from Junior Aid to being president of the county branch of United Way. By this time I have been appointed to the board of regents of the University of the Pacific and my contacts extend well beyond the world of women, yet my women friends from those early days were to become the ones who worked hardest on my two campaigns.

My preparation for and during my second campaign involved my taking lessons from a speech coach so that I could go on the political attack without looking unfeminine and scaring off the male voters. It involved giving a series of fund-raising luncheons modeled on those used by both Dianne Feinstein and Barbara Boxer, luncheons to which I invited all the powerful and affluent women in town, including key representatives of minority groups, such as Mary Delgado from STAND. Support of women candidates by women voters and feminist political action committees (PACs) such as EMILY's List is a key factor in any woman candidate's political success these days. The role of women as both candidates and supporters is bound to increase for the coming generation of women politicians.

This book ends with a brief retrospective on what I feel are my accomplishments and legacy and some personal reflections about how much fun I had being mayor and why, ironically, I have not missed it for a day since I left office.

Meet the Candidate

*A*long the stretch of beach in greater Los Angeles from Torrance Beach to Marina del Rey, there is a concrete sidewalk fourteen feet wide. This strip, also called "the bike path" or "The Strand" in some of the towns it passes through, runs for thirteen miles in front of the line of houses that face the beach and offers ample space for walkers, joggers, bikers, and roller bladers. Beyond it, the sand stretches for fifty yards out to the beautiful breakers of the Pacific Ocean. I grew up in one of those houses fronting the strip. In 1937, my mother's mother, a Scottish immigrant who came to California in 1886 at the age of six months and who left school after the sixth grade, bought a four-bedroom/two-bath house at 2222 The Strand, in the beachfront town of Hermosa Beach. Nana rented this house for a nominal sum to my parents, who moved there in April 1937, when I was two years old.

Mom and Dad had both grown up in Los Angeles, where Mom attended a girls' school, Cumnock, and my dad, Kryne Van den Akker, went to Los Angeles High. After one year at Mills College in Oakland, Mom transferred to University of California, Berkeley, from which she graduated in 1927. The focus of her college life was the Delta Gamma sorority, and she kept those Delta Gamma friendships well into her eighties. Dad went to Stanford and Stanford Law, where he graduated in 1932 after spending his second year at Harvard Law School. Mom and Dad were married in Los Angeles in 1931. My older brother Peter was born in 1933.

Growing up at the beach was no picnic. It seemed all the best games were for boys. I ran barefoot on the sand, chasing my brother and his friends who most of the time wanted nothing to do with the "little sister." He called me "fat," and I called him "stupid." Once, I asked if I could sleep in the other single bed in his room. He agreed, but in the middle of the night he yanked me out of bed and sent me off to my own room, for snoring he said. Other days, he would grab me by the throat and squeeze. I thought he would choke me to death. To this day, I jump when anyone touches my neck or shoulders unexpectedly. I learned to fend off Peter by lying on my back and kicking. Every night I checked under the bed to make sure he wasn't hiding there, getting ready to murder me in the night. Let's just say my childhood relationship with my brother trained me to be tough and self-protective, two necessary traits for success in politics.

After Pearl Harbor and the American entry into World War II, there was talk of Japanese submarines off the coast. Dad put up black covers on the windows to hide the lights from enemy eyes. The year before, he and I went door to door handing out buttons for Wilkie, who was running against Roosevelt. Dad joined the Navy and, after a training course at Harvard, was sent as a supply officer to Seattle, where he stayed until 1945. When he came home on leave, he would head for his favorite place, Catalina Island and the small harbor town of Avalon, where both his family and my mother's owned small vacation houses. That is where Mom and Dad met as teenagers, and they shared many a wild ride on an aquaplane or speedboat. In college, Dad won medals as an Olympic-quality swimmer and water polo player.

When I was about eight, Dad took up skin diving and wanted me to accompany him. He and I swam around the rocks and kelp by the casino, hunting abalone. I would spot them, show Dad, and he would dive down and pry them off the rocks. One day, I saw a small black one tightly fastened to a brick. I dove down seven feet, abalone bar in hand, but could not get my bar under the shell. The abalone only stuck tighter and tighter. After three or four tries, I gave up and brought the entire brick to the surface, abalone and all. Back on shore, Dad pried the abalone off for me. He liked my determination and imaginative solution. Years later, he would hearken back to those summer days when we went diving together.

I was undoubtedly the favored child. Dad would organize football games at the beach, with me the only girl among eight players. His team—himself, one boy and me—played against the other five boys. One time he grabbed three boys from the opposing team by the arms, neck, and back, all at once, and held them. Then he ordered the boy on our team to hold another boy, handed me the ball, and yelled "Run, Joanie, run!" I ran with all my might, but a fifth boy, a skinny, badly coordinated kid whom no one had thought worth grabbing, ran after me and tackled me. I was furious. Everyone else, especially my brother, was jubilant. I ran to the house in tears, but the game went on. Dad urged me to come back out and play, but I wouldn't. My brother laughed and exercised his middle finger.

I had almost no girl friends because none lived near us, but eventually I did meet one girl. We were both movie fans of course, and we liked to play cowboy and damsel in distress. I was a very romantic cowboy, strictly Hollywood, and my friend was a touching heroine. One day, her mother listened at the door and did not like what she heard, possibly our brilliant version of the dialogue from a steamy love scene. She called up my mother and told her to come right down and take me home. Mom came, accompanied by a friend of hers, and I remember striding home behind them still feeling like a cowboy, though somehow shamed. I never saw that friend again.

We left the beach and moved to a big house in Los Angeles in 1946, when I was eleven. Before we left, however, Mom and Dad gave me a dinner party at the local country club, as a going away present. At this time, I was in sixth grade. I knew that we were moving to a safer place, because once, earlier that year, when I was out on the street with a group of kids, one big, husky girl had told me "My brother is better than yours." I couldn't stand that. "No, he's not." "Yes, he is," she insisted, getting mean. "You wanna fight?" "Yeah," I said, feeling pretty scared since she was a lot bigger. Her brother and my brother and a bunch of boys formed a circle around us and yelled "Fight!" We went at it. She slugged me and I slugged her. I hope I made her cry. We separated and the boys screamed "Fight, you sissies." We went at it again. After it finally stopped, I remember lying on my bed with bruises and a black eye, feeling guilty. When my parents got home and saw me all messed up, I explained, "I got into a fight because this girl said her brother was better than mine." They smiled lovingly, but it was at that point that my mother said we were moving to Los Angeles, where I would go to a girls' school and things would be better.

The new house was in a nice, old neighborhood, Hancock Park, where Mom had grown up. It was huge: 5,500 square feet, with eight bedrooms, five baths, a paddle tennis court and a big terrace. It needed a lot of work when we moved in, but basically it was a magnificent Craftsman-style house, in the manner of the Gamble House in Pasadena, with a beautiful mahogany staircase, thick baseboards and window trim, stained glass windows on the staircase and in the library, and lovely garden look-outs. Over the next five decades, Mom gradually fixed it up. After Dad's death in 1976, the house was her greatest source of activity and pleasure. I look back on it now as the most beautiful house I was ever in. Back when I was eleven, what I liked best was my own bedroom in the front of the house. Peter selected a room way at the back of the house where he could have privacy. I know now that Pete hated leaving Hermosa Beach. He had adjusted well to junior high school and was a popular kid. He never liked Los Angeles. To this day, he goes biking along The Strand, eleven miles, from King Harbor to Marina del Rey.

The move to Hancock Park in 1946 followed my father's return from the service in 1945 and his assumption of the management of the family business, Dearden's. Nana, the Scottish immigrant with a sixth-grade education, had married Edgar Dearden, an English immigrant, who opened Dearden's furniture store in 1909 on Seventh and Main Street in downtown Los Angeles. Dad became president in 1945 and ran the business until his death thirty years later. Dearden's, which has stayed a family owned and managed corporation, now has seven stores in Southern California. Growing up, although my father did not pay himself a big salary and my parents did not seem wealthy, I came to take economic security for granted. Today, my brother Peter and I sit on the board of Dearden's as do two children of my uncle, Doug Dearden, Mom's brother, who managed the company after Dad died until his own death in 2000. The current chair of the board is Raquel Bensimon, a Sephardic Jewish immigrant from Tangier, who joined the staff in 1961 and whose brilliance Dad and Uncle Doug recognized and nurtured. Her son, Ronny, has succeeded her as president of the company.

After the move there was the question of school. One did not just enter Marlborough School, the most prestigious girls' school in Los Angeles. One had to be recommended. My sponsor was a sorority friend of Mom's, my godmother Jo Williams. I was tested, interviewed, and accepted into the seventh grade. The annual cost was $1,000, a stretch for my parents, possibly because it was also in 1946 that Dad bought the first of two houses he eventually owned in Avalon. In addition, the family by now included my two younger brothers, John and Doug, born in 1942 and 1945 respectively.

At Marlborough we all wore pastel uniforms, and we were all white Anglo-Saxon Protestants and Catholic—there were no African Americans, Hispanics, Asians, or Jews at Marlborough. At the end of my senior year, there was a minor scandal when it was rumored that one of the girls was one-fourth Jewish. In the seventh grade, my first year there, a teacher would sit with us at lunch and correct our table manners. One Wednesday, the day we had chocolate sundaes, I raised my elbow to pour on lots of fudge and was reprimanded. Every month we had a formal tea. We learned to write thank you notes and acceptances to formal parties. On the other hand, I was cheered as the catcher on the school softball team. The academic preparation, which became more rigorous from the ninth grade on, was adequate to qualify us for the colleges that we and our parents had in mind.

I had learned anti-Semitism at home, which reflected the attitude of that part of the Los Angeles business community where my father worked. His father, a Dutch immigrant who owned a jewelry store in Hollywood in the twenties, had the same prejudice. In eighth grade, for reasons that elude me now, I left Marlborough and attended the public junior high for a year. It was there that I reached a low point in bigotry, perhaps the start of what later became a long journey toward fair-mindedness. When a Jewish girl did something that annoyed me, I hissed, "Stop that, you kike." She was shocked and greatly offended, and she and her friends avoided me for the rest of the year. By the ninth grade, I was back at Marlborough, where I felt more "comfortable."

When I was twelve, in the seventh grade, my mother adopted Christian Science fiercely and completely. Dad hated it. A ruthless pragmatist, Dad would become infuriated at the dinner table when Mom would quote the teachings of Mary Baker Eddy: "Man is not matter, he is not made up of brain, blood and bones. Man is made in the likeness of God."[1] Dad would shake his head in disgust and say that was ridiculous. Mom fought back, but she never won because she would burst into tears and run upstairs. I often followed, but there was no comforting her. Peter got the picture better than anyone. "Mother's Christian Science is a way of standing up to Dad," he would say, "and I think her religion is a good thing."

For me it was hard. Whenever I had any physical hurt or painful feeling, such as loneliness or jealousy, I told myself that this was just Mortal Mind, an erroneous belief that needed to be replaced with Truth. I had to understand as best I could that I was made in the image of God and therefore perfect. I knew that it was really bad and wrong to cry. In my eighth grade year, when I was at the John Burroughs Junior High School, I developed a pain in my stomach. I tried to overcome it, to know it was not there, to know the Truth about myself, but the lump in my stomach grew larger. Mom and Dad probably took me to a doctor; I do not recall. One time when I was spending the night with my friend Dody Currie, I was so intensely uncomfortable that I could hardly walk. Dody's mom called my mom to report my distress. When the doctor operated, he took out a four-pound sack of fluid the size of a football, an ovarian cyst that, had it burst, would have been the end of me.

Back at Marlborough, perhaps as my own way of standing up to Dad, I began a series of small rebellions. Once I was caught chewing gum, which my father had forbidden. This infraction prevented me from running for a school office. I ridiculed the Spanish teacher and put Coke bottles in the waste basket of the English teacher's classroom, where we were forbidden to eat or drink. This behavior lowered my "personal adjustment" grade at the school so that I could not run for president of the senior class. On Halloween night of my senior year, my group of six friends decided to write obscene words on the school windows. Since the principal was Mrs. Mitchell, we wrote "Mitch the bitch" in soapy letters. Then we hung glowing lanterns that we had stolen from roadside construction sites all around the buildings and swore each other to secrecy. Mrs. Mitchell called us in the next day. "Who were you with last night?" she inquired. We did not lie about that. Everyone knew we hung out together. After school we went over to Bugsie's house and smoked and laughed for two hours. Mrs. Mitchell may have figured out who the miscreants were, but we were never accused or punished.

Marlborough had the last word though. I was not recommended for Stanford. Girls with lower grades got in, but I did not. Even Bugsie got in. I was devastated. Mom went to talk to Mrs. Mitchell, who told her "Joan isn't always the perfect girl at school that she is at home." The school had sent home warnings every time I was disrespectful, but neither my parents nor I thought these small wrongdoings would affect my future.

Talk about good results coming out of trouble! My father had insisted that I apply to Radcliffe as well. Fearful that I might bring discredit on the school at Stanford, Marlborough had gladly recommended me for

Radcliffe, which no one I knew from Marlborough had ever attended. Meanwhile, a Stanford regent, a friend of my best friend's mother, asked the president of Stanford, Wallace Sterling, to review my case. I flew up to Palo Alto for a personal interview with him. A week later, when his letter confirmed my rejection, Dad said, "Congratulations! Now you will go to Radcliffe and get a much better education." An amusing footnote to my history at Marlborough is that in 1992, at my fortieth reunion and during my first term as mayor of Stockton, I was given the "Marlborough Woman of the Year" award, the school's highest alumna honor.

Radcliffe was radically different from Marlborough. It scorned group think and gave weight to the individual. It taught that a person with a fine education ought to make the community a better place than she found it. Reading the great thinkers of the Western world (all men in those days of course), I learned that those who questioned or even rejected accepted authority were often those who changed the course of history. I had a new set of models—So long Mrs. Mitchell, Hello Galileo—and an emerging set of new values.

The section of Los Angeles where I had grown up, half a mile south of Hollywood and four miles west of Beverly Hills, had the highly materialistic values of Southern California. My immigrant grandmother, Mom's mother, showed off the new Cadillac she bought every several years and prided herself on her membership in the Ebell Club. However, my dad scorned the glitz—the country clubs and beach clubs and new cars. When I read Veblen's denunciation of ostentatious materialism as "conspicuous consumption" in my first year at Radcliffe, I recognized the strength of what Dad advocated, that the answer lies not in material possessions, but rather with individual responsibility. If you have a problem, it is your job to fix it. You need to take action in your own life and make it add up to something. Decades later, when Stockton was in a mess, I believed that I could change the course of the city's political history, and it was up to me to do just that.

One of my best friends at Radcliffe was Elsa Weil, a Jewish girl from Scarsdale, New York, who also lived on the third floor of Whitman Hall. Sitting smoking on the concrete stairs of Whitman late at night, we talked about inclusion and acceptance. She says now that when I met her, I claimed I had never met a Jew. That was not strictly true, but it conveyed how sheltered my life had been, and how steeped in prejudice. Elsa must have taken me on as a mission.

I arrived at college uncommitted politically, though I was from a hard-core Republican family, and I left two and a half years later a lifelong Democrat. And I am no longer a Christian Scientist. In my first year at Radcliffe I took the subway to the Mother Church in Boston every Sunday. At the end of my first semester, just before finals, I called my mother to say I was sick. While she was telling me to know the Truth, I passed out and spent finals in the college infirmary.

By sophomore year I had stopped attending church. The idea that man could be Mortal Mind and therefore Error was no longer something I would try to accept. Independent thinking, the importance of the intellectual life over materialistic values, greater tolerance, rejection of my religion—this was my legacy from Radcliffe. And this spelled success to my dad. When, after two and a half years in Cambridge, I told my parents I wanted to return to California to finish college, my father made no objection. Radcliffe had done its work.

Back home at the University of California, Berkeley, I reverted to my mother's values. I went through sorority rush and became not a Delta Gamma but a Kappa Kappa Gamma. Fitting in at the Kappa house was a big adjustment—back once more to group rigidity. Luckily, I joined other groups as well. I chose political science as my major, probably because of my interest in current events from the days of Dad's wartime service. What made my time at Berkeley memorable was Project Pakistan-India-Ceylon (or PIC), a group of eight students who had been competitively selected to be sent on a goodwill mission to Southeast Asia in the summer of 1956 and to live with students there. With four others I went to Calcutta, Dacca in East Pakistan (now Bangladesh), Lahore, and Bombay. The culture shock was enormous, especially the appalling poverty. This experience spoke loudly to me of the need to use one's life to benefit others.

After graduation I returned to Berkeley for a teacher's credential and then taught English at a public high school in Los Angeles and lived at home. At the age of twenty-two, teaching 160 students with very different ability levels in three different grades (tenth through twelfth), was overwhelmingly difficult.

By the time I was twenty-four and still not married, my mom said, "Why don't you stop teaching and join the Junior League?" She meant to be helpful, but she denied the value of the life I had chosen. I did not join the Junior League; instead I went to Stanford to work on my masters' degree in education and a credential in counseling—and to find a husband. It was my good fortune that friends from Los Angeles introduced me to Jim Darrah, one of their law school classmates. Jim drove over from Stockton to Palo Alto every weekend to take me out. He proposed in March 1960 in Lovers' Cove in Avalon. I said I wasn't sure, whereupon his mother invited me to stay at their home in Stockton for the summer. By August, after two months with his family, I was still wavering, and Jim ran out of patience: "If you don't decide by Christmas, it's all off." I decided the next day. We were married in Los Angeles in December, had a big reception at Mom and Dad's house, and moved to Stockton in June 1961.

I thought that my having grown up in Los Angeles would impress people in Stockton, a former "cow town" in the Central Valley, but nothing could have been further from the truth. In Stockton, among people who have lived there for several generations, the greatest good is to be born and raised in Stockton. Next best is to be from a small town in the Midwest. We bought Jim's Aunt Bertha's two-bedroom house, and I taught English and counseled high school students in Lodi, the town next-door. Jim worked in his father's law office. Two years later, when I became pregnant with the first of our three children, Jeanne, I quit work without hesitation. I had two more children, John and Peter, joined several community boards, and took courses at the University of the Pacific in the doctoral program in education.

My major activity at this time revolved around Junior Aid, a Stockton women's philanthropic organization of about eighty members, mostly wives of local business and professional men and comparable to the Junior League elsewhere, just the sort of group my mother had wanted me to join five years earlier. I called a former Kappa friend to sponsor me as a member.

New members were required to learn about Stockton and the surrounding area by spending one day each month at various sites, such as the port, the University of the Pacific, the Haggin Museum, city hall, the asparagus fields, and the wineries of Lodi. Through two major committees, ways and means and health and welfare, the organization raised about sixty thousand dollars a year which it donated to various civic groups. Junior Aid also held events such as rummage sales and large dances. For nine years I found all of this—the committee work, the organizing of volunteers, the phone calls, speeches before small and large groups—absolutely gripping. These activities and raising my children were the focus of my life from 1964 until 1973, when I was elected president of Junior Aid.

In the same year I was asked to join the board of the United Way of San Joaquin County. I served on that board for four years, the last two as its first woman president. I presided over meetings, recruited and motivated volunteers, and held retreats to set campaign goals. I also developed a management model: the buck stopped with me, and the proper relationship between an executive director and a board calls for the executive director to carry out the policy which is set by the board. The United Way presidency in turn led to my nomination to the board of regents of the University of the Pacific, where I served from 1976 to 1989, the year of my mayoral primary. Throughout these years, I developed a large circle of friends and acquaintances among the social, business, and educational leadership of the city of Stockton. I became a seasoned and respected public leader. Finally, it should be said that my status in the community derived from my being, by then, a judge's wife as much as it did as from my managerial talents, high quality education, and hard work.

At the same time that I was busy with the children at home and with my Junior Aid activities, I enrolled in the doctoral program in the School of Education at the University of the Pacific. Before long, I had to admit that this was too much, so I took a step down to work on the degree of specialist in education, which required a fieldwork project. Fatefully, I ended up in the office of Judy Chambers, then assistant to the president at the University of the Pacific, who needed someone to gather data for an affirmative action plan for the university. I liked Judy immediately but concluded that the job would take too much time away from home. When I went back to her office to tell her my decision, I found that she was desperate for help with statistics. "The only thing I know about tables is that they are good to put scotch on." She kept me talking for an hour and a half, during which she time refused two calls from the president. I gave in.

I found myself working with a committee under a difficult chairperson who would sometimes wait until everyone seemed to agree on a point and then oppose it. One night at home, to the kids' amazement—

this had never happened after a Junior Aid meeting—I burst into tears of frustration. Jim had the answer: Do not leave it to consensus—call for a vote! After that, no matter how complimentary the chair was or how friendly the committee, I insisted on a vote. Even at the last meeting, when goals, timetables, salary equity issues had all been agreed to, I looked to Judy and formed the silent word "VOTE." We did, the plan was approved, and subsequently adopted by the board of regents. It became an important standard in the recruitment, hiring, and compensation of women and minority faculty and staff. The chair got a big award from the university, Judy was promoted to vice president for student life, I got my degree, and soon thereafter was elected to the board of regents.

Through the University of the Pacific, I also became involved with an evaluation of a new neighborhood police facility in South Stockton. The grant that funded this pilot project required that it be evaluated, and the funding committee approached Professor Bill Theimer of the education department. Theimer recruited me as his research assistant, and for three years I interviewed police officers and neighbors and wrote reports. This experience had a powerful influence on my perception of police/community relations: When people feel comfortable and work with police (and vice versa) much can be accomplished; an adversarial relationship is counterproductive. My later pro-police bias owed a lot to this early study of police officers in action. Of course, I also got to know individual officers and came to like them, especially Julio Cecchetti, the chief, and a young lieutenant, Jack Calkins, who later became chief himself and was of great assistance to me as mayor. The affirmative action project for the University of the Pacific took about half of 1971; the police study began later in 1971 and lasted through 1974.

In 1975 my father died. It was also in that year that our family moved to a new and rather upscale residential enclave called Lincoln Village West on the north side of Stockton, where new development was taking off. The three kids changed schools then too, since we were now in the Lincoln Unified School District, which meant no more busing and a quite different—a whiter, more affluent—school population.

We now had a modern, four-bedroom house with a fifty-seven-acre artificial lake at the back and a two-car garage. I was well known, even prominent, and I had built up two key assets for any politician:

a long list of contacts among the affluent and influential people in the community and a set of skills, including fund-raising. It would be another three years before I ran for elective office, but I had already taken step one. I had been the campaign manager for Jim's long-shot election as a judge.

In the spring of 1969, after an unopposed primary election, Judge Max Willens, one of six judges on the San Joaquin County Superior Court, was indicted for bribery. This came as no surprise to most of us since Willens had a reputation for accepting money for fixing traffic tickets.

Normally, once the primary has taken place, an additional candidate can run only as a write-in candidate, which requires one hundred names on a nominating petition. Jim filed this petition, as did four other men. However, given various technicalities of the election code at the time, Jim saw a possibility of getting his name printed on the ballot—if he could get five thousand signatures (approximately 5 percent of the registered voters) on a petition. This was definitely worth a try, and he and I contacted about two hundred fifty people we knew and asked that they help collect signatures. Within ten days, we had an event in our backyard where these people turned in the signatures they had collected. We found we had more than the required number.

As it turned out, this petition was turned down, but there was excellent press—headlines in Stockton's newspaper, *The Record*,[2] when five thousand signatures were turned in and again when our petition was rejected. We were back to the write-in candidacy, but the publicity had been valuable for a young man who was not well known.

The next task was to educate people about how to write in a candidate's name. We ordered 60,000 small pencils that read, "Write in JUDGE Sup. Ct. DARRAH." Stu Auchincloss, Jim's close friend, organized "M kits." These were boxes that contained 1,000 (hence the "M") of each item: labels, envelopes, pencils, and brochures. Sixty volunteers took the kits, stuffed and sealed the envelopes, and returned them to us for a mailing to the residents of San Joaquin County. We needed endorsements from well-known sponsors throughout the six towns of the county, which meant phone calls to people we both knew from our organizations.

Jim and I also put on a "Ballot Box Social" at the civic auditorium with the help of several of my Junior Aid friends. *The Record* did not endorse Jim because, they said, Willens had not yet been convicted and indictment alone was not a reason to unseat an incumbent judge—in other words, innocent until proven guilty. Willens was later found guilty as charged. In the final week before the election, there were only two people, Bing and Ben Wallace, social and business leaders in Stockton, who thought Jim would be elected. They were right. Jim won by a two-to-one margin, with more votes than all the other candidates, including Willens, combined. It was a thrilling victory.

At thirty-seven, Jim became the youngest elected judge in California. His salary doubled, from $1,000/month working with his father, to about $25,000/year. We felt quite flush and took the kids to Disneyland. The day after Jim's election, as I was driving my children to school, I was stopped by a police officer for an infraction. "Are you related to the judge who was elected last night?" When I told him I was his wife, he waved me along.

Jim was following in his father's footsteps. Guard Darrah had been district attorney for San Joaquin County from 1924 to 1932, a very colorful era in Stockton history. He took on official corruption in county government. He had Sheriff William Riecks indicted for bribery and later proved the ballot box was stuffed in Riecks' re-election. Guard pursued a far-reaching cleanup of county government for which he earned the hostility of the power structure of Stockton. He never again won elective office. After a defeat for district attorney in 1932 and two unsuccessful campaigns for judge, he was narrowly defeated for the California Assembly in 1960. When I first met Jim, he was his father's campaign manager for the assembly seat.

I would not have gone into politics without Jim's wholehearted support. Given the conventional, middle-class expectations of the 1960s, his supportive attitude was surprising, to say the least. Especially in conservative Stockton, it was extremely unconventional for a woman to run for office. Indeed, when I ran for a seat on the San Joaquin Board of Supervisors in 1978, there had not been a woman on the board for forty-two years. Many men in Stockton, and in other places too, would have discouraged their wives from running for political office. The difference in our case begins with Jim's appreciation for my help in getting him elected to that judgeship.

Another factor has to be Jim's own particular temperament. For example, when Peter, our third child, was in fourth grade, he wanted to go to a Halloween parade dressed up as a dollar bill. I thought it was a ridiculous idea, but Jim and Peter made a big box and painted dollar bills on all four sides, and Peter marched in the parade as a dollar bill. That was Jim's modus operandi—to endorse whatever a person in his family wanted to do, regardless. So, when I became interested in running for county supervisor, Jim was for it. This was my first campaign for elective office, and he backed me all the way, even to providing coffee and Danish pastry for the 7 A.M. staff meetings at the house before he left for work.

My decision to run for supervisor came at a time when I had gone as far as I could go in nonprofit work in Stockton. Sizing up my assets as a candidate, I thought I looked pretty good. I had a good record, including a 17 percent increase in money raised by United Way under my leadership. The seat was wide open because Cliff Wisdom, the four-term incumbent, and unbeatable, had decided not to run. I had the names of five hundred people who had volunteered to work for my campaign. I had raised a significant amount of money. *The Record* endorsed me. I ran two full-page ads with 1,400 names endorsing my candidacy. On the down side, as the wife of a judge on the superior court of San Joaquin County, it looked to some people as if I could have a conflict of interest. I also had three children at home, and many voters took the view that my place should be with them, as the following story will illustrate.

On weekends during the campaign, when I was going door to door from 4 to 6:30 P.M. through all the precincts, Jim would pile the three kids (then ten, twelve and fourteen) into the car and go shopping for groceries. Jim would give each child a list at the supermarket and they all had a lot of fun. This particular form of family recreation, however, did not go unnoticed. The day before the election, the local paper ran a huge front-page article about my opponent's family and my family. It described Jim taking the kids to the supermarket. The reporter asked why he did this. "'It was a matter of necessity,' Jim explained. 'For about a week, we were sort of eating catch-as-catch-can until the cupboards were bare. Then it was up to me to get out and do the shopping.'" Throughout the article Jim is "the judge" and I am "Joan."[3] The companion piece on my opponent, Doug Wilhoit, led off with an account of his mother having been an actress in a film that starred Ronald Reagan: "No political overtones. Just fond memories," she said demurely. The article also celebrated Doug as a member a fourth generation Stocktonian family. Weeks after election day, at a meeting of Women Executives, the consensus was that this leaning of the press, especially in the story of "the judge" going to the supermarket at the eleventh hour to feed his family, had cost me the election. The bent of that story was obvious: It just wasn't right. The kids were too young. They needed their mother.

Warning me about the possibility of incurring negative press, Jim had suggested I take this reporter out to lunch. "She might have it in for you," he said. The reporter had been quizzing him about his role all through the campaign and Jim felt there would be a big article just before the election. He thought a friendly lunch might make her more favorable to me. I should have listened. In retrospect, I see my avoidance of that reporter as typical of a very foolish and even arrogant attitude toward the press which had plagued me for many years. I somehow had the idea that I ought not to talk to the press, try to please them or tell them my side of the story unless I was asked. It was my job to perform well, theirs to report fairly without coaching from me. Talk about a self-defeating attitude for a politician! For years after I became mayor, I was still inhibited and awkward about calling the press. Others, as we shall see, had no such qualms.

It must be said, too, that Doug Wilhoit, my opponent for supervisor, was a formidable candidate: A police officer and a very popular man from a well-known Stockton family, Doug ended up raising and spending more money on his campaign than I did. He could easily have won without the help of this reporter. To the end, I thought I would win. Contemplating my future office on the fifth floor of the courthouse made the last week before the election one of the happiest of my life. Election night brought a shocking defeat. The next day's headline read, "Wilhoit Beats Darrah in a Landslide."

Now what? At the time the premier authority on what to do with the rest of your life was Richard N. Bolles, author of *What Color Is Your Parachute?* In the spring of 1979, about four months after the election debacle, I attended a four-day workshop with Bolles in San Diego, where I learned the idea of "transferable skills." Looking inward, as directed, I saw that I enjoyed leading, motivating, organizing, and speaking; that I liked to be boss; that I wanted to work only part-time because of the children; and that I wanted to earn $10–$20,000/year. The next step in the Bolles plan was for participants to conduct an interview with a person in the same line of work that each participant thought he or she might enjoy.

Since I enjoyed being be the hostess at social events and I liked to go out to eat, I interviewed a restaurant owner and was informed that the job was not just greeting people at the door; it was also fixing the refrigerator and it took eleven hours a day. It sounded impossible. At lunch that day with the restaurateur, I broke my tooth and lost a filling. Back at the seminar, I took up Bolles' invitation to anyone who wanted to recount the day's experience, and before three hundred fellow participants I gave what proved to be a hilarious speech.

The next step in Bolles' program was to prioritize your skills and goals—from a list of twenty you take the top four or five—and do a second interview. I like motivating people and being in charge, I want to work part time, and I only need to make $10–20,000/year; what do you think I should do? A couple of people saw my question only from their point of view, such as a college president who thought I could do part-time teaching at night. Then I talked to David Catherman in the development office at the University of the Pacific, and he said, because he actually wanted to do it himself, that I should start my own public relations business.

Soon after my talk with Catherman, a good friend who had helped me during my supervisor's campaign, Patrick Johnston, announced his candidacy for state assembly. I wanted to help him, but I realized I could not perform fund-raising endlessly for every agency and candidate in Stockton; this time I wanted to be paid for my work. Pat's campaign chairman offered me $500 to coordinate a fall event. I followed my usual pattern of recruiting many of my old contacts, and we put on a marvelous Harvest Celebration. For the next twenty years, during his terms in office, first in the assembly and then in the state senate, Pat held that same celebration. Once elected (by only twenty-five votes!), he contracted with me to do a series of fund-raisers.

About the same time, the Women's Center of San Joaquin County received a grant of $7,500 from the United Way to start a shelter for battered women. The center, which became one of the most significant and powerful agencies in San Joaquin County, already had a rape crisis center, a program to prepare low-income women for employment, and a program to teach children to be aware of potential abuse. When I first heard about men beating their wives, I could not believe this actually happened, but I was interviewed for the contract and got the job.

I soon came to appreciate what a serious social problem domestic abuse had become. My first task was to convince the public that domestic violence was prevalent. I decided I needed a brochure to which prominent people would attach their names and photographs, verifying that this was a real problem. My son Peter had just broken his leg and was in Saint Joseph's hospital. When he would fall asleep, I'd rush downstairs to the hospital pay phone and make calls. I remember talking to Mike Smith, the director of San Joaquin County Health Services, who affirmed that we had a raging problem of domestic violence in Stockton. Back in Peter's room, in the adjacent bed, a woman was being threatened by her husband, a tough-looking guy who said he would "get" her if she did not do this or that. He gripped his fist and shook it at her. She was compliant, sweet, and docile. Thirteen-year-old Peter and I learned together how essential a shelter for abused women would be.

We needed to raise over one hundred thousand dollars for this facility, so I headed for the Stockton-area property developers, and I asked the first one for fifty thousand dollars. He said "Joan, that's an awful lot. Why don't you ask several of us for five thousand?" I asked if he would be the first to make a contribution, and he agreed. Once I got started, I raised forty to fifty thousand dollars, the county gave seventy thousand through the influence of Doug Wilhoit, and the shelter was opened within a year. That was the result of the brisk, efficient fund-raiser I had become. But the women's center changed me too. I met new people and began to think in different ways. The three women who ran the center became close friends of mine. One had a doctorate in French literature from Stanford, another a master's in women's studies from Webster University in Saint Louis, and another a bachelor's degree from Stanford. All three were remarkable women, and quite different from the Junior Aid crowd. I became an ardent supporter of the efforts and achievements of women, and these friends in turn have backed all of my endeavors.

With the aid of a part-time secretary, I ran Joan Darrah Public Relations out of an office in my home. In addition to the women's center project, I did a building fund campaign for Stockton Civic Theater, put on the 125th anniversary celebration of the San Joaquin General Hospital, and organized the opening of a new wing of the San Joaquin Historical Museum, the Helen Weber Kennedy Library. It was here that I learned about Mrs. Kennedy's grandfather,

Charles M. Weber, the founder of Stockton, and the man who built a home on Weber Point in downtown Stockton in 1848. This is the site of my major legacy as mayor, the waterfront project at Weber Point.

Had I stayed with my public relations business, my next move would have been to open an office outside my home and hire more employees. To be honest, that prospect just did not interest me. What I really was waiting for was another opportunity to run for public office. That chance came with the adoption by the voters of Stockton in November 1986 of the electoral reform known as Measure C. I had been one of the small group of people who drafted and sponsored this new way of electing members of the city council. When two other members of the group called to urge me to run for mayor, I decided to go for it.

3

Getting Elected

*Ralph White and Measure C: Closing Down the
"Monday Night Circus"*

*P*assage in November 1986 of the package of electoral reforms known as Measure C was the key factor in my decision to run for mayor.[1] Before those changes in the way members of the city council were elected, and hence in its personnel, the council was so contentious that it was an embarrassment to the city. With the new rules, a new day could come in Stockton politics. That day should have dawned two years after the passage of Measure C, with the primary of the next regular election cycle in June 1988 and the vote on a new mayor and council in the fall. I had started a primary campaign in the summer of 1987 and hoped to be elected in November of 1988. Instead, a legal challenge and subsequent injunction barring Measure C from going into effect put everything on hold for three years.

In the fall of 1989, the legal case was dismissed and the primary was held, followed by runoff elections for mayor and council seats. I finally took office in February 1990. In the interim, I not only started and stopped a primary campaign, I also ended up as the plaintiff in a lawsuit against the city to enforce compliance with the provisions of Measure C. In order to explain the basics of this rather complicated sequence of events, I must introduce the reader to the chief opponent of Measure C, Ralph Lee White, who some claimed to be its chief target.

White is the best-known politician in Stockton's recent history. Originally a civil rights activist and then a businessman and council member for sixteen years, he evolved from a social reformer into an intimidating power broker and a figure who came to epitomize the worst in Stockton politics. By the mid-1980s, I was one of a small group of people determined to bring about reform in the Stockton electoral process, which we believed we had accomplished with the approval of Measure C at the polls, only to be thwarted by the ensuing legal delay. Meanwhile, in September 1987, when White was about to recover his seat on the council, from which he had been removed by the courts, I brought suit against the city of Stockton to enforce the provisions of Measure C and thus keep White from returning to power. The story I want to tell is a complicated interweaving of large national issues, such as civil rights, and what became a personal battle between Ralph and me.

Ralph White was sixteen in 1959 when he moved to Stockton from Texas and went to work in the fields and orchards of the Central Valley. He soon left farming to become "a two-bit hustler, and a fence for stolen property. 'I was like the typical black kid. I wanted to be cool. But I was young and dumb and didn't know nothin'," he told an interviewer for *The Record* years later.[2] By 1967, he had started on his career as a civil rights activist and "young hot head" by getting the Community Action Council to support a training and recreation center for troubled teenagers that he called Project Identity. "White warned that militant young Negroes are on the verge of rioting similar to that in other cities recently...." He argued that such a center would "lessen the chance of racial rioting" in Stockton.[3]

In that same year, 1967, White cofounded Ebony Young Men of Action, a group that undertook a number of protest actions concerning minority employment. For example, they wrote to the state Fair Employment Practices Commission to complain that San Joaquin County had only 157 blacks on a payroll of 2,940, and 120 of these individuals were employed at the San Joaquin General Hospital. In another action, White's organization filed suit against the United Crusade and did not withdraw that suit until this organization hired a black person to a full-time position on its staff. They filed similar suits against both the Boy Scouts and the Girl Scouts. Stockton banks were challenged over unfair employment practices, as were other downtown businesses. At one point, noting that there were twelve thousand blacks in Stockton, Ebony Young Men threatened a boycott of a downtown shoe store, Leeds. On January 16, 1971, *The Record* reported "The U.S. Department of Agriculture has launched a 'top priority' investigation into a charge that the General Mills plant in Lodi is violating equal opportunity provisions in its federal contracts by discriminating against blacks in its hiring practices." Ebony Young Men of Action was the group that made this charge. The paper quoted a letter to White from the compliance officer of the U.S. Department of Agriculture assuring him that "you will be notified prior to our visit to the facility... ."[4] White was informed that his assistance would be welcome during their inquiry. The state of California began its own investigation of the Lodi plant at the same time. During the late sixties Ebony Young Men received supportive press for their many antidiscrimination initiatives, and White became widely known in Stockton, San Joaquin County, and beyond as a forceful activist.

White was soon well connected with the national black leadership. After he was elected to the city council, again quoting *The Record*, "White used his second annual testimonial dinner to bring [Jesse] Jackson to the [Stockton] Civic Auditorium, where he received a standing ovation following his talk." Speaking of White, Jackson told the audience, "He is a friend and a brother. I am here because I consider him an outstanding public servant."[5] Civil rights leader Julian Bond was a guest at a nightclub White owned. Powerful California Assembly Speaker Willie Brown became a prominent, long-term supporter and attended several of White's fund-raisers. White even appeared with Mohammed Ali in a staged fight in front of a delighted audience of nine hundred at the University of the Pacific.

In 1969, White ran for the city council and lost, but two years later the city had instituted district voting, which meant that each member was elected by voters in his district alone, rather than by voters in the whole city. This change in the electoral law, which Measure C would partially reverse fifteen years later, was designed to facilitate election of members of minority groups to the council, and in 1971, White and another African American, Jesse Nabors, became the first minority members of the city council.

Along the way White acquired wealth. He became the owner of several small businesses—a high-volume bail bonds business, a gas station/mini-market, and a nightclub—as well as several chunks of South Stockton residential property. But his real interest was power. Once elected to the council, White made himself a man to be reckoned with. Stockton began to experience a long residential development boom, beginning in the 1960s and lasting into the present, and city politics have been heavily influenced by land developers during those decades. White quickly found ways of making himself critical to a developer's chances of having an item passed by the council, and developers expressed their appreciation of favors granted, or anticipated, in the usual way, with campaign contributions.[6]

So successful was White at the power game that, in a piece on the most influential people in San Joaquin County in the summer of 1987, near the end of his tenure on the council, *The Record* reported the results of a poll of county residents that voted White the second most influential person in the county, ahead of Assemblyman Patrick Johnston, mega-developer Alex Spanos, and the Republican Central Committee chairman Philip B. Wallace. At the same time, respondents labeled White "negative," "corrupt," "obnoxious," "controversial," "outrageous," and "connected."[7] By the time he was forced to resign from the city council, White had become, in many people's eyes, the crudest and most outrageous member of a group known for its pettiness and its flagrant abuses of power. He was the star performer—clown, high flyer, and lion tamer in one—at the "Monday Night Circus."[8] The story of White's gradual transformation from respected and energetic young activist to a man many Stocktonians saw as corrupt and self-serving, unfolded over two decades, from roughly 1966 to 1986.

White's most famous escapade was a gesture in support of drug testing for senior city officials, police, and firefighters. "White leaves message in bottle," says the headline. "It wasn't exactly a public forum but Stockton City Councilman Ralph Lee White made good on his drug test pledge Monday night—he urinated in a specimen bottle before half a dozen reporters and photographers at City Hall."[9] Later that evening, the council adopted his drug-testing proposal by a 7 to 1 vote.

White was famous for his language as well. During an argument with Mayor Ronk, who was supporting another candidate in White's district at the time, *The Record* informed its readers that "White interrupted Ronk. 'I think you're a prejudiced son of a b—— as I told you before, and I think you're a little faggot and I told you that before, too,' White said."[10] White enjoyed his reputation for arrogance and bombast. "First you have to get [people's] attention," he explained. Taking on his favorite public role, advocate for the poor, he compared himself to Christ: "'I'm in a struggle just like Jesus was. When you're trying to help oppressed people, you're going to have a lot of people that's not going to like you because they don't want to give up none of their power.'"[11] Mayor Ronk was thrown off the council too, by the way, on a charge of forging travel vouchers. He claimed he had done so to recover expenses he had incurred investigating White's dubious activities.

By the fall of 1983, White had attracted such suspicion among the voters, even in his own district, that he lost his seat to Mark Stebbins, the candidate Ronk had favored over White. During that campaign White came up with an attack on Stebbins that made the national press. According to White, Stebbins was a fraud because he had told the Black American Political Association of California when he joined it that he was an African American. In order to discredit Stebbins with this association and in his district, White sent to Colville, Washington, for Stebbins' birth certificate, which indicated that Stebbins was white. Stebbins said he never had a copy of his birth certificate, if it said that he was white, then obviously his parents hadn't considered themselves to be black. But, for himself, Stebbins said, "I am black to the best of my knowledge and belief." He insisted, "I have never represented myself as anything other than black."[12]

Stebbins charged White with making race an issue in the campaign. In November 1983 Stebbins won the seat by a small margin. For the next three and a half years, until June 1987, White tried to reverse the electoral outcome.

White's recall campaign against Stebbins, based on the charge of fraudulent racial representation—Stebbins' calling himself black when his birth certificate indicated he was white—was launched *before* Stebbins was actually elected. In those days, district voters could recall a council member and at the same time vote for his replacement. Naturally, White's petitions listed White as the replacement candidate. On a vote in May 1984, Stebbins survived this recall by a 58 to 41 percent margin. The following October, however, White mounted a second recall effort, and in December of 1984, with the help of a thousand absentee ballots, he won back his seat by seventy-two votes.

Stebbins promptly filed suit over the absentee ballots. When Judge Frank A. Grande of the San Joaquin County Superior Court "addressed White's conduct in gathering the absentee ballots that eventually provided his margin of victory...Grande found that White had bullied voters, invaded their privacy, and even deceived voters into voting for him when they really wanted to vote for Stebbins." Grande ordered White removed from office for "election law violations," and noted, in what *The Record* called "a colorful and scathing opinion," that White had "bribed, harassed, and intimidated voters to secure absentee ballots."[13]

White retained his seat during an appeal to the third district court. When this court agreed that White should vacate his office, he appealed to the California Supreme Court, which, in June 1987, refused to hear the case. That was the end of it. Almost two years after Judge Grande's ruling, White was finally off the council.

The Record editorialized about White's political demise in pretty strong language: "A malignancy on Stockton's body politic has been excised. An embarrassment to the city's psyche has been removed....When Ralph Lee White burst upon the Stockton political scene in the late 1960s, he was one of the most effective civil rights leaders this community has known. [In later years,] instead of extinguishing the embers of racism, he fueled the flame. He abused people and process. His public persona became that of everything he fought against in the late 60s and early 70s: an arrogant racist."[14] Letters to the editor sputtered with rage: "I am sick and tired of ex-Councilman Ralph Lee White. He is a loud-mouthed, self-serving, self-centered, racist, bigot. He struts about like a peacock, pruning [sic] his feathers, protecting his kingdom, thinking everyone should see the world his way."[15]

White had been dismissed, and the council needed to appoint a replacement to his seat. The choice was between a businessman, John Nisby, and a school principal, Floyd Weaver. When the vote was tied 4 to 4, Weaver resolved the impasse by withdrawing in favor of Nisby. Two and a half years later, when I had to decide between Loralee McGaughey and Floyd Weaver as my vice mayor, I recalled the way Floyd had put public harmony ahead of personal advancement and selected him over McGaughey. Not long after Nisby's appointment— less than a year—there were rumblings that White was moving to recall him. This time, I brought suit myself to prevent his doing so, but before I get into that part of the story I need to explain the provisions of Measure C.

In 1984, a small group of citizens, including me, came together to discuss what seemed to us a crisis in Stockton politics. Out of these talks came a five-point proposal for electoral reform known as Measure C. The key provision of our plan was a change in the election procedure for the city council. Under the old system, in effect since 1971, council members were elected only by the voters in their own district. Under our proposal, there would be a district-wide primary in June, when several residents of one district would run against each other, to be followed by a city-wide election in November, when the two highest vote-getters in each district would compete for the votes of all residents of the city.

Whereas previously a representative was accountable only to his own district, from now on candidates would have to be concerned about the needs of the whole community. In the event of a recall, Measure C provided that the council would appoint the replacement. Additional provisions of Measure C brought in term limits for the mayor and council and redrew the council districts, reducing their number from a total of nine to six. The mayor would be the seventh council member and would be elected at large, rather than from the sitting members. Finally, in an effort to enhance turnout, Measure C required that council elections be held at the same time as elections for other city and state offices.

What problems were we trying to fix with these reforms? To our way of thinking, district voting had produced council members who were incapable of dealing effectively with the major issues in the city, such as crime, traffic, growth, and jobs. Competing against several other people in their own district, they dramatized themselves as advocates for the most local of issues and slighted matters of general welfare. The most extreme candidate attracted the most attention; compromise was not a virtue. Council members could typically not even agree on the wording of the minutes at a council meeting. They fought incessantly. They screamed at each other until two in the morning, while dismayed residents watched the proceedings on cable television.

With Measure C in place, the city-wide vote could defeat anyone like Ralph White, even though the district had nominated him. The issue during the campaign, especially since many believed that White would be voted out of office, was whether this arrangement would discriminate against minorities. Because each district retained the power to nominate, proponents of Measure C claimed that minorities would not be disenfranchised. Opponents protested that because city voters could select the less popular of the two nominees, they could subvert the wishes of the majority of district voters.

After Measure C won at the polls (in November 1986), a legal challenge was mounted against it in federal district court by the Mexican American Legal Defense Education Fund, a national group that challenges electoral systems in districts having large numbers of Hispanic residents but none in elective office. MALDEF, which found six residents of South Stockton to act as plaintiffs, won an injunction barring Measure C from going into effect, and the matter remained in limbo for three years. This period, especially the spring and summer of 1988 when the primary election for mayor and council was delayed, was hugely frustrating for many of us. It was also very expensive—the city spent $1 million defending the suit. Rumors at the time suggested that none other than Ralph White helped finance the opposition case. I regularly attended the court sessions in Sacramento, where the district court judge delayed hearing the case due, he said, to a crowded court calendar. The irony was that, when the judge finally heard the case, he dismissed it because the arguments against Measure C were too thin to warrant a trial.

At the same time as the legal attack on Measure C was dragging on, Ralph White was taking advantage of the delay to get back on the council by trying to recall John Nisby, whom the council had appointed to replace White after the courts sustained his dismissal. Prior to Measure C, vacancies were filled by special election in the district; afterward the council appointed the replacement. Ralph's idea was to proceed under the old rules, where district voters could cast ballots to recall a council member and at the same time vote for his replacement, the process he had used against Stebbins. *The Record*'s description of White's *modus operandi* in his move to recall Nisby tells the story: "When some polite but fast-talking signature gatherers implored residents in southeast Stockton to sign a petition earlier this week, most people were happy to oblige. Residents were told the purpose was to halt closure of a local fire station. But those who bothered to read the fine print learned that what they actually were being asked to support was yet another recall against Stockton City Councilman John Nisby. 'It was really done in a shabby way,' [said one woman]... when she lifted a paper covering the document's summary, she found it was for the recall."[16]

More people than merely the residents of District 9 were upset by this scam. Ron Stein, an attorney and the chair of the committee for Measure C, called me to say that the city attorney, Tom Harris, wanted to see me. I went to Harris's office and he indicated that a lawsuit could be filed against the city of Stockton seeking to enjoin the council from calling a special election. In view of my prominent role in the group that formulated Measure C, I might be the one to file such a suit. I would have a very good case, in his opinion. As I considered Harris's proposition, I could not get over what a terrible slap in the face to the whole city it would be if, after all the hassle of changing our charter and electoral process, the worst of the offenders were to defy the new law. I decided to sue the city and hired Robin Appel, a young, bright, gutsy lawyer, as my attorney. It was courageous of her to take the case—many people in Stockton still feared Ralph White.

On September 1, 1987, I filed my suit to compel the city of Stockton to implement the provisions of Measure C for replacement of a vacancy on the city council. When asked by the newspaper if the suit were aimed at White, I gladly admitted that I did not want him once again to bully voters into putting him back on the council in a special election. White accused me of looking for publicity in my recently announced bid for mayor. "If you want to get elected, attack Ralph White."[17] He also charged that my suit would get preferential treatment because my husband was a superior court judge. When the case came up on November 10, 1987, the court found in my favor. An outside judge, Robert M. Salasko of Merced, was brought in to avoid the appearance of favoritism. White did not attend the court hearing, but when he heard of the judge's decision, he reacted angrily: "It was a judge's wife that filed it. Black people have a hard time getting laws that are right for them anyway."[18]

The case was decided, but White tried an additional gambit. He claimed that he had obtained about twenty-five hundred signatures on petitions, enough to recall Nisby, and that he intended to file them soon. Since he was an affected party in the suit that barred the special election, he contended, he should be allowed to intervene. On October 28, 1988, Judge Salasko refused to reopen the lawsuit. This ruling dashed White's hopes of overturning the injunction against the special election. He subsequently challenged the decision in the California Third District Court of Appeals and was rejected. While he decided not to move beyond the appellate court to the state supreme court, he said he might bring a lawsuit against me and others who, he asserted, were conspiring to keep him off the council. "If it ain't a...conspiracy going on, what's going on?" he asked. "Black people are being deprived of their equal rights under the law."[19] It is highly likely that had I not filed this suit, White would have repeated his coup against Mark Stebbins; he would have recalled Nisby and gotten himself elected in his place. He would have been back on the council for another two years before the February 1990 election, the first runoff election to be conducted under Measure C and the one that put me in the mayor's office.

Considering appearances in court, depositions taken, and discussions with my attorney, I paid almost $13,000 in legal fees and was able to recover only $8,000 in the settlement of the case. But I look back on that suit with a lot of pride. I took a risky stand against a man I felt had become a dangerous and destructive politician and succeeded in keeping him out of city government. I hope that it was a factor in my successful election in 1990, although today many Stocktonians forget the earlier corruption and illegalities and hearken back to the entertainment White provided on Monday nights. "He's one bright guy," they'll tell you.

My ideas about politics led to a view of city government that was very different from the backroom boys' rules that many men in Stockton, as elsewhere, understood and used to their advantage. White understood them well—the boys and he could work together to get what they both wanted out of city hall. With the advent of Measure C and the subsequent elections, there has been an entirely new tone at the council. The proceedings now unfold with very little public criticism of staff or council members, one to the other; no public scandals; and no need for charges to eliminate people for illegality. With all due respect to White's theatrics, council meetings are not as colorful as they were in his day, but the council has taken giant steps forward in credibility and accountability.

Although I am no longer active in Stockton politics, Ralph White is. He has run for city council three times (1990, 1992, and 2000) and lost all three elections, although he qualified for the city-wide ballot each time. In 1990 he also ran for the Stockton Unified School Board and was defeated, and in 1996, he lost a bid for a seat on the San Joaquin County Board of Supervisors. He has also been one of the prime movers in recent efforts to have South Stockton secede from Stockton.

Another piece of mischief on White's part has been his campaign to reduce the city utility tax from 8 percent to 2 percent, a move which, if it were to succeed, could lead to significant layoffs in the police and fire departments. On the more constructive side, part of White's legacy is the continued presence on the city council of minority representation. He was the first nonwhite to serve, and his election was made possible by the move from city-wide to district voting in 1971. By keeping the nominating primary within the district, Measure C sought to protect and sustain minority access. Thus far, it appears to have succeeded. In the period under district voting prior to Measure C, 1971 to 1989, there were either two or three minority members on a council of nine, except for 1985 to 1989 when there were four out of nine. The four councils immediately after Measure C went into effect have included either two or three minority members out of a total of seven.

Fund-Raising: The Nuts and Bolts

After the lawsuit against Measure C was dismissed in June 1989 and Judge Garcia ordered city elections for November, my first campaign began anew. As we all know, a winning campaign demands money. I had learned a lot about raising money in my work for nonprofits, in my campaign for county supervisor and, of course, as a professional fundraiser in my business, and I knew that the key to successful fund-raising is that it be conducted face to face, one on one. You, the candidate, have to look the potential donor in the eye and ask for $500, $1,000, or more. To raise the really big bucks necessary for any successful campaign, you must personally ask another person for money. No one can do it for you. The donor wants to meet you and hear you make your case. The process is excruciating at times, but it is also indispensable.

Raising money takes guts because you open yourself to personal rejection, yet it is crucial to convincing the voter that you are the best choice. There are a lot of things to do in life, many of them more satisfying and less work than running for elective office. In order to declare a candidacy, you have to be able to feel that "I am going to kill myself to win this campaign." On election day there is one winner. The rest are "unsuccessful candidates."

Personal contacts are invaluable, and I cannot stress too strongly the importance of being active in community organizations. Aside from serving a cause, this is how you meet people. Come campaign time, these people know you and will be your donors and your volunteers. They are the ones who will go door to door for you, send out endorsement cards, put up your lawn signs, stage your events, bring friends to attend them, and ultimately vote for you. Women do not have access even now to all the organizations men can join, but there are plenty of places women can get a start.

As I have said, the first big organization I joined was a women's group, Junior Aid, which raises money for needy causes by putting on large social events. I put a lot of energy into Junior Aid, including chairing several major events, and was ultimately elected president. Getting this office did not happen by chance. I wanted it and, when my turn came up, I recall being sure I suggested a woman for the nominating committee who was favorable to me.

During the years I was involved with Junior Aid, I seemed to have a compelling need to be very social. I was uncomfortable unless several Saturday nights in a row were lined up with an activity: dinner with friends at our house or theirs, a trip out of town, a community-wide fund-raising event. Jim and I put on frequent dinner parties, including a big luau in our back yard. I don't know if all this entertaining helped me get the presidency, because I had also held three big committee chairmanships in Junior Aid, and I deserved to get the top job, social or not. What I want to say is that there were several years of a certain restlessness that was best satisfied by either giving or attending parties. This socializing brought me into contact with a large number of people and helped me to become known in a city where I was not born and raised but where I wanted to play a major leadership role.

It was at Junior Aid that I met Elizabeth Rea, a third generation Stocktonian and the wife of a savings and loan executive. She served as fund-raising chairperson for my 1978 campaign for the county board of supervisors. At the time, having been prominent in the campaign to build a major sports center in Stockton, Liz was the best-known woman fund-raiser in the city. She was also well connected to the business power structure and had been for generations.

When Liz Rea agreed to help me I thought my worries were over. I assumed she would go out and raise big bucks for me. However, instead of giving me fish for a day, she taught me to fish. She gave me a list of potential donors, told me to go out and ask for donations, and told me how much to ask for: "They don't know you, Joan. They need to meet you. Ask them for money yourself. Only the candidate can do this." She was right. Almost everyone she referred me to was willing to see me, and most contributed. It was really quite amazing, but frightening too. In spite of its reliance on private-sector funding for a great many things, our culture still makes a person feel very awkward asking for money. I was lucky to have Liz as an expert and loyal mentor, a woman who had been a role model for me when I joined Junior Aid and who stuck with me as the chairperson of both of my mayoral campaigns. This loyalty was not in the least weakened by the fact that I was a registered Democrat and she a staunch Republican. The offices of county supervisor and mayor of Stockton are both nonpartisan; candidates run individually rather than as nominees of a political party. Thus it happened that later while she was working for me to become mayor, Liz was doing her best to elect Republican candidates to statewide and national office.

In addition to working with Liz, I knew several other women from Junior Aid who started a fund-raising organization known as ALS/SOS (Amyotrophic Lateral Sclerosis Society of Stockton) to benefit people with ALS or Lou Gehrig's disease, with which one of their husbands was afflicted. ALS/SOS staged marvelous, elaborate fund-raising events for the next twenty-two years. I cochaired several of them, and strengthened my relationships with these very talented women who later assisted me in many ways during my mayoral campaigns.

As a fund-raising contractor with the Women's Center, beginning in 1978, I developed a formula for putting on a major event. First, I selected a site, the home of a prominent person whom other people would like to meet. The house itself needed to be beautiful and located in a "good" residential area. Second, I established a committee to promote attendance at the event. Although volunteers intensely dislike asking for money, they will sell tickets and urge their friends to sit with them. Third, I formed a committee to secure auction prizes, including some high-end ones, such as time at condominiums at vacation resorts. My final task was to personally solicit sponsors, donors of $500 or more, whose names would be listed on the invitation and who would be recognized at the party.

Although the committees met for a couple of months, the most intense activity occurred during the last two weeks. The day of the event became the culminating moment of the campaign: the day to get your money in, to have your friends lined up to attend, the last date to contribute. The committees worked particularly hard in the last week of the Women's Center campaign, both to encourage attendance and to secure auction prizes. Because the event was always at a place that was a big draw—the lakeside home of a doctor or the gardens of a developer—I made sure that a line drawing or a photograph of the site appeared on the front of the invitation. This pattern became the model for the major fund-raising events of my political campaigns.

During the eight years I worked with the Women's Center, I put on thirty-three events and ran eight major fund-raising campaigns. Among these events were several that continued to be given for years after I started them, including a Dickens-of-a-Christmas and an auction where businesswomen in the city could auction their business services. We often had a huge dinner and auction where I utilized the winning combination of a large event and one-on-one solicitation. I never had an auction at a political campaign event, however, and as far as I know no political candidates have an auction. The question of who is giving what to whom gets untidy. In addition to coordinating fund-raisers, my association with the goals, programs, and leadership of the Women's Center sensitized me to such issues as rape and domestic violence, pay equity, child care, and abortion rights, all causes that I would address as a politician.

As a professional fund-raiser, I also developed a formula for one-on-one solicitation. Before calling on the potential donor in person, I wrote a letter describing the importance of the cause and explaining the need for funding. I indicated that I would like to see this person in his (yes, almost always it was *his*) office and I would be making a follow-up phone call to set a date. Because I knew most of the potential donors personally, or was known to them through the board of regents or my supervisor's campaign, they were usually willing to see me and often to make a donation.

One such donor for Women's Center causes, the president of the Williams Group and a wealth-transfer specialist, gave me a list of business leaders I should contact when I ran for mayor. He advised me to begin my letter by saying, "I have just been visiting with our friend Roy Williams and he believes that you and I feel the same about business concerns for our community. I would like to talk with you about these concerns and my campaign." These contacts proved to be a very lucrative source of funds. Roy was also the person who advised me to sign up for the Toastmasters program in order to improve my public speaking.

While I was a consultant for the Women's Center, I attended courses on how to raise funds from major donors sponsored by the Fund-Raising Institute, an outfit affiliated with the University of Indiana, which offers courses in Northern California. One excellent instructor was Kim Klein. Talking about one-to-one solicitation, she explained that people give to people on their own economic level, and they give to people they know personally or through a friendship or business network. If you do not know the person you intend to visit, try to find someone who does know that person to come with you. Kim advocated sending a letter in advance and getting to know the potential donor's secretary, the one who will make the decision whether or not to let you through the door. To identify major donors, she gave us very specific instructions. Look at disposable income—does this person have money for frequent, spontaneous, unplanned vacations? If yes, it is likely that he can afford to give to your cause. She told us always to ask for a specific amount. Do not worry if the amount seems too high; the donor can always give less. Always express sincere appreciation for the donation, as you will surely be back asking for assistance again. Giving money and being thanked, she explained, provide the donor with warm, pride-enhancing feelings, some of the only ones the donor may have that month or even that year. Thus, by enhancing the donor's self-esteem, you are doing him a great favor! Finally, remember that you are in his office for one and only one reason and that is to get the money. Write that down at the bottom of your folder: "Get the money." Resisting donors will give a hundred excuses why this is a bad time. Listen. Then get the money. Once the donor states an intention to give and has been thanked, then determine when and how the money is to be given. Never feel even the slightest bit guilty for asking for a donation. The rule of thumb is that the average donor can give five times more than the amount he does give.

Shortly after this course, when I was fund-raising for the shelter for battered women, I wanted to see a wealthy businessman, a charming fellow but one who was not known for his generosity. I did not know him personally, but I did know a friend and neighbor of his who was interested in helping the Women's Center. She called for the appointment and we went together to his office, gave our pitch for the shelter, and asked for $500. What followed was nearly an hour of reasons why he could not possibly make a donation: He was overcommitted to a number of other charities; his wife had been very ill; his business was in a period of significant, stressful change. All of the excuses were stated in such sincere and compelling words that a less trained fund-raiser could have simply left. Instead, I kept thinking, "Get the money."

Finally, I resorted to a cheap trick. I called on the friendship between him and his neighbor. I said, "She cares about this project and she is your friend of many years; give for her sake." He sighed, shrugged, and then succumbed: "I will donate two hundred and fifty dollars, but nothing more." "Great," I exclaimed. "How generous." He grinned. When I asked how he would like to make the payment, he pulled out his checkbook and wrote the check on the spot. On the way out he showed us a large training room. "My nineteen salesmen are having record-breaking years," he confided to me. When we left, my colleague turned to me and in a very concerned voice said that she hoped that we had not taken advantage of him. I reminded her of Kim's rule: People can normally give five times more than they actually do.

First Mayoral Campaign

My first campaign for mayor was demanding, exciting, and extremely busy. In one day I would have a 7:00 A.M. campaign committee meeting, make calls setting up sessions to ask for large donations, have a working lunch with my campaign staff, go door to door with volunteers for two hours in the late afternoon, and attend a council meeting that evening. The pace was frenetic and I thrived on it. As long as I kept bringing in the dollars, day in and day out, the campaign would stay on track and victory would be mine on election day, or so I hoped.

In many ways, campaigning consisted of doing what I had been doing for nonprofits for the previous twenty-five years: organizing volunteers, giving speeches, planning events, chairing meetings, designing brochures, and doing one-on-one solicitation. In these areas the ground was familiar. What was unfamiliar was the electoral process: the polling, identifying issues, deciding on a major theme, finding the necessary staff, learning the techniques of negative campaigning—how to do it as well as how to take it—and anticipating how to deal with the traumatic stresses of election night. Moreover, in politics, although there is an organization of campaign workers, the role of candidate is very much a solo performance—"I will bring change to the city of Stockton, I need your money, I am not the wimp or the fool my opponents say I am."

When I became a candidate for mayor, the people of Stockton had been angry at the antics of the city council for ten years or more. This anger is what brought about the 1986 adoption of Measure C by a 2 to 1 margin. When Measure C's chief architect, Dean Andal, decided not to run, two other promoters of Measure C urged me to go for the job. I was ready. I was in a stalemate on a contract with my major client, and with the advent of a new electoral process and a new council, there would finally be an opportunity to address long-standing major problems in the city. I discussed the idea with my husband, Jim, and we both thought I had a good chance of winning. I would run as an outsider, an alternative to the regulars of the "Monday Night Circus."

As mentioned previously, shortly after Measure C was approved by the voters, a case was brought in federal district court to enjoin the city from implementing its provisions. As long as the case was pending, no municipal elections could be held, but most thought that the case would be settled in time for the next election cycle to proceed two years later. Accordingly, I declared my candidacy, set up a campaign committee, opened a headquarters, recruited my daughter Jeanne, then twenty-two and a graduate of the University of California, Santa Barbara, in political science, to be the campaign coordinator, and started to prepare for a June 1988 primary. Six men, but no other women, also declared candidacies: a political consultant, who had been a state assemblyman, a mechanic, a retired Air Force enlisted man, an attorney, and a small business owner. The sixth man was Al Bonner, a member of the Stockton City Council and a past-president of the Stockton chapter of the NAACP.

To the dismay of many, Judge Edward J. Garcia decided to further postpone hearing the case against Measure C, with the result that municipal elections could not proceed. I will never forget calling Jeanne to tell her the disappointing news. "Oh, Mom, I'll have to stop, but I had the headquarters all fixed up," she replied, the discouragement all too evident in her voice. Not until the fall of 1989, when Judge Garcia dismissed the case for lack of evidence, could elections for mayor and council go ahead.

The first two questions one asks in a political campaign are "What are my chances of winning?" and "What issues are on the voters' minds?" My pollster, Joe Shumate of San Francisco, found that a stunning 83 percent of Stockton voters rated the city council as doing a poor job. Even more said that it was time for a change in city government. Sixty percent believed that council members were "somewhat-to-very unethical," and some 80 percent believed that our most serious issues were drugs and crime. A third issue was Stockton's unrestrained residential growth. Of the six candidates for mayor, I had the highest name recognition and the best favorable-to-unfavorable rating, by a margin of 8 to 1. Shumate advised me to pound home the theme of change and the idea that drugs and crime were devastating our city and then to convince the voters that I was the candidate who could best bring about change.

I produced a brochure, "A Change for the Better." "Drugs are rav-

aging our cities; we must end this plague," it asserted. "Criminal elements terrorize our community. I want to bring honest, effective government to the city of Stockton." Readers saw a stern, concerned photo of
me before the microphone on the steps of city hall. I also listed the names
of 150 community leaders—major business leaders, representatives of
the city's several ethnic groups, political leaders, even the popular supervisor who had defeated me for that job nine years earlier—as supporters
of my candidacy. This brochure was mailed to a targeted audience of
approximately 35 percent of the 80,000 registered households, those where
someone had voted within the last two years and those where newly registered voters lived. Such a limited initial mailing is recommended by the
professional mailing house for two reasons: the high cost of printing and
mailing and the likelihood that, though registered, the other 65 percent
will not vote. A second brochure proclaiming "New Ethical Leadership"
included more biography and five photos; it stressed the same themes:
fighting crime and drugs, promoting well-managed growth, and improving Stockton's image.

A third mailer was designed to capture the absentee voter. It included
an absentee ballot application form, a letter from me, and another brochure: "Are you a Victim of Stockton's No. 1 Problem: Drugs and Crime?"
followed by a five-star program for drug control based on my research
with city law enforcement and the county drug control agency. In this brochure, Police Chief Jack Calkins spoke of the decreased number of police
officers and the consequent lack of new programs. "Thousands of
Stocktonians are victims," said my brochure. "What has the current city
council done? Decreased the number of police officers." The polling had
told the truth. When the primary results came in, they were labeled "decisive:" Darrah, 43 percent, Bonner, 24 percent, and Doug Carter, the political consultant, 17 percent. The remaining three together received 15 percent of the vote. The ballot would list two candidates, Bonner and me.

Running as an outsider, I had the luxury of taking the high road.
Only when Bonner accused me, in ads late in the campaign, of wanting
to start at the top, having no experience, being the perpetual volunteer,
and answering critical questions with "I don't know; I'm not sure" did I
come back with a negative ad. It noted Bonner's excessive travel expenditures over a four-year period, the second highest of all nine council
members. "Is this the kind of experience you want?" I asked. I had obtained this information from the deputy city manager, who seemed only

too ready to expose Bonner's excesses. Travel abuse had become a source of embarrassment for this council.

The Record endorsed Bonner, citing his experience, his "stronger, steadier, surer hand." The newspaper conceded that "his sometimes abrasive, superior, know-it-all attitude can-and will-annoy." The paper said I had slick, quick and forceful responses to the expected questions, but that I was hesitating and noncommittal in responding to the unexpected. This was evidence of my inexperience in city government.[1]

When a candidate asks the question "How much money do I have to raise?" my answer is always "As much as you need to win, and then a lot more." First, there is the cost of polling to show you your chances and to identify the major issues. Then comes hiring the consultant, crucial to your success, and the paid campaign manager and the volunteer coordinator, without whom you will not have time to make the calls for dollars. There is the cost of operating a headquarters, so the campaign will not be run out of your house, and the expense of all the publicity material: the brochures, lawn signs, billboards, get-out-the-vote fliers, the television ads, the radio spots.

From the beginning, I set up a fund-raising structure identical to the one I had developed in the past: a committee, an event, and individual solicitation by the candidate. Our fund-raising committee was chaired by a prominent man, a politic choice in our conservative community since my campaign chairperson was a woman. Committee members were not expected to solicit for funds, because most people hate to do that, but they were encouraged to promote attendance at events. We set priorities for contributions which were beyond the price of the event, including sponsor categories of $1,000, $500, and $250. I then made calls, asking people to be sponsors. Donors had their names listed on the invitation, or were publicly recognized in other ways, and they received complimentary tickets. These events always had a theme, wonderful food, and were at homes that were a draw. Clever invitations designed by volunteers were sent to from 1,000 to 1,500 people. My first campaign for mayor raised and spent $100,000, twice as much as my opponent's did. My fund-raising expertise was the salient reason for my success. Of those candidates who prevail on election day, 80 percent have raised more money than their opponents.

Who donates to a political campaign? Once upon a time I thought it was people who wanted to see good government. Not so. First and foremost, donors, especially the big donors, are people who have a special interest. The candidate needs to identify who those donors are and gain access to them. In city government they are all those people—the businessmen, unions, lawyers, contractors—who do business, directly or indirectly, with the city. At election time, they put their money on candidates they think will win. In our city of 240,000 persons, there are probably two hundred donors who will regularly give over five hundred dollars to a political candidate. I knew many of these people from the volunteer organizations and boards I sat on before I ran for public office. There are also your relatives. In my first campaign report, 20 percent of my total of $19,000 came from relatives: $2,500 from my mother and $1,000 from my uncle. I had no idea they would give so much. Close friends also give and so do people who have worked with you, people who know and trust you and believe in your leadership.

However, being a skilled fund-raiser was both my greatest strength and my greatest liability. My opponents just could not stop commenting on how much money I raised and how I was buying victory. In his negative ads in the last week, Bonner headlined, "Ability Speaks Louder Than Money." When I had raised twice as much as Bonner, the city clerk was impressed: "I've just never seen money come in like that before."[2] My campaign raised far more than had been raised in any previous city election. In response to criticism, I always argued that the amount of money coming from as many sources as mine did showed broad-based support.

The marvelous thing about a campaign is that it rises to a climax, election day. The votes are cast. The results are known. The candidate either wins or loses and it's over. Many other things in life take years to show results, and then they can be inconclusive. There is an old saying, "I've been poor and I've been rich; rich is better." I say the same for elections: "I've lost and I've won; winning is better."

After the polls closed on election night, the campaign workers came to the house for a party and to await results. A photographer for *The Record* came by for pictures for the next day's story. When a candidate has a big lead, he or she goes downtown to the county courthouse where the official election results are being tabulated and the several reporters and photographers gather to interview and photograph the winner. It is an exciting and heady moment. The next day's news carries an upbeat statement of the gleeful, successful candidate, who is very relieved and trying to act cool. The unsuccessful one stays home on election night;

volunteers drift away, she goes to bed bewildered and dejected and the next day she feels like she's been hit by a truck. There are some caring phone calls from family and close friends. Letters of consolation follow for the next few weeks, and the failed politician tries to figure out what she's going to do next.

On my first mayoral election night I was fairly confident because a recent poll had shown me with a considerable lead over Bonner. The volunteers, back from getting out the vote all day, were at the house drinking, eating, and carrying on; however, as an experienced candidate, namely one who had lost an election previously, I knew that only the final results counted. The polls closed at 8:00 P.M., and right away, despite conservative absentee ballots that came in first, the results were terrific. I took an early and strong lead. When *The Record* called, I said that I was "hopeful." By 10:00, I had a significant lead. With 126 of the city's 142 precincts reporting, I had racked up 64.9 percent of the vote to my opponent's 34.7 percent. It was time to go to the courthouse for the interviews and flashing cameras. An entourage that included my husband, campaign chairman, campaign manager, and other friends joined me as I accepted congratulations and responded to reporters' inquiries. The headlines the next day read, "Darrah Wins in Landslide." I like this word applied to me. In my supervisor's race, my opponent had won "in a landslide." The final count had me at 58.2 percent compared to Bonner's 41.5 percent.

Inauguration and Settling In

Hallelujah! I had been elected mayor. This was an opportunity for a gala event, my specialty. I wanted the inauguration to mark the beginning of a new era for Stockton. It should have drama, dignity, and style, be open to everyone, and it should be cheaper for the city budget than past receptions. Let's include people other than the usual donors and developers, I thought, wanting to be very inclusive.

I approached the deputy city manager: "What budget does this event come out of?" There was no line item in the city budget to cover the cost of renting the Stockton Civic Auditorium for a reception for the mayor and council members. In other words, we would have use of the auditorium for free. This made me uncomfortable because I knew others in the community paid a hefty fee for the use of this facility.

"What about the food?" I inquired. Food was ordered by and budgeted through the city clerk's office. On my way to talk with the city clerk, I ran into the city reporter from *The Record* and invited him to come with me to hear about the plans. The city clerk had already lined up a master of ceremonies, a man I liked a lot, luckily. She had also arranged for hors d'oeuvres with Bernadette at Cal Deli. Someone on her staff was handling all the arrangements for the reception. There was not much for me to do, but at least I hoped for a good story in the paper about the entire city's being invited to a wonderful event. Two days later, a humiliating, front-page spread appeared: "Mayor plans lavish party to take office."[1] This was my first post-election press.

When it came time for the rehearsal, I gave orders to the city council as I had to the volunteers for my nonprofit events—"You stand here; you put this over there!" and so forth. I had asked each council member to select a judge to swear him or her in that evening, and all fourteen of us lined up for practice. Everyone was cooperative except for Council Member Panizza, who kept looking up into the rafters above the stage while I was giving directions, a small portent of things to come. I also told each council member to speak no more than one minute, which I thought was generous. It was my way to be inclusive with the council as well as the citizenry. The staff worked out appropriate staging for the television cameras. The key moment was to be the presentation to me by the outgoing mayor, Barbara Fass, of the three-foot gavel with the names of past mayors engraved on the head.

The evening was dynamite. Ed Coy, the master of ceremonies, was dashing in his tuxedo and performed brilliantly. The council, especially the women, were all dressed in their finest. I had a new, white linen suit for the occasion with shoes dyed to match. The vocalist arrived at the last minute, purse in hand, just in time to sing "Look Out And Touch." Seven robed judges simultaneously swore in the council. Lastly, Barbara presented me with the gavel and each council member gave a one-minute speech. After the official business was taken care of, two thousand people happily scarfed up the hors d'oeuvres and hung around to congratulate the newly sworn-in council members. Of course, my shoes were excruciatingly tight by that time. The evening had marvelous TV coverage, the best that Stockton politics had ever had, and *The Record* the next day was favorable as well. The new era seemed off to an auspicious beginning.

As I watch the short videotape of that first inauguration, I have to laugh. Here am I, the expert at putting on grand events, who did not even arrange for my own coordinator to run this extremely important occasion the way I knew it should be done, much less for private donors to pick up the cost. Worse, I was so much the political novice that I gave a polite, wimpy little speech in which I thanked Barbara Fass and then the two coordinators just as we did at Junior Aid events, rather than give a rousing pep talk for the new day dawning in Stockton politics. Most of the council members gave excellent politicians' speeches. I did not sound like a politician at all! Panizza's resistance at the rehearsal should have warned me that politics was different from the polite world of nonprofits. But I did not get it—not that night, not for a while.

For the same reason that I wanted a large public party to mark the beginning of a new era in Stockton city government, I wanted the mayor's office, the room itself, to be a place to be proud of. What I found was a dark room at the far end of the city manager's complex, on the second floor of city hall, with a small adjacent office for the single secretary who was assigned to the mayor and the six other council members. Both rooms were shabby and depressing. In the mayor's office, the brown rugs were ripped, the walls were yellow from years of cigarette smoke, even the light fixtures were ugly. Other than one desk with a Formica top and a bookshelf, there was no furniture. There may have been a plaque or two on the bare walls, and in the middle of one wall there was a door which led to nowhere. The mayor's office was shared with the council—there was no separate space for council members' desks, books, or phones, no private place to make a call or meet with a constituent. I was determined to change this whole scene. If Stockton were going to take itself seriously, the mayor had to have a presentable office. Happily, Alan Harvey, the city manager, agreed.

There was no budget for renovations either, but the city manager was allowed to spend up to $20,000 on his own authority, without council approval. Since Harvey supported the project, he and I assumed I was free to spend the $20K on redoing my office. The deputy city manager and I talked about redesigning some space for the use of the other six members of the council. We chose a room about half the size of my office, and one of the council members took on the job of fixing it up for herself and her fellow members.

Work began. Blue rugs were installed in my office. Union carpenters removed the door to nowhere and filled in the space in the wall. The ceiling was lowered and light fixtures were added. One wall was paneled; the others were painted off-white. The plastic furniture was removed. A friend of mine knew someone who had inherited furniture from her grandmother that she could not use. Would I like some pieces? You bet I would. After the renovation was finished, her brother delivered an armoire, a small antique desk, and an antique display cabinet. In the new space for the council, we installed six, good-quality, modular desk units, each with its own nicely upholstered chair, bookshelf, and telephone. In an attempt to retain the décor appropriate to the building's 1920s architecture, we selected some embossed green wallpaper and old-fashioned light fixtures for the council room.

Then one day a newspaper reporter happened to be in the city manager's wing. She inquired about the remodeling, gathered figures on prices, interviewed several council members and wrote an article representing the whole effort as extravagant. When the council members spoke later to this reporter, I learned to my surprise and dismay that several council members were quite happy to disparage my improvements. "I'm very disappointed it's so expensive. I'm also appalled and embarrassed," said Councilwoman Sylvia Sun Minnick. Panizza concurred: "I'm not keen on seeing the taxpayers' money spent in this manner. I don't think it was necessary."[2] Another member complained that the city manager had gone over his $20,000 limit. He had, but he insisted that there were two different projects, one for the mayor and one for the council, which meant that not $20,000 but $40,000 was available for the remodeling project.

The former mayor, Barbara Fass, said of her former quarters, "It was an office, not a palace." The director of the San Joaquin County Taxpayers' Association observed that "the honeymoon period for the council is going to be over real quick" if public money is spent on "this kind of behavior. I think it's damaged them already."[3] Two weeks later, the council unanimously passed a motion by Mel Panizza: Any item of remodeling or decorating to be done to the office of the mayor or council members must be brought before the city council for its approval. The tiniest or most routine expenditure had henceforth to be put on the agenda and brought to a vote.

The idea was to put me in my place, but I did not mind. By then I had my office looking the way I wanted it, with the gorgeous antique furniture, especially the armoire, where I kept the many reports, plaques, and gifts that a mayor acquires while in office. I used the desk that my father had used in his law office in the 1930s in Los Angeles, and chairs that my father-in-law had used in his office in Stockton from 1934 to 1988. I put up photos of my children on the wall, my framed degrees from Berkeley, Stanford, and the University of the Pacific, my two favorite plaques, one designating me a member of the board of regents of the University of the Pacific and the other for being first woman president of the United Way of San Joaquin County. I bought three white, ribbed, plaster columns four feet high and one foot in diameter to use as plant stands. And on the wall opposite my desk, I hung my favorite art object, a framed quilted tapestry that represented the struggle of the Hmong people when they were forced out of their native land, swam the Mekong River, and were befriended by soldiers on the other side.

Four years later, I purchased from local artist James Bell a two-foot by five-foot painting of Stockton's waterfront with Mount Diablo in the distance, as seen from the Hotel Stockton. Bright golds that flood from the blue sky down through the clouds and reflect on the river give a sense of expectation and excitement to the city's remarkable geographic configuration. I hung this painting in place of the Hmong work in the office and took the Hmong piece home. Above the antique table I hung a mirror that was set in a frame of white wood and Portuguese tiles that I had brought back from Lisbon. To complete the new mayor's office, I bought a beautiful, solid oak round table for two-thirds off its regular price, during the closing of Quinn's stationery store downtown. This was the table I used for conferences and staff meetings.

Certainly, one of the best things about being mayor was having this office. I loved it, and the city needed it. Many visitors came through there—the Consul General of China, numerous groups of students, trade missions from around the world, the president of Iris Manufacturing, U.S.A., who came to see whether he wished to build his manufacturing plant in Stockton (he did), and many others. When these visitors came into the mayor's office I was proud to welcome them on behalf of the city. I got some flack for the renovations from the council, but it was worth it to me. I used to retreat to my office during the recesses in the middle of long council meetings, when the other members would go to the Round Room, off the chamber. I felt safe and important in my office.

4

First Term

Relations With Council and Staff

The Departure of Alan Harvey: Politics Is Not Junior Aid

I have made much of my "transferable skills," the techniques I acquired in twenty-five years of work with nonprofit organizations and in my own business. All that fund-raising, committee work, and speech-making served me well when I got into elective politics. Even when I lost the race for county supervisor in 1978, my skills had not let me down, and in my first mayoral campaign they proved invaluable. What was absolutely different about being in politics was the way personal relations worked. In nonprofits the goal was to be polite, work together, accommodate differences and achieve commonly agreed goals on behalf of the organization. In politics, goals were personal, not organizational, and personal relations were often abrasive and unpredictable.

At the outset of my first year as president of United Way, the board had a three-day goal-setting session, and for the next year focused on achieving these goals. I presumed politics worked the same way. In my first two months as mayor, the city manager and I set up a goals-setting session at which six of the seven council members developed a mission statement and a set of goals for the city. I felt completely comfortable with the results and nicely in charge. What I didn't get was that the member who attended only part of the session, Mel Panizza, had his own agenda, and he turned out to be the *de facto* leader of the council.

At this time, my chief aim was to avoid bickering and open conflict among members of the council. What I did not appreciate was that conflict is vital to politics. A healthy democracy responds to the competing demands of many constituencies. Issues are complex; unanimity is not always possible. The vote is usually split and the majority wins. Had I understood this I would have spoken up more forcefully, as was my right and my responsibility. As it was, I tried to model the Junior Aid leader role—queenly Joan in charge of a harmonious team. This was definitely not how the other council members saw things. Sylvia Minnick and Beverly McCarthy each had her own agenda. Panizza wanted to be in charge. He and Loralee McGaughey, who had known Floyd Weaver from the previous council, had been political friends for many years. They lined up Nick Rust to form a voting bloc, known in some quarters as the "gang of four." The leader of that bloc and, at times, my most formidable adversary was Mel Panizza.

The city charter gave the mayor only two specific powers: to preside over council meetings and to nominate the vice-mayor. It was council policy and not the charter that gave the mayor the power to appoint committees, a power the council could therefore always revoke. Within the first month, the council established four standing committees. I interviewed each member to determine committee preferences. I did not nominate myself for any of the committees, yet another instance of my inexperience, because major policies were initially developed from within the committee structure. After one year in office, I decided that I wanted a voice on the budget and finance committee, so I nominated myself as a member of that committee, which Panizza chaired.

Panizza ruthlessly opposed me. Abruptly, during a council meeting, he announced that he thought the mayor should not be a member of any standing committee. On the spot, the council voted to implement this change. I was stunned and humiliated. If I fought back there would be open conflict. Worse, the council could deny me even my committee-nominating power. This change robbed me of any influence on the formation of budgetary policy at the committee level. It took away my confidence as well.

A further obstacle to cooperative teamwork was the Brown Act, a California law which states that a majority of city council members cannot meet together in private, away from the public eye. It even discourages conversations on political matters by two or three members. Although the intent of the Brown Act may be admirable, its effect is to promote the isolation of council members and to discourage necessary working relationships. It goes without saying, too, that people do talk to each other, but the fact that conversations on topics of public business are illegal creates an atmosphere of uncertainty instead of cooperation. The result in our case was a further erosion of my mayoral authority.

Learning my new job meant unlearning old ways of dealing with people. My effort to carry over the executive director/board chairperson relationship from the private sector to city hall meant that the mayor, the equivalent of the chairperson of the board, had to work well with the CEO, the city manager. This was why I worked so hard to get along with Alan Harvey and help him keep his job at a time when a majority of the council had made up their minds to get rid of him. Second, an ongoing battle developed between me and Thi To Can Nguyen, a Stockton resident who attended almost all of the council meetings during my two terms as mayor and did her best to raise hell. In my efforts to deal with her often outrageous behavior, I had to rely on the advice of the city attorney, another chief staff person. I became unwilling to dispute or even to question the ineffectual procedures that Tom Harris, the city attorney, recommended, and I was consistently far too accommodating to the city manager, Alan Harvey.

Many large cities across the country have a "strong mayor" who is not only the chief policy maker but also the administrative head of municipal government. Stockton, like most California cities, has a "weak mayor." The council, which includes the mayor, sets policy and hires the top staff people—the city manager, city clerk, city attorney, and city auditor. Once hired by the mayor and council, the city manager is the chief administrative officer of the city, having the power to hire and fire city employees, roughly two thousand persons in our case. When I was in office, the city manager's salary was approximately $116,000; the mayor got roughly $15,000, and council members received half that amount.[1]

As I have said, the Stockton City Council, derisively known for years as the "Monday Night Circus," had a history of bickering and inefficiency. In such an atmosphere, it is hard to recruit good city managers and they do not stay long when hired. They are either fired or they leave for better jobs. In the period from 1980 to 1991, there had been five city managers in Stockton. Alan Harvey, the fifth, was in the job when I took office. I had been mayor barely a week when a department head confided to me that many of the department heads were afraid for their jobs because Harvey was so abrasive and unpredictable. Rumor had it that the old council had almost fired him and that he never took a vacation for fear he would return to find his job gone.

I wanted to get along with Harvey, who struck me as bright, energetic, and knowledgeable. He had been eager for me to win the election. He was also tall, well-built, attractive, and had a terrific voice. There was a male energy about him that was vital, but more than a bit unnerving. When Harvey explained issues at staff meetings, he would grip my forearm strongly in his hand as he lectured at me. I disliked the grip, but I let him do it anyway. Maybe I thought it was a "guy thing" or that I would appear too "touchy," as my mother used to say, if I removed my arm. In retrospect, I regret allowing this public bullying.

Another thing that made it tough to get along with Harvey was his habit of yawning in my face. Here I was, the elected mayor of the city; I had spent two and a half years of my life getting elected; literally hundreds of volunteers had worked on my behalf; over $100,000 had been donated to help get me the job. And here was the city manager standing in the hallway of the city manager's complex, no doubt with other staff around, giving me his version of some issue. I would prepare to respond. As I began to speak, he would take in a long, full-chested yawn and then blow his foul-smelling breath right smack into my face.

Harvey talked a good line about the proper relationship between the city manager and the council. He wanted a full and equal partnership, a team. The best demonstration of partnership would be to move his seat in the council chambers to the dais, where he would sit with the council during its meetings. At first I went along. What could be better than having the top administrator pull his weight equally with the council? Council members Weaver and McGaughey, who had dealt with Harvey for a year on the old council, would not hear of it. No, he could not sit up on the dais with them. I was worried that he would be hurt by this rejection, and I wanted him fully on board. We all had to get along.

On my own, I scrutinized the council chamber and found a table centered in front of the dais but below it. I asked him to come with me to look at the chambers and showed him the prescribed location. He could not sit up on the dais, I explained, but here was another place he could be comfortable. He was upset. He strode about. He fussed. I spent at least an hour cajoling and humoring him, and easing him into his new place. This was absurd. He was an employee of the council and the city of Stockton. He could damn well sit where we told him to.

Harvey's trouble with the council was clear from the start. Soon after the election that brought in five new members, including me as mayor, he set up a series of "study sessions" to introduce new members to the several departments. Some of these sessions went well, but at the meeting with the planning department, Harvey introduced material that others immediately challenged as needing to be discussed in open session. When Loralee McGaughey called him on it, he became red-faced and silent. At another such session, he introduced the subject of an elaborate new computer system he wanted installed at city hall. Panizza left abruptly, claiming that this was not an item for a non-public session. In despair, I wailed, "Mel, please come back." He refused. The meeting ended.

More than once, Harvey referred to Floyd Weaver, the newly elected vice-mayor, as "a son of a bitch." He said this in the presence of other staff people and I listened. In those days, my *modus operandi* was to do everything to avoid open conflict. Others had different ideas. Although a majority of the council wanted Harvey fired, rumor had it that they would wait until after the November elections of that first year, 1991, when three members—Minnick, Rust, and McGaughey—had to run for re-election. Well before election time, however, the council decided to conduct an evaluation of Harvey in closed session. I met with him several times in advance to talk through his misgivings and encourage him.

We gathered in the Round Room and each council member evaluated him on a number of criteria. Because Harvey had a way of dominating meetings and often in so doing, shooting himself in the foot, I asked him not to speak until each member had his or her say. After each of us had spoken, some favorable and some not, Harvey informed us that obviously this relationship (between himself and the council) was not working, and he wanted out. In effect, he resigned. I was shocked. I had hoped he would rise to the occasion, hear the council's complaints, agree to make changes in his style, and persuade the council to keep him on. Instead, he walked out of the room and went to war. He hired an attorney to negotiate a good severance package, and the council hired its own attorney to get off as cheaply as possible.

The Record dramatized the subsequent conflict in a series of editorials that described Harvey as a victim and the council as power-mongers. In his parting shot Harvey described the "Gang of Three," led by Panizza as "dirty-mean, flat-mean, ugly-mean people."[2] He described Panizza as a "master manipulator" who had accumulated power in city hall by positioning himself as chairman of the powerful budget and finance committee. Panizza denied the charges, as did the other two. McGaughey was quoted in *The Record* as saying that "Alan Harvey has lied to so many damn people he can't even remember how many lies he's told."[3] Rust said that Harvey should have swallowed his pride and done what the council wanted him to do, which was pretty much my position. Although at the time I had hoped Harvey would shape up and stay on, I was soon glad he had left. Indeed, he should have gone long before. Under Harvey, we would have continued to wrangle for months.

Undoubtedly Panizza was instrumental in Harvey's demise and thus in my political education. Although I had been acutely aware of the dysfunctional relationships between Harvey and virtually everyone else—the city attorney, the city clerk, the council itself—my intention had been to work with him. I expected to change his ways, to get him to work more harmoniously with the others at the Monday morning staff meetings, and to cool his temper. Panizza's approach was to get rid of the guy, not by firing him but by exploiting his temper and provoking him to resign. The kill was effected at the closed evaluation session. Incensed by harsh criticism, Harvey seemed to resign on cue, and the only legal hassle that followed was over the severance package. I say "on cue," but it could also be the case that Harvey was just as calculating as Panizza. Aware that he was about to be fired, he may well have resigned to prevent that from happening.

Panizza personally, and the council in general, got some bad press, a small price to pay in exchange for the opportunity, which happily we used very effectively, to give the city new management. Harvey's successor, Dwane Milnes, was his complete opposite—competent, professional, diplomatic. Under Milnes, the city set a course of stable, sensible government and maintained that course for close to a decade. No amount of niceness from me or anybody else could have done that.

Mrs. Nguyen, the City Attorney, and Gracious Me

Standing at the podium in the council chamber, short of breath, her long, graying hair pulled back, her large-framed glasses in her hand, Mrs. Nguyen told her story again. She spoke clearly, deliberately, with a strong Vietnamese accent. "They kidnaped me, beat me up, handcuffed me, brought me to the mental health department, locked me up there, drugged me, and humiliated and terrorized me for five days and nights. In spite of all the evidence—bruises, cuts, and swelling spots on my body—dozens of people have seen them, including the city council—the D.A. refused to press charges. He said there was no evidence, based on the police report."[1] Her arrest and incarceration came about, she explained, because of a conspiracy against her by the police and mental health departments of the city. Although this incident occurred the spring before I took office, Mrs. Nguyen became the wayward celebrity of my political career. Recalling my time as mayor, people in Stockton often remember "that little Asian woman who used to come to every one of the council meetings and blast Mayor Darrah."

Thi To Can Nguyen,[2] born in Vietnam in 1931, was arrested in her apartment on Stadium Way for creating a disturbance on April 7, 1989, and taken to the county mental health crisis center for evaluation. She was held against her will for five days. Soon after her release, she began coming to council meetings. During the five minutes allotted for citizens' comments at the beginning of each meeting, she berated the police department, Mayor Barbara Fass, my predecessor, and the city council for (as she saw it) this abuse.

Barbara assured me that Mrs. Nguyen's allegations had no basis in fact, but when I took office I reviewed the case. After a careful check of police records, I concluded that the officers' actions that night had been justified. Nevertheless, Mrs. Nguyen continued her attacks. Every week she filled out the card to request to speak in the period for citizens' comments. She was there on February 26, 1990, at the first council meeting over which I presided as mayor, and she was present at almost all of the meetings for seven years thereafter. Of approximately three hundred fifty meetings, she came to probably three hundred twenty.

On one typical occasion she held up *The Record*, which carried a report of a forthcoming conference called "Take a Look at Stockton," which was being sponsored by the Stockton Chamber of Commerce. She did not have the $135 to attend the conference. More important, she wanted to dispute the rosy picture of the city being marketed by the promoters. She looked right into the eyes of council members, her voice rasping and full of invective. "I am deeply disturbed by the conference... You claim you do a good job," she said with a menacing sneer. "Let's look at me," and she was off on an account of being harassed and terrorized by crime and criminals. Who were these criminals? "Police and mental health criminals who collaborated with special interests," she claimed. She named the officers responsible for her arrest and noted that they were still in the police force. Two had risen in rank.[3]

What to do about Mrs. Nguyen confounded me. I wanted to tell her to sit down and shut up, but that would not be gracious. Besides, she had her right to speak like everyone else. She also had moments of acute insight. The advice of the city attorney was to allow her to speak only on matters over which the city had some control, but she was slippery. During a citizen comment period, she announced that she had written to the San Joaquin County Grand Jury to request the investigation of fund mismanagement in the Stockton Unified School District. I interrupted her, saying she should not speak about an item over which the city had no jurisdiction. "You do [have jurisdiction]," she responded in a clipped, authoritative voice. SUSD was in the city after all, and it had a serious impact, even if it was administered independently. One had to acknowledge her common sense on that point. The budget, she said, showed a surplus, yet the SUSD administrators complained about a deficit. She called for the resignation of the entire administrative staff of the Stockton Unified School District.[4]

At times she sounded unbalanced, as when she appeared before the council suffering from shortness of breath and extreme exhaustion. "Last night, no, the night before last night, they turned my watch one hour late so that I would not be on time yesterday. This morning when I opened my eyes in the parking lot behind Lyons, I remembered it was the day they forced me out of my house. The buttons on my coat were opened and unbuttoned." Holding up her hands, she said, "Twice they cut two of my fingernails." She continued with a rehash of the old incident and concluded, "You, Mayor Joan Darrah, you are heading the crime committee. I hold you responsible for crime and criminals condoned and protected in the city police and the county mental health departments. They have ruined me completely. I stand here trembling because I am sick. Yes, no job, no home, nothing."[5]

As the months went by, Mrs. Nguyen spoke out even more, especially on such issues as the homeless, the actions of the police department, and low-income housing. In addition to the five minutes allowed her under citizens' comments, there would be seven or eight further items on the agenda on which she wished to speak. Many of them were on the "consent calendar." These are items on which the city staff anticipates no discussion or controversy whatever. Not so with Mrs. Nguyen present. She took them off the consent calendar and then would speak about them as they came up. After cursory attention to the issue purportedly under discussion, she would launch into her tirade about police abuse, frequently reverting to her own experience in the spring of 1989.

Frustrated as I was over her insults and interruptions, I could not silence her. My job was to control her. The business of the city had go forward; the council meetings needed to proceed efficiently. I appealed again to the city attorney, Tom Harris, for help. His only advice was that I had to keep her on track. One evening, when the question of whether "community service officers" (auxiliary police personnel) should be allowed to give parking tickets arose, Mrs. Nguyen defeated Harris's policy suggestion.

As it happened, she had received a number of parking tickets. She viewed this as an instance of police harassment, prompted, she said, by her having criticized the police department in public. When I interrupted her to clarify the issue—doing my best to keep her on track—she grabbed her five parking tickets off the podium, waved them in the air, and shouted, "They use parking tickets as punishment against people who criticize the police." Again, I interrupted her and restated the issue, namely the role of community service officers. She shouted back that she had five tickets and no money. The tickets would increase to thirty-five dollars each, and if she did not pay she would go to jail. When I reminded her again, she reiterated, "I need to tell you the problem. Parking tickets are used as retaliation on people who criticize the police." Trying to clarify her argument once more, I said, "So, you are saying we need to hire the right kind of person to enforce our parking laws." She agreed, noting that you need the person on top to hire the right people. Then she started in again on her April 1989 experience. "That is not the issue," I said." Yes it is," she screamed.[6]

Her harangues exasperated some people who watched the council meetings on the local cable channel. My campaign chair, Liz Rea, asked, "Isn't there anything you can do about Mrs. Nguyen?" Again, I turned to the city attorney for more guidance and this time he came up with the five-minute rule. I could limit her time to five minutes, but I would have to limit every other speaker's time on the same issue as well. On one occasion, in June of 1990, when the important issue of the city budget came before the council, I did limit everybody's speaking time to five minutes. A well-known political activist yelled that this was the most unfair thing he had ever seen in government.

I wanted to find a way to allow Mrs. Nguyen basic citizen's rights and at the same time to ensure that the people's business was being conducted in an orderly way. Especially given my political inexperience, I needed more and better advice from the city attorney than I received. I should have demanded that he find a city code or write one that could help control her. Only two years later did he discover a passage in one of the municipal codes that indicated that a person could be sent out of the council chamber if he or she became "boisterous," a mild word indeed for Mrs. Nguyen's tirades. The only requirement was that I give her a warning before asking her to sit down or to leave the chamber. Had I known of this provision from the start, Mrs. Nguyen would not have taken council time nor abused our patience to the extent she did.

The other point the city attorney made repeatedly was that a lawyer could take up Mrs. Nguyen's case. He could argue that her civil rights had been violated, charge the city with unfair treatment, and sue for damages. To me, the thought of the city's having to pay cash damages to Mrs. Nguyen, who had so abused her right to speak, was outrageous. That was the other reason that I did not take stronger action to suppress her outbursts. I sure did not want a lawsuit.

After about three years, Mrs. Nguyen began to develop physical disorders. She would talk about our poisoning the air so that she could not breathe. She described bruises around her shoulders and her back. She would stretch out her arms and ask us to look at her injuries. In fact, she volunteered to lift her shirt to show them to us, and I felt awkward explaining to her that such exposure was inappropriate. She used to be very healthy, she claimed, but now she was a broken and old woman because of us. "Shame, shame on you," she would shout, as I urged her to wrap it up and take her seat.

I contacted the head of the county's mental health department because I believed that serious harm could come to Mrs. Nguyen if she was left on the streets. The mental health director and her assistant met with me several times and explained that under the law they could not incarcerate a person against her will. There was not sufficient evidence to show that Mrs. Nguyen was harmful to herself or to others, the criteria for involuntary institutionalization. They did, however, give me some further insight into the possible workings of Mrs. Nguyen's mind when they suggested that a person with a mental disorder could often derive a lot of energy from it. It became a sort of high. If such a person took medication, she often became calm and reasonable, but she lost the excitement and the energy that the disorder provided. Hence, like many mental patients, Mrs. Nguyen did not stay on her medication. They felt that if she were locked up, medicated, and then evaluated, she would be a very credible witness in court and would probably get herself out again in short order. At that time there was an attorney in the public defender's office who had a record of persuading judges and juries to let mental patients return to the streets. Once again, I was stymied.

I got much harder on Mrs. Nguyen at the council meeting just after my mother, who was dying of cancer, moved to Stockton. All at once my genteel persona vanished. In my grief over my mom, I lost patience with Mrs. Nguyen's crap. At the beginning of one meeting, she violated the rule of making announcements only concerning upcoming events. Without warning, I turned off her microphone. When she persisted, I said, "You need to sit down." She refused. Enforcing the provision barring boisterous behavior, I said that she could not speak any more that evening. She started yelling. Looking to the back of the room at the two Stockton police officers who routinely staffed meetings, I said, for the first time in four years of tolerating her harangues, "Officers, will you please have Mrs. Nguyen leave the council chamber." They came forward to the front row, where Mrs. Nguyen always sat, and helped her gather up her considerable paraphernalia—her shopping cart with clothes and food and books and papers—and led her out of the chamber. She shouted, "That woman is a law and crime violator." However, being escorted out by the police restrained her wild behavior. Everyone was delighted.[7]

I was not the only one who got tough with her. In early 1996 the chairman of the board of supervisors, George Barber, shouted at Mrs. Nguyen, kicked her out of the chambers, and told her to go back where she came from. This outburst caused an uproar. Representatives of several community organizations, including the Asian Advisory Committee, came before the board of supervisors and demanded that Barber make an apology. However, having received some three hundred calls of praise from the community, he never apologized.

Mrs. Nguyen started living in the Tuxedo Street Post Office as of early 1995, when she seemed to have lost the use of her car. A few times she came to council meetings with bruises on her face. There was some speculation that she had been sleeping on the high tables that are provided at post offices and had fallen off. When patrons came in at night to use the post office, she was there and she spoke to them. For a while the post office tried barring the door, but then customers complained that they could not get their mail at night, so the doors were left open. On one or two occasions, Mrs. Nguyen herself barred the door. Once during the day, when I went by that post office, a clerk complained, "In the morning there are cups of urine around the ledges of the post office. It's disgusting." I agreed, though admittedly most homeless people are not that tidy.

Finally, Mrs. Nguyen went too far. In September of 1996, three months before the end of my term, I received a letter from an eighty-four-year-old woman saying that Mrs. Nguyen had physically attacked and verbally assaulted her at the Tuxedo Street Post Office. I turned that letter over to the police. Even though Mrs. Nguyen was present for my final council meeting in December, doing the same old tricks of taking items off the agenda and blasting the council during citizens' comments and screaming, "Shame, shame on you, Mayor Darrah and council," soon thereafter she was arrested and held for observation. She was found guilty of assault and of disturbing the peace and was sentenced to confinement for sixty days.

The new mayor and council that took office in January 1997 had a short respite while Mrs. Nguyen was doing her time. But sure enough, once back on the outside, she returned to city hall. Again, she took items off the consent calendar; again, she took up her harangue. Fed up with her disturbances, the new council adopted an ordinance banning speech by anyone who "is unduly repetitious or engages in extended discussion of irrelevancies." The ACLU immediately objected that the new ordinance "leaned too far in squelching speech."

In February 1999, two years after I left office, Mrs. Nguyen's brother, Hoang Nguyen, came to Stockton to collect his long lost sister and take her back to San Jose. He claimed he had tried for many years to find her but could not. An article written by *The Record* librarian for the *Mercury Viet* newspaper had finally tipped him off to her whereabouts. Taking her leave of Stockton, Mrs. Nguyen warned that she would continue to watch "local criminal animals" and might return one day. Meanwhile, she was keeping an eye on all the folks from San Joaquin County to the White House. On the day of Mrs. Nguyen's departure, Public Defender Elaine Swartzenberg told *The Record* "Nguyen was perfectly adapted to street life and deserved to be left alone."[8] There was more than a grain of truth in that statement. As of this writing, Mrs. Nguyen is back in town, and back at the podium, but thanks to the new ordinance regulating disruptive behavior, the chamber is a more orderly place these days.

Though long gone from the mayor's office, I am occasionally asked about Mrs. Nguyen. "That little Asian woman used to really get to you, didn't she?" She irritated some, but for others she was a source of amusement, much as Ralph White had been in the old days. Some people actually enjoyed the drama that Mrs. Nguyen created, especially the personal conflict with me. I coddled her excessively, especially in the early years, and she took advantage of it. That ended when I stopped being Ms. Gracious and when I finally was given the right legal tools to control her.

The Agenda: Crime and Drugs

Cleveland School: A Defining Moment

It was in August of 1989 that I had Joe Shumate of San Francisco conduct a poll to show my potential as a mayoral candidate and to identify issues of foremost concern to the voters. His results, as I have said, were dramatic. By far the most important issue for residents of Stockton in the summer of 1989 was crime, with drugs a close, and closely related, second. I wrote my campaign literature to stress those topics and I spoke about them at every opportunity. Once I was in office, they were my top priority.

At this time, many American cities were experiencing problems with crime and drugs that approached crisis proportions, yet in Stockton the distress was even more acute than elsewhere because in January 1989, six months before the Shumate poll, there had been a horrifying "massacre" at a public elementary school here. The Cleveland School shooting made national headlines for days. Although many Americans were waking up to stories of violence in the papers and on television in those days, Stockton felt itself to be in a special position. Dating back to the 1930s and off and on since then, Stockton had been known as "a wide-open city," and this reputation continued to be a sore point for many of us. The consciousness of this past, together with the recent spectacular disaster at Cleveland School, made for a deep pessimism in the minds of Stocktonians, many of whom felt that nothing could be done about these matters, a feeling that in itself became a serious obstacle to change. It was against this background of actual violence, Stockton's legacy as being "wide-open city," and the continuing popular perception of an intractable crime problem that my administration set to work to change things. But first, here is the story of Cleveland School.

"The laughter and frivolity of lunchtime recess turned into a horrifying nightmare of terror and death Tuesday when a heavily armed gunman shot and killed five children and wounded 30 others at Stockton's Cleveland Elementary School. The tragedy is thought to be the worst of its kind in California history and one of the nation's worst ever."[1] Patrick Edward Purdy, a twenty-six-year-old loner with a criminal record, but with no felony conviction that would have prevented him from buying a gun, entered the school yard and started spraying bullets into a crowd of first, second and third graders with an AK-47 that had been adapted from a semiautomatic to a fully automatic rifle.

Shortly before he entered the school yard, he had loaded his car with explosives timed to blow up at the moment he started firing, an apparent diversionary tactic that suggested careful planning. Leaving the bleeding bodies on the paved playground where they had fallen, Purdy then pulled out a pistol, which he had bought less than three weeks earlier in Stockton, and killed himself. As "hundreds of people converged on the school...it became a scene of bedlam, death, hysteria, and the desperate efficiency of rescuers," a scene made more chaotic by the presence of many television camera crews, in addition to the medical helicopters, ambulances, fire trucks, and police vehicles.[2] All of Stockton went into shock.

Two days later, when the school reopened, buses competed for space with television trucks. The shooting had become a national media event, and of course a major story all over Northern California. Because the school's population was 71 percent Southeast Asian, there was tentative speculation at the time that Purdy may have had a racist motive, but no evidence was ever found to support that theory. He had himself attended the school twenty years before, but that fact led nowhere as well. He had also been described in a psychiatric report of April 1987 as "a danger to his health and others."[3] People here had no answers. The whole thing was as baffling as it was devastating. Speaking to *The Record* three days after the event, the Stockton police chief, Jack Calkins, said of Purdy, "He had a problem with alcohol, a problem with marijuana and a distinct dislike for everybody—not a particular race, all of them."[4]

In response to the Cleveland shootings, the Stockton City Council passed the first ban on assault weapons of any city in the country. This was far from an easy thing to do. The night the council discussed it, a large and insistent group of NRA members and supporters lined up to speak against the ban; yet the council adopted it unanimously. The Stockton ordinance was followed by a state ban and ultimately a national ban on the kind of assault weapons that this madman had used. The community raised over $100,000, which became a college scholarship fund for the victims' siblings, money that Mayor Barbara Fass successfully protected against later pressure to use it for other projects. In spite of these responsible actions on the part of city government and the public, the story made Stockton infamous for the degree of violence alone. The sad and less marketable truth was that we had a crime problem like any other city. An even sadder truth was that we ourselves believed we had a much worse problem than the other cities, that somehow Stockton was an especially seedy, crime-ridden and lawless place.

An essay-length article in the *Los Angeles Times* in the mid-1980s entitled "Stockton: An Inferiority Complex on a Rampage" described Stockton's image problem with considerable amusement. It noted, for example, that the antics of the city council ranged from the merely silly and incompetent to the sensational: silly in that the members are "a bunch of buffoons" who "might go on for 45 minutes about whether they're going to have a ten-minute recess;" sensational in the case of former Mayor Randy Ronk, who admitted to falsifying travel vouchers "only to recoup money that he had spent during a secret investigation into alleged City Hall corruption that was never proved." The *Los Angeles Times* writer noted that Stockton had an exceptionally high unemployment rate and "a city crime rate that is fourth highest in the state." Claiming that Stockton sleaze went way back, the article reported that, as Stockton grew in the 1930s, it boasted not only "magnificent buildings such as the Hotel Stockton," but also "one of the biggest, toughest, most wide-open Skid Rows in the West."[5]

Even by the late 1990s, the *San Francisco Chronicle* could not resist pointing to the leaden lining in Stockton's cloud of success. "Stockton Strikes Gold," read the headline of July 18, 1998; the subhead read "Merchants, Residents Delighted to Host 49ers."[6] The front-page story glowed with enthusiasm over the arrival of the San Francisco football team at its new summer training camp at the University of the Pacific in Stockton. It glowed, that is, except for the final paragraph of the story, in which the writer abruptly changed his tune: "The one glitch on Stockton's resume, although everyone here rejects it, might be the issue of crime. This reputation seems to have taken root since a gunman opened fire with an AK-47 assault rifle on a school yard full of children in 1989." This was a reputation that has dogged the city for many years.

Even *The Record* sounded the same note in the summer of 1998. Announcing a $38 million contract for a new multiplex cinema and the restoration and renovation of the Hotel Stockton, a wonderful piece of news for the city, the paper quoted the familiar prophet of doom, in this instance a man named Cudney: "It [the movie house] will be just another waterfront derelict like downtown Stockton... Put it under the freeway. Nobody's going to go to it anyway.... Who's going to come downtown to see a show?"[7] By the summer of 1998, this man sounded like an old grump whose knee-jerk pessimism was out of step with the growth in public confidence, but that is a measure of how much things had changed in the decade since I took office in 1990. Earlier, this sourpuss would have sounded like the voice of common sense.

Police Funding Committee: A Popular Tax Increase

As I have mentioned, the polling results from my first campaign, in the summer of 1989, had shown that crime needed to be the next mayor's top priority. Shortly after I took office, I paid a visit to Jack Calkins, the handsome, articulate young lieutenant whom I had first met in 1972 while I was doing the evaluation of the neighborhood police facility project. He was now the Stockton chief of police. We talked about the city's crime problem and how it might be addressed.

The police department's current difficulties, he told me, had begun two years earlier when a hiring freeze was imposed. In 1987, in order to cover a shortfall, the city transferred $750,000 from the capital improvement budget to the operating budget. The following year, to avoid a repetition of this misfortune and to find ways in which the city could save money, the city council ordered an efficiency study by the consulting firm of Cresaps, McCormick, & Piaget. Cresaps suggested a freeze on the hiring of police officers and fire fighters. At the council meeting following the release of the Cresaps report, Mayor Barbara Fass had to fight to keep control of angry public safety officers. After a stormy, confrontational session in which the most powerful unions in the city raged against the Cresaps report, the council voted to approve its recommendations, including the freeze.

Calkins told me that the hiring freeze, which had resulted in a one- to two-million dollar reduction in spending, had been hard on the force. In 1986, there were 268 sworn officers. By 1989 there were only 245, a ratio of 1.2 officers per thousand persons, which he thought too low for safety. In May 1989, the department hired one officer, the first in twenty-seven months. Although the city manager, then Alan Harvey, had authorized additional officers in the budget, he had not provided funding for them and so, of course, none were hired. In response to my questions about what could be done about the crime problem, Calkins assured me that no new programs, such as community-oriented policing, bike patrols and walking beats, could be instituted without additional officers. Police were already struggling to answer calls for service.

At the second meeting of the council after I took office, I proposed the creation of a police funding committee. In addition to the Cleveland School shooting, the recent fatal beating of a police sergeant and the shooting the year before of two deputy sheriffs underscored the need for more sworn officers. Having done some research, I was able to point out that Stockton was forty-two officers below the state average for cities its size, while drug dealing and violent crimes had risen in recent years. "What kind of safety is this for the officers? What kind of safety is this for the citizenry?" I asked.[1]

My intention was to appoint the committee myself, but council members Panizza and Minnick recommended that each of the seven members of the council appoint one person. This was a good idea, and it helped assure council support for the committee's final recommendations. The committee chairman, one of the best appointments I made as mayor, was Michael Heffernan, a local mortician with a winning personality whose business was located downtown and who thus knew more than most about crime in that area. One afternoon, he walked me around his neighborhood, pointing out the drug users and the boarded-up shacks where they hung out. Chuck Bott, a former mayor and council member who understood municipal finance, was another good appointment. I served on the committee, as did Sylvia Minnick, the member for the downtown district.

The committee gathered a lot of information on the police department's current staffing, projected needs, and job performance and then studied ways by which an increase in the number of officers might be financed. The chairman was a genius at keeping us together and on track. We met weekly for five months (for something like five hundred hours altogether!) At the council meeting of June 4, 1990, we presented our three-part recommendation:

- Hire 62 more police officers over the next three years at a rate of about 20 per year;
- raise the city's 6 percent utility tax to the level of 8 percent by 1993–94 (an immediate increase of 0.5 percent to be followed by .75 percent increases in the next two years);
- use the hotel/motel tax revenues of $484,000 over the next three years to buy and upgrade equipment.

The tax increase was the key recommendation, and only a newly elected city council still on a honeymoon in a city with a pervasive crime problem could ever have put it through. An alternative to council action would have been a special ballot measure to obtain voter approval of the tax, but this would have required a two-thirds majority. It could have taken two or three elections to prevail, and the need for additional officers was immediate. As committee member Chuck Bott said to the newspaper, "When you get down to it, there is no other source of revenue that is available to the city that could implement the program right now."[2]

For adopting this tax increase to fund the hiring of additional police, the council received its best editorial support in all the years I was mayor: "Council Gets A+ on Adding Police."[3] When I left office, the valedictory editorial noted that the real power of the mayor lay in persuasion and consensus building between the council members themselves and within the community at large. Citing the establishment of the police funding committee as an exercise of that power, *The Record* called it one of my lasting legacies to the city. Indeed, this action was pivotal to Stockton's ability to confront its crime problem. Our sworn personnel increased from 254 in 1989–1990 to 308 in 1991–1992, with an additional twenty-two scheduled to be hired in 1992–1993. Eight more officers identified specifically for the downtown area were paid for from reductions in costs elsewhere and from other general revenue sources.

The new recruitment and hiring plan at the police department enabled the city to put walking beats and bike patrols downtown, to institute community policing, and to adopt the very successful Safe Stockton, a comprehensive anti-crime program, which included putting police officers in the schools. The result was a dramatic decrease in crime over a four-year period (1990–1994). This decrease, especially striking in the designated Safe Neighborhoods, in turn legitimized the increased budget allocation to the police. In 1990, the council spent 57 percent of its operating budget on public safety (police and fire). By 1996, we were spending 66 percent, with the police department's receiving 80 percent of the additional funding. Chief Calkins wrote to me in early November 1990 to thank me for my efforts on behalf of the Stockton police department: "You assumed responsibility for what most people perceive as an almost unattainable task. Although many would see it as support of the Police Department, and I agree it was that, most importantly, I think it was support of this community.... We truly appreciate everything you have done."[4]

I kept that commitment to public safety throughout my seven years in office, and I believe it was the most important and successful commitment I made as a politician. I listened to the citizens of Stockton, took action on their demands, and gave them what they wanted. In all my campaign material, when I ran for reelection in 1992, I noted the increase in police personnel and the Safe Stockton program. I sent an eight-by eleven-inch endorsement card, featuring a photo of former Police Chief Jack Calkins and myself, to 64,000 households. The card quoted Chief Calkins, "Fighting crime is Joan Darrah's #1 priority.... She deserves your support on November 3."

It would be some time, however, before polls registered a increased sense of personal safety on the part of the citizenry. In fact, the polls I conducted for my reelection campaign in 1992 showed that people still put crime and public safety at the top of their list of concerns. What I think did happen in 1990, with the police funding committee and the new programs mounted by the department, was that people saw me as aware of the crime problem and working to solve it, but for them to feel personally safer would take more time, more substantial programs, and more work by city government.

STAND and "A Mayor Who Is Not Afraid to Make House Calls"

At a meeting of the U.S. Conference of Mayors in January 1991, I met President Bush's assistant for municipal affairs, a man who had once been a city mayor and who claimed that the way to get reelected was to go to people's houses. When he ran for reelection himself, he had taken out a huge ad in the local paper saying, "I'm a mayor who isn't afraid to make house calls," and he listed the houses he had visited during his term. It sounded like the sort of thing I could do too. I got my chance two months later when a woman named Mary Delgado telephoned me in the mayor's office. She was distraught about the drug problem in her neighborhood. She had called other city departments to no avail; I was her last resort. She wanted me to come to her house.

Mary lived on Sixth Street, just south of the fairgrounds, a part of town I rarely even drove through. Not only was it not on my regular route, it was dangerous. She was agitated when she opened her door, pleased and surprised that I had come but angry that her street was so out of control. Mary did not mince words. A pretty woman with dark hair and eyes, she spoke directly. "Look," she said, with a mixture of appreciation and impatience, "I like my house and I don't want to move, but living here is almost impossible.... You are the first person who has been willing to come." She then described a truly appalling situation. The Delgados lived at the end of a short street off a major thoroughfare, Airport Way. It was gang territory. She could not drive down her own street without being stopped by crowds, cars, and drug dealers. At night, bedlam ruled. Sounds of gunshots, beatings, and racing stolen cars kept the residents awake. The homes on Sixth Street were turning into crack houses. It was terrible trying to get out to the main street with so many cars and people crowding the street, buying and selling drugs.

Mary described the scene at Garfield School on Sixth Street, two blocks from her house. Garfield was linked with another North Stockton elementary school; Garfield had classes kindergarten through third, while grades four, five and six were bussed to the other school. This meant that the very youngest children were in the midst of a daily drug scene so bad that even those who lived within a block of the school had to be escorted there by their parents; it also meant that children nine to twelve years old were harassed by drug dealers as they waited to board their bus. A heroin syringe was found in the sandbox at Garfield. Mothers were afraid that their children would contact the AIDS virus while playing in the school yard. Across the street were derelict apartment houses with decaying exteriors and debris in the front yards. The addicts who lived in these apartments hung around on the streets buying and selling drugs. Adjacent to Sixth Street was a large city park with a baseball diamond; the whole park had become too dangerous to use.

I felt I had to provide an answer for Mary. This just could not go on. But there was no mechanism in city government, no procedure or program that could respond to a neighborhood besieged. What I fell back on was the power of the group process that I learned in my volunteer days. I said that we should get the neighbors together and discuss the problem. At my own expense, I printed 500 flyers, which Mary delivered to neighbors, announcing the first "town hall meeting" to be held in the auditorium of Garfield School. Forty people showed up: mothers, some with children; school personnel, including teachers and the principal; the owner of the rotting apartment house; and perhaps two police officers. When I asked the residents to describe the problem, there was an avalanche of stories about how destructive and demeaning it was to live in a neighborhood out of control. They vented and I listened, but by the end of the meeting no clear course of action had been identified. They all wanted someone to clean up the neighborhood, and that "someone," they assumed, should be the police.

All I could think of was to have another meeting and bring more city representatives and more council members. Again, Mary and I did the flyers, and this time there were a lot more people, maybe one hundred fifty, occupying the seats in the Garfield School auditorium. There were also school board members, three council members, and representatives from the police department. Once again two hours of angry storytelling ensued concerning the ravages of drugs in that neighborhood. And the thrust was not just about drugs. It was about basic, ordinary safety. The attendees told of cars speeding down Sixth Street where many small children lived. Again, no solution was identified. I excused the police department, saying it was understaffed; officers were doing all they could. And I set up a third meeting.

By a fortunate accident of timing, I had picked up a videotape created in Macon, Florida at the June 1991 meeting of the U.S. Conference of Mayors. In Macon, too, people had been infuriated and overwhelmed by the drug problem. What they did was to rise up, put on hard hats, and hold a march where they carried signs saying they were not going to be controlled by druggies. They proclaimed that they would take charge of their own neighborhood. By a series of actions—people writing down the license numbers of cars whose occupants did drug buys in the neighborhood, lighting up their streets at night, yelling at and harassing the drug dealers, and most of all by simply coming together as a powerful force that was organized and intent upon its objectives, the Macon people got results; they cleaned up their neighborhood. They had enough financial support from businesses to buy their hard hats, but it was the residents who were taking the action, not the police, and certainly not government officials. There was a quality of a vigilante body in what they did.

After the video had been shown, I asked, "All right, who will step forward? Who will organize this neighborhood?" People looked at one another; no one raised a hand. Yet I could feel in the air that they were inspired by Macon's success. Again, I asked for volunteers. Finally Mary stood up, then Virginia and James Gorman, then the Johnsons, and others. In voices that reflected how utterly fed up they were with the whole frightening mess, they got the ball rolling: "All right...OK...I'll help."

A police sergeant named Mike Ries was present that night. He said he had seen neighborhoods in Oakland and San Jose that had organized with the help of the police department and had driven out the drug users. He volunteered to meet with the Sixth Street group. Mary tells the story of first hearing about Ries and thinking, "Oh good, he is Hispanic like me," but he turned out to be blond and blue-eyed, Ries not Ruiz. Mike picked up my tape that night, and I never saw it again. Police departments discourage vigilante groups.

I was not able to attend that first meeting, but I went to the second. In that short time, the group, which now called itself STAND (Stocktonians Taking Action to Neutralize Drugs), was on a roll, so much so that the volunteers did not want me there. I was clearly *persona non grata*. It was their issue now, and they were in charge. As in Macon, they began with a plan to have each person in the neighborhood keep a sheet of paper on which would be recorded the license plate numbers of cars whose drivers were doing drug deals. So intimidated were the residents by the pushers that for a long time they were afraid to call the police department directly to report the numbers. Instead, they called them in to the STAND committee, which in turn called the department. This reporting provided the police with the information they needed to obtain search warrants and make arrests for drug sales. It reduced narcotic transactions in the neighborhood. So did the special police unit assigned to patrol the STAND area each day. The message that was coming across was that the community had to take the leadership and the police would be there to help.

STAND next took on the school district. As with the city, the people at the top, including the superintendent of the Stockton Unified School District, initially brushed off the STAND effort. Determined to be heard, STAND members brought footage they had filmed at Garfield School to a school board meeting. As Mary Delgado described the viewing that night, "You could have heard a pin drop, they were so embarrassed."[1] There were pictures of drinking fountains covered with green mold, of glass and garbage littering the ball field, of pot holes and broken fences and rain coming through the roof of the school library, and of a kitchen stove in the school that was so dirty you would not even want to clean it. School board members also saw ten-, eleven-, and twelve-year-olds being approached by drug pushers as they waited for their bus.

The budget officer for the school district promised that these things would be fixed but he needed time, at least two weeks. When nothing happened during that time period, STAND volunteers got out their cameras again. The repairs swiftly followed. Another action by STAND that came later was a lawsuit against the landlord of a Sixth Street apartment house who refused to evict drug-dealing tenants. STAND won its suit and got a judgment against this man for $120,000, which he appealed. In the meantime he evicted ten families from his building.

STAND was an organization of neighbors working together with several police officers. City government itself could not become involved until we had a new city manager. Alan Harvey, the old city manager, had departed in January 1991, and it took us a year to replace him. After an intensive national search, we appointed Dwane Milnes, who started work in January 1992. A couple of months later STAND contacted my office to request a meeting with me at city hall. Although things were going better, the STAND representatives brought a long list of requests: Street lights should be fixed, street barriers needed to be installed to block drug traffic, and so on. I invited them back and asked Milnes to join us. He took extensive notes during the meeting and promised that a plan would be forthcoming from city government to more adequately meet the needs of this neighborhood. It could not be just the police department and the residents; other departments would have to become involved. It was at this point that city government took its first steps toward creating what became a comprehensive response to citywide crime.

Time dragged on and, although there was a noticeable reduction of crime in the area due to the police sweeps, Milnes had not produced his plan. Meanwhile, my reelection campaign was heating up and poll results indicated that, once again, drugs and crime were the main public concerns. After a frightening showing of only 33 percent support for me in the June primary, my consultant told me bluntly that without a credible plan for meeting the crime problem, I would never be reelected. I went to Milnes and demanded that his office produce a plan for addressing crime in this city, and do it fast.

Meanwhile, STAND served as the model in other neighborhoods that were crying out for help from the city. On a hot summer night in May 1992, I went to a church, Saint George's, in the southeast sector of the city, where I listened to three hundred angry residents who believed that city officials, including the mayor, were unresponsive to their calls for help. "If you don't want to work for us, we'll get somebody in here that does," threatened a lifelong Stockton resident. I responded with uncharacteristic combativeness: "When community members get mad, scream, demand action and don't let up—that's when you get results.... You are going to be cleaning up this neighborhood, and I will be here to help you do it."[2] Just days after the Saint George's meeting, Milnes produced Safe Stockton, a plan that included all the departments of city government, not just the police department. Much of it had been drafted by the deputy city manager, Donna Brown, under whose excellent leadership it eventually was to make a significant impact on many aspects of Stockton's problems with crime.

Safe Stockton had two major components, "Safe Neighborhoods" and "Safe Schools." Initially the STAND and Saint George's areas were identified as the Safe Neighborhoods. They had the all-important ingredient, an organized group of residents who were aggressively working with the police. Extra police were assigned to these neighborhoods with a mandate to eliminate the blatant drug activities. Arrests were made whenever possible, and a zero-tolerance policy resulted in hundreds of citations for violations, including loitering, drinking in public, curfew violation, trespassing, and traffic violations.

An interdepartmental committee from city hall, which included representatives from all city departments, met monthly to address complaints.

The public works department fixed broken street barriers, repaired street lights, and removed graffiti. The community development department sent code enforcement officers to haul away junk cars, garbage, and debris. Each of the two neighborhoods was assigned a senior community service officer who acted as the liaison between the police department and the neighborhood. The program was soon expanded to include two more neighborhoods.

Safe Schools, the second part of Milnes's plan, assigned uniformed police, called "school resource officers," to several of the most troubled schools. They served as mentors and teachers of the DARE classes, and they made home visits and patrolled the neighborhoods around the schools in the mornings and when school let out in the afternoon. An ambitious after-school recreation program was also developed at several Stockton schools.

Statistics were kept. Every year there were marked decreases in crime in the Safe Neighborhoods: in the first year, an 11.7 percent decrease; the second year, a 16.2 percent decrease; and in the third year, a 24.8 percent decrease. By the time the program had been in operation for six years, there had been a 71 percent decrease in crime.

Even more important, the members of these neighborhoods had become "empowered." They initiated employment programs for youth. They raised funds to put up lights on the exteriors of homes of the elderly. Several hundred residents regularly held huge barbecues in the park, where prizes were given out, games were played, and the police and fire departments put on demonstrations. Funding for home renovations in these areas was made available by the city's housing and redevelopment department, which allocated a portion of its HUD funds for the purpose.

All of this activity operated under the heading of "community policing" at its most basic level. The California Department of Health Services recognized Safe Stockton with the prestigious California Healthy Cities Project Special Achievement Award only three years after the plan was initiated. And when the Academy for Educational Development, a unit of the U.S. Information Agency, made a short list of U.S. cities for visits by delegates from over twenty foreign countries who were to study American drug control programs, Stockton was frequently on the itinerary.

In early 1991, when Mary Delgado called me to ask for help in her neighborhood, she had been able to find no one in city government willing to respond to her calls for help. By August 1994, Stockton City Hall had become such an authority on these problems that the city, under the sponsorship of the League of California Cities, put on a two-day Safe Cities Conference to show other cities how to combat crime and clean up neighborhoods. The celebrated Molly Wetzel, an Oakland, California, activist who teaches residents how to bring suits against corrupt land-lords, praised the city for encouraging neighborhood activism and other progressive methods of preventing crime. "I consider Stockton one of the more advanced community-policing programs I've experienced, within California and the nation," Wetzel told *The Record.*[3]

Four years later, *The Record* applauded STAND for broadening its role into that of a nonprofit housing developer, buying and renovating rundown houses and then assisting local residents to obtain the funds to purchase them. "STAND should be a model for all of San Joaquin County," *The Record* editorialized.[4] Discussing the success of this renovation and rental program, Mary Delgado stressed the benefits to the neighbors of having family units move in; the program in fact requires that the rental family group have at least two adults and two children. Finally, STAND persuaded city hall to change the ordinance governing noise at outdoor concerts, such as those at the nearby fairgrounds. Nowadays, the band moves indoors after 10 P.M.

Of my achievements as mayor, one of those I feel best about is the reduction of crime. The city had to shuck its crime-ridden reputation in order to attract business and jobs, which were desperately needed. The council had to bite the bullet and spend money. To get more police offic-ers, we needed to raise city taxes. We also needed to keep crime reduc-tion as a top priority, which we did. Stockton was fortunate to have a city manager with vision, one who appointed a police chief committed to community policing concepts, and a deputy city manager who could de-sign and implement a plan that worked, and that even received state and local awards. We had a city newspaper that printed success stories, and there were many of them. And we had neighborhood leaders who were determined and courageous. Gloria Nomura from Saint George's received the California State Crime Prevention Volunteer of the Year Award in 1994. Two years later she was elected to the Stockton City Council.

Looking back, I am proud that I made that first house call. At least in the case of STAND, it created a momentum that eventually gave strength and resolve to the neighborhood and instilled the belief, for the first time, that the people themselves might be able to make things better in their own lives. A Garfield school counselor wrote me, saying "Never have we had such a large number of parents/neighbors and such an influential panel here before.... The people are organizing and for the first time [are] willing to risk their lives for the improvement of the neighborhood.... Never since my experience in the U.S. Army have I seen people make such a serious commitment."[5] Even though the area affected by the efforts of STAND has seen a dramatic decrease in major crimes, the problems that it and the Saint George's group are dealing with will likely never be resolved once and for all. They will continue, and so must our response. Mary Delgado is still making phone calls to city hall.

A Visit to Taylor School: Follow-up to a Drive-by Shooting

At 4:15 on the afternoon of August 30, 1994, Nicole Martinez, age thirteen, was riding with her boyfriend and her older sister in a car owned by Nicole's family. Their car was stopped at an intersection when two young men in another car drove up beside it and asked to speak to Nicole. Her boyfriend said, "No." The two cars pulled away from the light together and several blocks later one of the boys in the other car, aiming for the boyfriend, missed him and shot Nicole in the head. The second car fled and Nicole's boyfriend called an ambulance. When Nicole went into surgery less than three hours later, her doctors expected that if she lived at all she would have major brain damage and be blind. Ralph William Perez, age fourteen, admitted to the shooting, in which he used a gun his mother had acquired after someone shot at her two months earlier. Perez was tried as a juvenile and convicted of attempted second-degree murder.

The press at the time saw the shooting as "the latest incident in a continuing escalation of youth violence throughout San Joaquin County." The former director of the Stockton Youth Gang and Drug Prevention Program spoke for many people when he said, "We've gotten to the point where people can't ride in their cars and avoid [violence]. Violence in our city seems to be on the rise. I think it's in direct relationship to the reduction in gang-prevention programs." People speculated about the possible connection between the shooting and drug-related gang activity, but the newspaper the day after reported that "police...don't believe the shooting was gang-related."[1]

It was, however, an obvious example of violence by and against kids. "For Stockton's young" wrote Mike Fitzgerald in *The Record* two days after the shooting, "the fear of random or senseless violence has become part of growing up. They fear guns; they dread being around shoot-outs or drive-bys, the stray shot, the ricochet." He quoted young people ranging from ages ten to fourteen who had seen so much gun violence that they had become afraid of being shot in their own bedrooms, not to mention on the street or in a car. Certain houses were particularly dangerous, they told him. This feeling existed even in the affluent neighborhoods where his readers might think children feel safe, Fitzgerald was told by a ten-year-old, "When I'm outside playing I'm always worrying 'cuz I hear this is a bad place and I'm afraid I might get shot outside.... It's happening everywhere."[2]

A teacher from Taylor Elementary School, Lori Sartawi, called my office to say that her fifth-graders were extremely upset about Nicole's shooting. Although they did not know her, they had tried to contact her in the hospital, hoping they could help, but Nicole was still in critical condition. The shooting unnerved and alarmed them. It was just like what they experienced in their own lives. It made them feel confused and helpless. They wanted to talk to the mayor.

I went to the Taylor School to meet with these children. The first thing I saw as I entered their classroom were big, colored sheets of paper, two-feet by three-feet, on which ten of the twenty-five children in the class had related instances of violence in their own families. Each child had signed his or her statement and taped it up on the wall:

My cousin was with his friends. Without warning, he was shot. —*James C.*

My uncle was shot in the chest. He wasn't doing anything wrong. —*Sona*

My dad and uncle were attending a birthday party. One was shot in the chest and the other was shot in the leg. —*Nicole*

My cousin was in his car at the stoplight. The car near them opened fire. My cousin died. —*Jessica*

When my uncle was at a birthday party, he was shot in the chest. —*Noemi*

My cousin was walking to his car. Quickly a car passed. My cousin was shot in the head. —*Shiro*

When my brother was at a party in Quail Lakes he was shot in the leg. —*Jonfred*

My brother's best friend was shot in the back. He wasn't doing anything wrong. —*James H.*

When I was two years old my father was killed in a drive-by in Stockton. —*Lawane*

My sister's friend was at a house. A stranger entered the house. She was stabbed in the chest. —*Audrey*

Then I was seated on a chair. The children knelt on the floor in a semicircle around me, looking up with expectant, trusting eyes. One boy carried in a beautiful, yellow chrysanthemum and gave it to me. The teacher said, "You are our only hope." I wanted to say something that would be a help, but I wanted it to be honest and to respect the children's sadness. They saw me as a person who might make things better—for Nicole, for themselves. I wanted to have an answer for them. If only I could have said that we had tough and effective programs that would wipe out gun violence. But we did not, so all I could do was identify with their sadness. "I feel very sorry about Nicole, too," I said, and then I promised to work every day to make Stockton a safer city.

At the moment, my words seemed like a weak, inadequate response to a profound request. Listening to the children at Taylor that morning, I seemed to hear them say that, in their world, there was very little protection for the innocent, very little social control. However, they were pleased that the mayor had come to their school and that she seemed to care what happened to them and to Nicole.

Another answer to the children's distress that day came from Officer Larry Roberson, a police officer who was assigned to Taylor School as a school resource officer (SRO). He told me: "What I am doing is a big part of the answer.... I connect to these children and teach them how to live safer lives." This thoughtful, sensitive man was one of several officers who were assigned to the schools of Stockton to be friends, mentors, resource officers, and teachers of a series of courses on anti-drug and anti-gang activity. It was gratifying to have him there at that moment.

My visit to Taylor School that day may have helped those children to feel that their lives and their fears mattered to the mayor, and thus to the powerful people of the adult world. The experience certainly had a profound effect on me. Face to face with those kids, almost half of whom told of violence in their immediate families, I felt their pain in a way one never does reading a story in the paper. Their language—"My uncle was shot in the chest," "The car near them opened fire. My cousin died"—is direct and moving, utterly different from the way politicians and professionals talk about "society's ills."

After that day I became a vocal advocate for programs to reduce the violence in these kids' lives, especially the expensive School Resource Officers program which I championed at council meetings, at organizations, and at meetings in other cities. I always voted to allocate funding for these officers, which was considerable, and which increased as more officers were placed in more schools. The hope is that these children, as adults, will join their neighbors and community police officers to make their neighborhoods safer.

Five years after that fateful August afternoon, *The Record* came out with a long article on Nicole.[3] She was alive, her brain was fine, and although a bullet remained lodged in her skull, her sight had returned and she had become an evangelist carrying a message to young people to stay away from gangs and drugs. Nicole's story, which of course she could not tell at the time she was shot, was that of a kid who grew up in the company of addicted parents and their friends. Nicole's mother was one of the drug customers of Helen Perez, the aunt of Ralph Perez, the gunman who had shot Nicole.

Nicole and her friends all belonged to gangs—her gang lived on the south side of town, their rivals on the north and west side. She would gladly have given her life, she said, for the honor of her gang. But the experience of being shot and nearly left blind for life had opened her eyes. She was now a member of the Victory Outreach Church. Her life and sight had been spared, she thought, because God had work for her to do warning kids away from drugs and gangs, kids just like those in Taylor school that morning who, unless someone led them away from it, would themselves be involved with the gangs within a few years. Nicole eventually married a young man from the rival gang and both had become passionate missionaries to the young people in Stockton. At the time of this writing, Ralph Perez, at age nineteen, is about to get out of jail. He too is a changed person who plans to devote himself to helping young kids.

Taylor School is less than a mile away from Garfield School, down the street from the home of Mary Delgado, the woman who started

STAND. Nicole grew up in a similarly dangerous neighborhood. Now Nicole has joined the ranks of citizen activists. One can only hope that she will succeed in persuading children and teenagers that the protection that gangs offer is really no protection at all and that their well-being lies elsewhere.

Downtown Cleanup: Early Days

"The downtown area is dead, and Stockton needs to wake up to that fact." This statement, rumored to have been made by one of Stockton's major developers, conveyed a widespread public attitude: downtown was not only dead, but it deserved to die because it was just one big, dirty crime scene. At the time I took office, in February 1990, a casual pollster would have heard a version of this view of downtown Stockton from many of residents, especially those who lived in the northern suburbs and never went into the old city center at all.

It would have been hard to exaggerate the need for attention to the downtown area. Crime, drug dealing, vagrancy, loitering and panhandling were common. Stores on the major streets were empty. Office space went begging. There was pervasive decay. The major economic powers of the city, those developers and bank executives who were profiting mightily from suburban residential development, showed no interest in investing in downtown, but only complained about the crime and deterioration that existed there. In truth, it was the extensive development in the outlying parts of the city, which had been going on at a relentless pace since the late 1940s, that was responsible for the decline of the city center. Since that time too, many Stockton politicians who funded their campaigns with contributions from the real estate development industry had been loathe to impose any but the most minimal conditions on this massive suburban growth. They too, in effect, had abandoned the downtown.

In 1990, however, the widespread cynicism began to be offset by a new feeling that things could change. The newly elected city council, with five new members out of seven (of which I was one), was the first council to be elected under the provisions of Measure C. Having been elected in a citywide vote, the council, now made up of citizens whose mandate was to be concerned about the problems of the whole city, could throw the weight of city government into the fight against crime and blight. A huge pent-up popular feeling that the city should "do something" about the problems of the downtown area finally exploded.

The council meeting of April 8, 1991, was the most important ever held, at least during my seven years as mayor, on the subject of Stockton's downtown. The chamber was jam-packed with businessmen, including a number of heavy hitters from key institutions in the area. They came partly in response to an article in *The Record* two days earlier that quoted several respected downtown leaders as saying that dopers and prostitutes were "winning the battle for the streets.... The reason businesses are leaving downtown and abandoning downtown is that it is so nasty down here. People won't come down here to shop. The perception is it is dangerous and nasty—and it is nasty."[1]

Strong language, and the speakers at the meeting were even stronger. They objected to the blight in the streets, to the panhandlers and the winos and drunks who, they explained, were outpatients from the mental hospitals. They protested gang activity and the robbing of old men sitting at bus stops. One speaker said that her company paid armed guards to patrol the areas, and still "they are so brazen they won't leave." A radio station owner talked about blatant drug deals, about people urinating in doorways, and about crime, drugs and vagrancy. With a mixture of anger and despair, the speakers informed us that "nothing has happened to make it better." There were prostitutes and condoms and needles everywhere. The council listened to some pretty graphic stories.

The most stunning news came from the president and publisher of *The Record*. This venerable institution, which had had its editorial offices in downtown Stockton since its founding in 1895, was threatening to move out of the downtown area over the issue of safety. The publisher informed the city council that the paper was "looking for a location that has an environment that is safe for all its employees."[2] We knew that if *The Record* found the downtown unsafe for its employees, no one else could be expected to stay there, much less to move there from elsewhere. Downtown renewal would become all but impossible.

Another theme echoed by the speakers that night was the futility of recent studies concerning downtown problems, studies paid for by taxpayers, the recommendations of which had led to pitifully small improvements. One attorney cited a 1967 study on downtown revitalization and the area at the head of the deep water channel; here we were in 1991 talking about the same problems and coming to the same conclusions and nothing had changed except in the direction of further deterioration. It was apparent that the city planning commission needed to make downtown its top priority. While the city had approved 28,000 units of residential growth in the outlying areas, its priority should have been downtown revitalization.

The president of one of the big banks, a prominent and powerful person in the Stockton business world, joined this chorus of outrage, remarking especially on his concern for the safety of 150 employees who worked at the bank's downtown location. Other speakers sought to persuade the council that what was needed was a coordinated program which would include the city, the police, the county, business, and the courts. More teeth must be put into the laws, and they needed to be enforced. It was common knowledge that if a vagrant or criminal were picked up on a downtown street he would be back on the street again within a few hours. People wanted to see a joint effort between the city and county health services, the California Alcoholic Beverage Control Board, the police and the city manager's office. Finally, the council was asked to provide for ten new officers downtown and two supervising officers, officers who would walk beats and ride bike patrols, and also for a commitment from the city to enforce narcotics abatement. The speakers that night gave the new council an earfull, and they conveyed a great sense of urgency. Businesses would be closing—old, reputable businesses—within the month if immediate action were not taken. It was an intimidating group of presenters.

We appointed a sixteen-member task force to develop a public/private security plan for downtown. The first focus of discussion clearly had to be police presence. Although the council had agreed at the meeting of April 8 to begin immediately to pick up parole violators and to identify bars, hotels and other businesses that were nuisances, *The Record* reiterated the call for more police. To this, the police chief objected that, with the budget in its current state, the police department would have to wait four months, until July, to beef up downtown patrols and make the requested arrests. However, the cry for "Now!" was too loud.

The task force recommended the hiring of eight additional officers and a sergeant at a cost of $500,000. There was such tremendous pressure on the council to make this happen that we took this action without identifying a source of funding. I questioned this course on July 1, when it came before the council. Shouldn't we find out where the money will come from before we proceed? What impact would this expenditure have on the rest of the city departments? My questions were received with sneers from the audience. The council voted for the addition of new officers and then instructed the budget and finance committee to come up with the required half million dollars, which was accomplished by putting a hiring freeze on all other departments and severely clamping down on expenditures for supplies and maintenance. The public response was enthusiastic. *The Record* voiced the opinion that the choice was between biting the bullet now and paying a lot more later to prevent crime, to add police officers, and to make up for lost revenues. "Public safety has to come first, they argued."[3]

Equally responsible for the deteriorating condition of the downtown were the owners of properties who were making a tidy profit on their flophouse tenants. The *status quo* suited the slumlords just fine. Two groups took up the fight against these landlords. SMAC (Stanislaus and Main Action Committee) was led by Tom Migliori, the owner of a cleaning establishment whose family had been in business for almost half a century. One downtown street corner, bounded by Stanislaus and Main streets, had four particularly disreputable hotels. At the Bronx Hotel, a woman who had been smoking cocaine in her room jumped from the window; on another occasion, three people were shot outside the hotel. A hotel clerk had been arrested by undercover officers on charges of receiving payments from prostitutes. When Migliori asked business owners in the area to join him in lawsuits against the four hotels, they all signed on. Another group, SCUMLORDS, filed small claims law suits against the owners of two other hotels. Both of these groups took their cue from a local judge, Rolleen McIlwrath, who had originally told Migliori about Molly Wetzel, the woman from Oakland who had cleared her neighborhood of crack houses by filing small claims actions against them.

"Bronx Hotel SMAC'd with $115,800 Penalty," read *The Record* headline of January 31, 1992. Judge Richard Mallett agreed that the hotel was "a nightmare of drug dealing, prostitution, and public drunkenness as well as robbery, rape and kidnaping" and awarded damages to twenty-one business owners and five employees.[4] The sixteen-page opinion detailed the abuses at the site, including a homemade drug delivery system that sounded like some quaint village device. The dealer, who lived on the second floor, lowered a basket on a string to the sidewalk where a customer filled it with money. The basket was raised to the second floor, the money taken out, the drugs put in, and the basket was lowered to the waiting customer. At first, the judgment was set aside on the condition that the hotel owners take steps to clean up the hotel, but eighteen months later, Judge Frank A. Grande ordered the owners to pay $150,000 to SMAC on the grounds that they had "flagrantly violated the terms of the agreement."[5] A total of $3,100 each was paid out to some thirty business owners in the area. Migliori donated his $3,100 to a drug treatment program. A few others donated to the police bicycle patrol, but most of the recipients kept their money. The rest, some fifty thousand dollars, went to attorneys' fees. The city subsequently bought the Bronx Hotel and remodeled it as a single-room occupancy facility for low-income tenants.

The bike patrol was an instant success. It is hard to describe what a boost it was to see police officers in their helmets and uniforms, short-sleeved shirts and shorts, patrolling the streets of downtown on their bicycles. They had an immediate effect, too, resulting in a 21 percent decrease in crimes against persons in the latter months of 1991, compared to the earlier months of that same year. By 1994, arrests in downtown had dropped by almost one-third. In the central core area, where the major banks and office buildings were located, arrests declined 42 percent between 1990 and the end of 1993. Arrests for vice crimes, mostly prostitution and narcotics, were cut by 70 percent. Tom Migliori noted that "in the thirty years I have been downtown, I have never seen it look so good. The whole picture has improved."[6] In a review of the downtown conditions in March 1998, a police lieutenant was quoted as saying that downtown Stockton had become "astronomically safer" than it had been seven years earlier, in part because of the bike patrols begun in 1991. From 1994 to 1998, serious crime fell 35 percent in and around downtown, compared with an 18 percent drop citywide. Again, the bike units were given credit.

Despite these improvements, basic change occurred slowly. At the behest of the council, Lyn Krieger, an especially effective administrator, was hired by the city to work on downtown problems. She initiated the expansion of the "redevelopment area"[7] to a size that would entitle Stockton to more federal funding. She also coordinated the joint application by the city and the county to give the downtown area an "Enterprise Zone" designation, which we finally received in 1992 after a long and competitive effort. I remember Lyn's wheeling into the council chamber a huge cart load of files and documents that were required for the enterprise zone application. This designation entitled businesses to receive tax incentives that served to stimulate investment.

Lyn also initiated the facade improvement program, and she worked with developers to get tax credits for renovations of the Bronx and Phoenix Hotels, two of the former prostitution and drug hangouts that were on SMAC's list. A major bank, Union Safe Deposit, built new administrative offices in downtown. The Salvation Army constructed the Silver Crest Apartments for senior citizens. A downtown developer renovated an indoor shopping mall. Lyn also was the key staff person for the waterfront renewal project (see "Redesigning Stockton's Waterfront" below). Lyn and her staff worked extensively with a group of citizens on the renovation of the Fox Theater, a beautiful old theater built in 1930 that had fallen into disrepair. Friends of the Fox and city staff coordinated a gala opening in October 1995, featuring stars from Beach Blank Babylon out of San Francisco. Two years later the Fox was drawing hundreds of patrons monthly to downtown.

The Children's Museum was also established and became a major venue for activities for the city and the downtown. A thriving farmers market opened downtown and continues to attract shoppers every Friday afternoon. The Downtown Business Alliance invited national leaders to Stockton to discuss the formation of a business improvement district. Uniformed hospitality guides, who are employees of the alliance, now walk the streets giving directions and providing safety.

Despite all of these successes there were disappointments as well. A major senior housing project fell through when the developers failed to secure tax credits from the state. A sports center/entertainment corporation based in San Jose that had development rights for a ten-acre parcel along the waterfront changed its mind about locating in Stockton. The Pasadena developers for the Hotel Stockton, a magnificent hotel at the head of the channel, were not able to get investors to provide funds for renovation. Blocks and blocks of empty storefronts and graffiti-marred and aging buildings still confronted the casual visitor or would-be investor with a spectacle of neglect.

A particular challenge was the Gateway, the block at the foot of the ramp that leads off the freeway into the city center and the first sight one sees upon entering the downtown area. The area contained three rundown hotels used by druggers and transients. Groups of loiterers and derelicts gathered outside the hotels waiting for drug deals, or just hung around. Potential investors remarked to Lyn Krieger that there was no way they would put a dime into a city where no one had the authority or the interest or the resources to clean up a block like this, particularly when it was just two blocks from the police station. A study by Gruen & Gruen in 1991, commissioned by the private sector, identified this area as the one most in need of cleanup, and in 1992 the council committed itself to doing the job.

As a first step, we declared it a "master development area" so that buildings could be acquired through eminent domain. In closed session the council labored over possible new uses for the site—a visitor center, an office complex, an entertainment facility. None of these ideas was financially feasible, with the only alternative being a big gas station and a fast food outlet, although this required the demolition of both hotels and an adjacent Mexican restaurant, Arroyo's, and moving the hotels' low-income tenants elsewhere. When we began the relocation, the city was hit with two lawsuits, one by the tenants and the other by Arroyo's. We settled the first and won the second. The demolition of buildings, including asbestos removal, caused additional delays. Finally, in the spring of 1999, the wrecking ball came down on the old brick hotels and the restaurant, which have been replaced by a large 76 gas station and a McDonalds. The Gateway project, an attempt to refurbish one city block, is testimony to the exorbitant amount of time, almost a decade, it can take to make change happen in a deteriorated downtown, even when the major policy makers, the city council, and the investors all agree on the preferred outcome.

The sense that the downtown atmosphere was improving was certainly one of the city's proudest accomplishments during my tenure in office. It happened as a result of collaboration between several groups—the council, the city staff, the police, downtown merchants, and hundreds of volunteers. With a very limited amount of federal redevelopment funding available and a recession in the early 1990s that constrained private investment, progress was painfully slow. Yet things would definitely have gotten worse had the business leaders not come to the council that day in April 1991.

Whether it is so in other cities, I cannot say, but in Stockton the one thing that had to change before any large scale, long term improvement could be affected in the downtown area was the public perception that the downtown was dangerous, too dangerous to walk around in, at times too dangerous to drive a car in. The first thing the city council had to do was provide a stronger police presence. Beyond that, there was the issue of funding. Urban renewal on this scale is very expensive. Always there was the hope for a silver bullet, the big investment that would raise the general economy and lift all boats. After 1998, this appeared to be happening when a major private investor committed $38,000,000 for a cineplex in downtown Stockton that included $15,000,000 to renovate the Hotel Stockton. Together with the completion of the Weber Point Events Center, this could have been just the kind of catalyst the city needed to initiate and sustain major revitalization. *The Record* chose to be optimistic: "Indications continue that Downtown Stockton is going to be a happening place in the months ahead."[8] Unfortunately, that particular deal came apart, but others are coming along.

The most telling statement that I know about the importance of downtown renewal came from a man who had been involved in many aspects of civic affairs in Stockton, from the Children's Home and the Boy Scouts and Girl Scouts to the Downtown Business Alliance and the Waterfront Task Force. In a speech accepting the award for "Stocktonian of the Year 1995," Don Geiger said: "I am a strong believer that the downtown is the soul and heart of the city. The vitality of a downtown affects how people in the community view themselves.... Downtowns have an importance far beyond their practical boundaries and physical structures. Cervantes once wrote, 'Every man is the son of his own works.' I believe that is not only true for individuals but for communities as well. Communities are judged by—and created by—what they have done."[9] As the process of rebuilding Stockton's downtown continues, I am persuaded, as Geiger is, that Stockton will itself be spiritually rebuilt.

Statistics: Seeing Results

In an age of daily polls by the major media, the public has become accustomed to thinking in numbers and percentages. In Stockton a dramatic drop in crime statistics during and since my time in office has had several important consequences, but first and foremost it has changed people's perception of how safe they are. We had crime, like any other city, but we also had a major hang up about what a dangerous and wicked place we lived in, what one *Los Angeles Times* reporter called Stockton's "inferiority complex." Whatever else was wrong, Stockton had a serious problem with civic self-esteem. Improved crime statistics over the last decade have eased that anxiety. Another important result of the improving crime statistics is that they have led to support for the higher utility tax and for an increased proportion of city tax revenues allocated to police and public safety programs. Both the perception of greater safety and the public support for higher expenditures have been essential to creating a new reality.

The perception of Stockton as "a wide-open city," to which I have referred earlier, goes way back. From our founding and early prosperity at the time of the Gold Rush, when miners and later agricultural workers came to town from the Sierra and the farmlands on weekends for a little "rest and relaxation," Stockton had been known for its gambling, saloons, prostitution, and cheap hotels. That was history, but it lingered in people's minds.

In the recent past, there was the sensational Cleveland School "massacre" in January 1989, a story that was carried on national television for several days. One year later, TV commentator Peter Jennings selected Stockton as the focus of a primetime ABC News documentary on gun violence. Although Jennings insisted that Stockton was simply a prototype of most American cities, the program talked about six gun murders that had occurred in Stockton and mentioned none in other cities. Stockton was made to look just like what Jennings said it was not, "the gunshot capital of the nation."[1] In 1989, there were two fatal shootings of deputy sheriffs, and in 1990, a Stockton police sergeant was bludgeoned to death. These violent events attracted the attention of major television stations, especially those in Northern California. *The Record*, then owned by the Gannett Corporation, reported constantly on crime in the city. Unfortunately, the police beat is the quickest and easiest source for a sensational story, and that was Gannett's stock in trade. After *The Record* was bought by the Omaha World Herald Company in November 1994, a more balanced and thorough coverage of city affairs became the norm.

There was a sense of helplessness in Stockton at the time I took office. People seemed to feel that crime was out of control, *and* that this was peculiar to Stockton. Except for a fairly good Neighborhood Watch program, there was no effective citizen involvement in crime prevention. Residents looked to the police department to deal with crime, and the police department, hampered by a decreasing number of officers due to recent efficiency cuts, had its hands full.

In the last twelve years—seven during my tenure as mayor and five since I left office—the public perception of safety in Stockton has changed dramatically, and I give much of the credit to improved statistics. To repeat, these positive statistics reflecting the decrease in crime in Stockton had the effect of justifying council actions, especially the utility tax increase, that might otherwise have lost public support. And it was the new tax that enabled us to institute new programs in high crime neighborhoods, which very quickly showed dramatic decreases in crime. By 1992 residential burglaries were down 50 percent in one targeted neighborhood and 75 percent in another; assaults decreased 28 percent in one neighborhood and 35 percent in another. As the newspaper rightly noted, "Complaints about the utility tax increase have been few because Stocktonians can see the results."[2]

Again in 1994, *The Record* reported that robberies and assaults had dropped in the city of Stockton, where the police department's expansion had been possible, whereas in those areas of San Joaquin County that were not incorporated within the city boundaries, crime had increased because the county had been forced to cut law enforcement.[3] Without these results, the council might have backed away from the tax increase, especially since the business community regularly complained about the potentially negative impact of our utility rates on recruiting new businesses, although even business leaders had to acknowledge the crucial significance of the image of Stockton as a crime-ridden city. Indeed their own document, "Vision 2000," published in 1995, pointed to Stockton's higher-than-average crime rate among comparable cities as the single greatest deterrent to businesses locating here. Our improved statistics muted their protest against the higher tax.

Early in my tenure as mayor I noted that the police department and sometimes the newspaper reported crimes as raw totals rather than as a percentage of population. The national standard, as set by the F.B.I. Crime Index, reports the number of crimes per 100,000 persons, known as a "crime rate." Our reporting method made our crime scene look worse than it was. Since our population was increasing, I strongly urged that statistics be reported in crimes per population both by the police and by the newspaper. In a memo of December 30, 1993, Police Chief Ed Chavez noted the advantage of measuring crime relative to population: "While there has been a slight increase in the actual number of motor vehicle thefts in the ten-month 1993 period compared to the ten-month 1992 period, the rate of motor vehicle thefts per thousand population has declined." On June 14, 1995, Chavez again gave a crime rate comparison based on the F.B.I.'s Uniform Crime Reports and noted that our crime rate decreased 10.7 percent overall from 1990 to 1994.

What the statistics also proved was the effectiveness of community-based policing. This system is best exemplified in the Safe Neighborhoods program, where Neighborhood Betterment committees worked with the police; the results were large decreases in crime. Community/police collaboration is an approach to crime that has had impressive benefits in cities across the country in the 1990s, and it was fully adopted in Stockton during my tenure as mayor. This approach took as a starting point the premise that the police simply could not do the job alone; the residents had to be their partners. Because our police chief met regularly with the publisher of the paper, the editorial writer understood the importance of community-based policing. In 1995, *The Record* noted a 29 percent decrease in crime in the Safe Neighborhood areas with this comment: "Community-based policing is working. It needs to be expanded and will be."[4] Such a statement supported the council's yearly increases in the police budget and concurrent decreases in other budgets.

Statistics began to put Stockton in a favorable light compared to other California cities. Stockton was not alone, as we sometimes thought, nor were we a crime-ridden anomaly as portrayed by Peter Jennings. In fact, by 1996, we looked better than many other California cities. From 1994 to 1995, our rate of violent crime not only dropped 15 percent, but we had less violent crime than San Bernardino, Oakland, Los Angeles, Inglewood, Riverside, and the geographically comparable San Joaquin Valley city of Fresno.[5]

By 1997, we compared favorably to California as a whole. Headlines proclaimed, "California Crime Rate Way Down, S.J. County, Stockton Joins Trend." The accompanying article pointed out that Stockton's crime decrease in the first half of 1997 over the same period in 1996 was significantly higher than the decrease statewide. The state's decrease was 8.2 percent and Stockton's was 13.7 percent.[6] "Upon reflection [*The Record* noted], Stockton is not as safe and crime-free as it could be or should be.... But we know of no city that is as safe and crime-free as it could be or should be.... Nor do we know of any others that have put forth the united effort and recorded the declines that Stockton has. The credit goes to the entire community, from the city council that had the courage in the early 1990s to increase the utility tax to pay for more police to the volunteers in schools and community centers to the Neighborhood Watch captains."[7]

This same commitment to crime reduction and the allocation of city resources was made by my successor in 1998 when he said, "People need to understand that the crime rate is dropping. It's an expensive proposition but a needed one. The last council and this council have worked very hard to make sure we spend where we need to spend to get the crime stats down, and Chief Chavez and the department have just done a magnificent job."[8]

Among the most reassuring statistics is the annual homicide rate. Whereas from 1990 to 1997, it was a yearly average of fifty, in the first six months of 1998, there were only five. An editorial reporting the homicide statistic began, "There is a revolution under way on the streets of Stockton. Crime is down—way down—in Stockton." It ended, "Because of its cultural and ethnic diversity, Stockton has been called California's model city for the twenty-first century. We might add that it's also becoming a model for community and police partnerships in crime reduction."[9]

Over the decade of the 1990s, the statistics on crime in Stockton were nothing short of terrific. Every year the crime rate decreased. I encouraged printing these statistics in our weekly council bulletins; I brought attention to them at council meetings before the TV camera. I celebrated them at every opportunity. I believed that our crime problem, serious as it was, had been distorted and misunderstood. We were more like other major cities than we thought. The numbers have since verified that hunch, and more. As the story was told in the papers and on the streets, the concept that Stockton was getting safer became part of the collective consciousness of the city.

5

Getting Re-elected

Gay Issue: Stockton Is Not San Francisco

*I*t was May 1992, and my reelection campaign was getting into in high gear. Sorting through my phone messages, I saw a call from Elaine Albertson, who wanted to schedule an appointment for herself and her friend Barbara to talk about a gay pride march. Everyone is now aware of the extensive gay and lesbian community in San Francisco and of the gay pride marches held in June every year that are often led by prominent politicians. Gay men and lesbians are elected to public office in San Francisco, and politicians solicit the support of this powerful constituency. Sections of the city are predominantly gay. Restaurants, theaters, retail establishments all cater to a very visible and dynamic gay population in the city.

Not so in Stockton. There are no openly gay areas, no gay restaurants, only one gay bar, and there had never been a gay pride march. Politicians do not show up at gay events. I know of gay men who are active in the AIDS prevention program of San Joaquin County, and I have participated in a candle-lighting ceremony and the march on AIDS Remembrance Day. From time to time, I see an announcement of a meeting by PFLAG (Parents and Families of Lesbians and Gay Men). But Stockton is not friendly or even neutral toward gay men and lesbians. There are fundamentalist churches here with memberships in the thousands which bitterly denounce homosexuality. Many politicians, especially those up for reelection, would have refused to see Elaine.

When she and Barbara entered my office, I found myself face to face for the first time with a transsexual. Elaine was a tall, broad-shouldered woman with long blond hair and an extremely deep voice. As a young male, she had been an eagle scout and a scoutmaster. She now owned her own business, a resumé preparation service. She asked whether

I would have any objection to a gay pride march along Pacific Avenue from the Weberstown Mall to the University of the Pacific, basically through the heart of Stockton. Her group, the San Joaquin County Gay Community Alliance, wanted to promote harmony and constructive relations between all groups in Stockton. The march would take place on Sunday, June 14.

Elaine asked that a certificate of recognition for the group be presented at a reception to be held after the march at the University of the Pacific. I endorsed their plan, thinking that this would be a positive move. More openness and inclusiveness was always a good thing. The march was not expected to be large enough to require a police escort, so there was really no need for a parade permit nor for permission from the mayor. In fact, as far as I could see, this would be just a group of people walking along the sidewalk. I indicated that I thought it would be all right. It should be said here that my younger brother Doug was a gay man who had died at age thirty-nine, eight years previously, not from AIDS but from heart disease. Doug lived in Los Angeles all his life. Most of my friends in Stockton had never met him.

When news of the upcoming parade hit the paper, I was quoted as saying that it said a lot about the gay and lesbian community that its members wanted to be a positive force in the larger Stockton community and that they hoped to contribute to a sense of unity in a multi-cultural city. The next Monday night, June 8, 1992, forty angry people representing several churches and other organizations awaited me in the council chamber. One after another, they attacked me for my support of the march and asked the council to revoke the group's permit. As I sat listening to them, I felt for the first time the intensity and violence of homophobic hatred. It was very frightening.

The first speaker said he had come to Stockton eight years ago with his five children because he thought Stockton was a great place to raise a family. He was now sorely disillusioned. Not only was he concerned about the violence and the breakdown of morality, but he was also extremely distressed that the mayor would see gay pride as a healthy thing. To him, this seemed "like an oxymoron. It is not a healthy lifestyle. It does not uphold family values. I object to lending vocal support to this movement."

The next speaker told it from the businessperson's perspective. She claimed that businesses in Fresno had been vandalized when the owners opposed gay activities. She concluded her statement with a personal threat: "I am surprised that in an election year you would present yourself as favorable to homosexuals." Next came a speaker who said that gay marches were marked by public nudity, obscene acts, and open advocacy of pedophilia. Next, a public school teacher and mother of three told us that gay people were aggressive and predatory. She said the purpose of the march was to elicit support for homosexuality and to recruit new members. She asserted that homosexual behavior was compulsive and addictive and was accompanied by a series of health problems. Next a licensed vocational nurse reported data from a questionnaire that, she claimed, found that gay people more frequently expose themselves than heterosexuals, they make more obscene phone calls, and they engage in more criminal activities, such as shoplifting.

After the nurse sat down, another speaker arose and attacked what she called my "endorsement of homosexuality as a positive force." Noting that medical books had now reclassified homosexuality as an "alternate sexual orientation" rather than as a disease, he asserted that this view was totally wrong. Homosexuals, he told us, are guilty of extreme promiscuity; they have a high incidence of STDs and AIDS, and they use drugs at a much higher rate members of the general community. Next came another nurse who spoke about Stockton's image: "Our city does not have a very good name. I don't believe this march is going to help." She invoked our country's history, asserting that the Founding Fathers had not promoted homosexuality. She believed that the mayor of the city should set a better example, lest innocent people follow my lead. A teacher offered additional "medical information" to the effect that homosexual men have "gay bowel syndrome and gonorrhea," and concluded with the remark, "When Mayor Darrah praised the gay march as positive, she was right in one respect, HIV positive."[1]

These wild and vicious statements were interrupted by the sudden arrival in the chamber of two gay men, Craig Arivett and Troy DeVore, who had been watching the council proceedings on television. They came down to City Hall to tell the meeting "that several people in the gay community were leading very normal lives." Arivett, who spoke first, thought the majority of the world's cities had liberal ideas toward homosexuality. DeVore said, "I am gay and proud of it. I am not going to be ashamed. We did not choose it. I want to let the straight community know that we are different and there is nothing wrong with it." When these two sat down, the testimony returned to its earlier themes, now in a specifically religious context. The next speaker told the story of Abraham and Lot and referred to Sodom and Gomorrah, the biblical cities destroyed by God because of their bestiality. He had a good friend who was gay and chose not to practice it. He asserted that most Stocktonians were God-fearing people who believed in heterosexuality. The final speaker summed up the opinion of the majority of the group: "Homosexuality it not a lifestyle. It is a death style. It should not be in Stockton."[2]

I was shocked and unnerved by this long, hateful harangue. I also felt very intimidated. There was an undertone of violence and viciousness in the speakers' voices. As I listened to these forty people, I had a sense that they might be the tip of an iceberg. There could be hundreds or maybe thousands of people in Stockton who had this angry and irrational view of sexual difference. I still endorsed the march at the end of the meeting: "Organizers want this march to be positive. A positive effort is OK."

On June 10, four days before the parade, *The Record* printed a column by Mike Fitzgerald, whose thoughtful views about human sexuality I had never heard before in Stockton: "I am glad local gays are parading Sunday. It is time Stockton grew up in its attitude toward homosexuals." Fitzgerald thought that each person's sexuality was unique or should be; that sexuality can flower as self-knowledge is gained; that sexuality sometimes blossoms beyond social norms. For example, to drink white wine with fish is nothing more than a convention based on the majority of tastes. Fitzgerald concluded his column by saying, "Our challenge in life is to match our wines and entrees to our real tastes. If we conform to the taboos of 2,000 years ago, we are in real danger of living a fake life. I am not saying Sodom and Gomorrah should be two of the county's five new cities. I am talking about personal growth that takes you in your own true direction. The benign differences that result are something to cherish and delight in, not to stigmatize and suppress." Fitzgerald called on Stocktonians to look at the march as a learning opportunity and encouraged the citizens to try to understand their gay neighbors. He also invited Stocktonians to telephone him and give him their views.[3]

As Fitzgerald later commented, a monsoon followed. He attributed many of the phone calls to a disc jockey on a Christian radio station who read the column over the air and urged listeners to call Fitzgerald. A torrent of emotional callers thundered the fundamentalist view. Homophobia ran rampant, he reported four days later in a follow-up article, and he related that some of his critics had inquired, "If we tolerate gays, will we then tolerate child molesters?" Other callers believed that homosexuality was a choice and that therefore their children could be seduced. Fitzgerald himself was even personally attacked. "Have you come out of the closet yet?" inquired one Christian menacingly.

Other callers, however, noted the fear that surrounds the issue of homosexuality, and they objected to the intolerance of the anti-gay speakers at the city council meeting. Some gay people who phoned in tried to correct some misconceptions. "I don't think any one of us chose this lifestyle," said Jerry, a gay man. A Stockton lesbian insisted that she and her friends were good people "regardless of what happens in our bedrooms." For Fitzgerald, a housewife got it right when she said, "This is just the beginning of many obstacles of prejudice we as a community need to conquer." Endorsing the march, a straight therapist said gays are doing our community a favor: "It's addressing an inequity that exists between us, and it's the only way that we're going to come to the unity and wholeness that will get us beyond the conflicts that we have."[4]

The Gay Pride Freedom Walk went very well. About a hundred gay people and their supporters marched down Pacific Avenue. They were greeted with cheers from bystanders, and motorists sounded their horns in approval. The organizers were pleased by this mostly friendly response. Troy DeVore, who had spoken at the city council meeting, was delighted: "I am so pumped up. It was perfect." Marchers carried signs with messages such as "God loves Her gay and lesbian people" and "Free to be gay." Participants seemed to believe that they had shown the residents of Stockton that the gay community was part of the total community. Although most of the bystanders along the half-mile route acted friendly, some did not. Three members of Victory Four Square Gospel Church carried signs reading, "You don't need equal rights. You need Jesus."[5]

I did not attend the march. I was out of town. I authorized the certificate of recognition and asked two of the more liberal members of the council if they would present it at the reception. They declined.

This all happened in the summer of 1992, four months before I came up for reelection. I had just run against five men in the primary and finished first, but I had received only 33 percent of the vote. Although the runner-up got only 27 percent, these results meant that two-thirds of the voters might vote against me. I knew that there were thousands of members of fundamentalist churches in our city with powerful leaders who could be mobilized against a given candidate. That same year, in his campaign against Patti Garamendi for U.S. Congress, Richard Pombo had made a big point of the fact that two homosexuals sponsored an event for her. Pombo beat her in a very close race.

I went to see the minister of a large Christian church in Stockton to ask him for his support. He has a way of introducing a visitor to his Sunday morning services, simply noting that person's presence, which gives his endorsement. This minister, a longtime friend of a major Stockton businessman and developer who was an important backer of mine, was ready to support me. He stated his conditions directly: If I were interviewed on the Christian radio station, I would be asked no questions about my stand on abortion; second, I needed to understand that homosexuality was a wrong against God as expressed in the biblical story of Sodom and Gomorrah. I was not to say anything that would suggest otherwise. The minister also told me a story to further clarify the line he expected me to take. One of his parishioners had come to him and told him he was gay. The minister told me that he had talked him out of it—the parishioner now had a wife and several children. Inwardly I flinched at this repression, but outwardly I only nodded, cowed by the threat of defeat on election day.

There have been no more gay marches in Stockton since the Freedom Walk of 1992. As mayor, I always attended the AIDS vigils and candlelight marches and often spoke and read the names of victims of AIDS who had died. I also always went to the civic auditorium when the AIDS quilt was in town and invariably my eyes filled with tears as I looked at those squares made by the loving friends and families of departed gay men and lesbians, and I remembered my brother Doug.

I believe to this day that Stockton would be a far richer city if gay men and lesbians were welcomed, but they are not. As a politician, I endorsed their actions to a degree, but in an election year I was scared to go full bore on their behalf. On election night, with 64,000 votes cast, I won by a mere 1,300 votes. An angry, organized fundamentalist opposition could have defeated me. A politician, some say, is not the leader out in front, but the observer who grabs the baton as the march goes by. Let there be many in the future who step forward for justice.

Learning To Speak: Getting Tough, Staying Sweet

Two weeks before my first mayoral primary in November 1989, when the League of Women Voters put on its candidates forum, I was one of six candidates for mayor. The debate took place in the broadcast studios of Continental Cablevision in Stockton. I had selected my outfit carefully, according to the prescription I learned in a speech class at Delta College. A speaker needs to dress colorfully and carefully apply more makeup than she would normally use. I was wearing my royal blue suit, a white blouse with a high neckline, and large, blue, matching beads. My glasses even had royal blue frames. Regrettably, they were reflective, so that as I spoke there were always four lights shining on them. My hair had too much red in it. As the television color dimmed, the color faded. In some lighting my makeup was good; however, as the lighting changed, I sometimes appeared to have too much on my face and not enough on my neck.

Each candidate was allotted a three-minute introductory speech. Smiling and friendly, I applauded the League of Women Voters and Continental Cablevision for trying to bring better government to Stockton. I had learned from my mother the importance of paying compliments, but I was hesitant and slightly breathless, and my jaw was tight. My lower teeth protruded more than usual. You could actually see the gold fillings. I said I had done polls and learned that the residents were appalled at the city's drug and crime problem. I voiced outrage that our city had fewer police officers now than it had two years ago. I came across as very serious, in fact, as harsh. I said that I planned to bring good leadership and well-managed growth and to attack drugs and crime. My mouth clamped shut. There was no smile.

When asked what I would do to build an effective council team, I responded that the council members needed to understand one another. We should spend time together as a body. I would initiate workshops where we would establish our goals and create a long-term plan to work together to achieve these goals. At the end, I did not smile, nor did I look at the camera. In my closing statement I was relaxed in the beginning, again complimenting the folks for coming to the meeting, then I closed with a strong statement: "I plan to bring to Stockton the leadership that it needs and deserves." There was no smile, no eye contact, a closed jaw. Despite this uptight performance, I won the election.

I had been warned about my speaking style. At one of my fund-raisers, a friend and donor to my campaign, told me I needed to learn to speak better. He advised me to attend Toastmasters,[1] which I subsequently did every Saturday morning at 7:00 A.M. for a year and a half until I was elected mayor. Two years later, during my campaign for reelection, another friend, a woman who worked at the local cable company and was well versed in the subtleties of constructing a public image, told me, "You're a nice woman, Joan, but you need to speak in a way that conveys your warmth and humor." She knew of a speech coach in San Francisco who had helped her boss with a speech for a Rotary Club meeting. As it happened, I had heard this excellent speech, so I signed up to study with Dawne Bernhardt.[2] She charged $150 an hour and the round trip drive from Stockton took four hours, but I knew my campaign was in trouble after I received only 33 percent of the total vote in the primary. Any help I could get, especially in this vital area, I was eager to have.

I liked Dawne immediately. A woman about my age, she was outgoing, attractive, well dressed, articulate, caring—all the things a role model should be. "How would you like to come across?" she asked me at our first meeting in her office suite on the tenth floor of a Montgomery Street building.[3] "Like Dianne Feinstein," I responded, "intelligent, articulate, knowledgeable, strong in my views yet caring, decisive yet open, in command of ideas, with some of Barbara Boxer's verve." Dawne followed up, "From the feedback that you've been getting, how are you coming across?" My answer was that people saw me as intelligent, caring, concerned, and gracious. Dawne laughed a little laugh. "What would you like to add?" I said I had been criticized for coming across as tentative and indecisive, then as harsh when I felt backed against the wall. "How long ago was that feedback?" Dawne inquired. In a poll taken in March, I explained, out of four hundred respondents, seventeen said that I came across as indecisive and eight as invisible. My campaign committee has advised me to be more definite, yet not to raise my voice when I was trying to make a point. I sighed and said, "I think I have figured that out though. I need more specific evidence for my statements."

I had been quite puzzled when my good friend Ann Hethcock, the one from the television station, told me I could use help in giving speeches, because in my long history with Junior Aid, United Way, the Women's Center, and in public relations activities I had often been told I came across as a good speaker. What seemed to have happened, beginning that first night at the League of Women Voters candidates forum, was that I felt a political leader had to be serious and tough so I tried to change my public persona.

Dawne watched the tapes of my council meetings and suggested, "Your persona is not a problem. You were clearly in charge and running the meeting." That was a nice surprise for me. In a high, slow voice, I said, "Oh, thank you very much for that." She noted that in a crisis situation people tend to do more of whatever they are good at. If you are decisive, when pushed you become even more decisive. She advised me that it's better to switch to a different part of your style: Disarm your audience with a one-liner. She said that I appeared defensive and came on as overly definite when I was challenged, but I didn't need to be that way. She said that I should change my style at this point in a presentation and that the best way to do that was to change my body language. Instead of leaning forward, I should lean back, let my shoulders drop, and exhale. She suggested that I blow out all the things that were bothering me and inhale the support of the people who were there in support of me.

Dawne talked about having an open mouth and open eyes. "Whenever you are backed into a corner, open your mouth and open your eyes, because the flight/fight syndrome is to clamp our mouth and close our eyes. You and I both have a small upper lip, and it's hard to see our teeth unless our mouth is open, and that's what gives us the accessible rather than uptight, the approachable rather than the defensive look, no matter how we are feeling inside."

I felt I had a habit of clamping my mouth shut. Dawne commented: "Some of the time you clamp it; most of the time you just close it. We have to correct this. Let your mouth open a little. When you are up against a wall, your jaw sets harder." I had noticed from the videotapes she had taken of me speaking that sometimes my eyes were only partially open. With a laugh I asked, "Should I get an eye tuck?" She had not noticed a problem with the eyes, just with the mouth. "Open eyes, open mouth, no matter what people hit you with," she replied.

Dawne videotaped two of my speeches, one for a downtown fundraiser and the other for the first of my Women Leading Luncheons. She urged me to use stories to make points, as the great communicator Ronald Reagan himself had taught us. She noted my use of long sentences and extended effort at graciousness. "You need a lot more punch to your talk," she said and advised me to think in terms of bullets, to write in terms of bullets, and to speak in terms of bullets and this way I would come across focused and strong. Instead of saying, "I want to give a progress report on the last two years," say, "We've come a long way." Dawne also instructed me to drop auxiliary verbs and introductory phrases. "Keep a light touch—your tone doesn't always have to be heavy. Your record speaks for you. You are riding the crest of a good wave," she counseled. To which I responded, "I feel like I'm drowning."

Her effort was to lighten me up: "Trust those one-liners.... Whatever bubbles up inside, just go for it." I must have looked spacey, because she often said, "Am I coming across?" Dawne was fond of saying that "style follows content." In a room filled with supporters, she saw 60 percent of my role as that of cheerleader. She advised that I start with, "This room is filled with winners," and my excitement would follow. At first, during my practice with Dawne, I would thank the preceding three speakers in my Women Leading luncheon with about a minute and a half of elaborate, highly complimentary phrases. Dawne was unimpressed: "Let me hear you say that more quickly, in shorter phrases," When I did, in a mere twenty-seven seconds, she responded, "That brought goose bumps." I worked at the new style—the cheerleading, the one-liners, the short sentences and colorful stories—and tried to leave out the phony graciousness.

Working with Dawne made me proud of what I had accomplished. She was an esteem builder. I would write out a speech in advance and deliver it to her. As we talked it over, I saw that the two years of my first term had yielded several achievements, and I got excited about them. She urged me to drop generalities and focus my speech on specifics, such as my five-star program for fighting crime. It had been designed when I was a candidate and became a reality while I was in office. How had I arrived at this program? Dawne asked. Not quickly. I had done extensive research and talked to several people including the Stockton police chief. Since being in office, I had implemented these five stars. "This is what I promised the citizens of Stockton, Dawne. I'm delivering on my promises." Dawne caught this and said, "This should be your speech. Call attention to the success of your record. It's amazing that you are not saying this, Joan. It's very impressive."

She advocated my having in the audience the key women who had cleaned up their neighborhoods, women who would lend credence to the strength and power of women's leadership. I mentioned that I had other goals: well-managed growth, a balanced budget, more efficiency and economy in government. "I really have done them all," I said, and she responded, "My friend, you are selling yourself short. Your opponent is attacking you on not getting anything done." She urged me to talk about the record of the ex-city manager, who was my opponent, and to say repeatedly, "Frank Fargo was fired." She loved the alliteration.

One day in Dawne's office I grumbled about having to speak before a men's group, Sertoma. "What do they do; what do they believe in?" she asked. I did not know. Very severely, she warned me to never speak before a group unless I could compliment the group or its members on at least three things. She suggested that it would be even better if I could refer to things that the group did that were consistent with what I was trying to accomplish. Establish rapport, she said. She recommended that I should have an advance team gather this information about each group to whom I was going to speak. If I had the time, I should take representatives of the group to lunch. I would need to figure out what the group's primary interests were and then reflect on those interests in my presentation.

I had that chance when I cochaired a breakfast for twenty-two black ministers during my reelection campaign. There had been disharmony between two ministerial organizations, and the breakfast was set up to promote unity. In fact, I had been asked to give a speech on unity. I invited five of the ministers to lunch to get their thinking on this subject. They explained what they meant by unity by giving an analogy of disunity—a chain that breaks when its weak links fail. They referred frequently to Dr. King and to the Bible. I wrote my speech with their figurative language in mind and tried to give it some of the emotional force I had heard in Sunday sermons by black preachers whose churches I attended while campaigning for mayor.

Vice-mayor Weaver and I paid for the breakfast. We had gone to a great deal of trouble to arrange the time and place for the meeting and to select a location that was agreeable to all. The breakfast attracted a much larger crowd than we had expected, thirty ministers and some guests. When I arrived, much to my surprise, I found Frank Fargo at the door greeting the ministers. There was nothing I could do to about his presence, but when he started to walk into the breakfast area, I said with a snarl, "Frank, what are you doing?" "Coming to the breakfast," he answered. "Oh, no you're not," I replied. "I was invited by Larry Thomas," he insisted. To this I retorted angrily, "You are not invited by Vice-mayor Weaver or myself. Get out!" Petulantly he replied, "I paid my money." I was shocked to hear this since everyone present was our guest. "Get your money back and go," I ordered. I glared at him. He left, and I was livid. I marched up to Reverend Thomas (who had run against me in the primary and also written a very hostile letter about me in the newspaper) and informed him that Frank was not invited. Thomas left in a huff. Then I sat down and did five minutes of Dawne Bernhardt exhaling, releasing much anger and bringing in some good thoughts. It worked. I got over my anger and prepared to deliver my speech, a speech in which I talked with feeling about the need for unity in Stockton. I quoted the Bible and Dr. King. I did my best to speak in a common language. The speech was very well received. I was given a plaque that has folded, praying hands in brass, which I now keep on the bookshelf in my office. The event ended with our standing in a prayer circle and holding hands, for forty-five minutes.

Dawne was not the only person who gave me advice on speaking. In preparation for the League of Women Voters debate between Frank Fargo and me, four men friends coached me: Terry Hull, a property management executive; Bob Whittington, the former publisher of *The Record*; Don Parsons, a certified campaign consultant whom I had hired as campaign manager; and my husband, Jim.

Terry had seen the tape of the first candidates forum. Whereas I thought I came across as serious and factual, Terry described my performance as "shrill." In a practice debate, Parsons asked the questions, and Bob played the part of Frank on the attack. I did not stay friendly. I got defensive. All four men said I just could not come across that way. No matter what happened in the debate, I had to smile and be nice, as well as to appear knowledgeable, factual, and friendly.

When I told Dawne about their opinion, she agreed that I should not come on as Ms. Serious. Being overly serious would put people off, Dawne warned and added, "Your serious is more serious than you realize; it's the jaw and the way you set your mouth. The medium of television makes people scrutinize you more carefully. You have to look pleasant but Fargo does not. The old boys don't have to. And there is from time to time a bit of a twinkle about him, a bit of a Santa Claus, and kind of a grandfather." "You can't afford that tight-lipped look," Dawne warned.

I chose my outfit for the debate carefully. In fact, I even took a trial wardrobe consisting of two suit jackets, one blue and one dark gray, and four blouses, a pink, a paisley, and two white ones, to show Dawne. She thought the combination of the pink blouse and blue suit was cutesy. One white blouse was too fluffy. The paisley blouse might be too loud, so that was out. At first, she thought the best combination might be the pink blouse for softness and the gray suit for authority. She worried about the white blouse. White can glare. She advised me to check with my friends at Continental Cablevision to see if the new cameras could carry white. "It's very important that you are focusing on this," said Dawne. "The world in which you live says that women have to be concerned with style. You have to come across as a woman; yet at the same time, you are the mayor of your city, so it's right that you focus on clothes as a way to help you with your image." I ended up with the white blouse and blue suit. Glare was not a problem.

The debate was very important to the campaign. We had pages of damaging material about my opponent, but Parsons did not want me to focus on this issue first, lest I come across to our conservative community as a shrew. He wanted Fargo to fire the first shot, a shot to which I could retort. The debate absolutely had to offer that moment when Frank would open himself up for attack. I had practiced the words over and over again, always with a smile: "Frank was fired" and "*The Record* in 1969 stated that Mr. Fargo's leadership has been unsatisfactory. We need a city manager of greater competence, initiative and vigor" and "Frank, in order to compensate for your budget deficit, you suggested a utility tax, and even a personal income tax." Slinging these calculated insults with a smile was like rubbing my stomach and patting my head. As a woman raised to deny difficulty, to look for good in everyone, and to always get along, I had a lot of anxiety about the role of attacker. It took intense concentration even to fasten these facts in my mind.

The debate was held in the council chamber.[4] Three of us—Frank, the moderator, and I—sat on the dais. Parsons was seated in the first row, next to Fargo's campaign consultant who I believed to be my enemy, a woman who I felt had tried—unsuccessfully—to slander me in my first campaign for mayor. While answering the moderator's questions, Frank and I took small stabs at one another. He suggested the council was working through the department heads and not the city manager. I countered that. Fargo talked about the history of Stockton's double-digit unemployment. I said he was living in the past, that we had new companies in town that were hiring several hundred new employees. Fargo said that vacancies in public safety had not been filled, and I pointed out that we had hired sixty-two new police officers. He said I had extremely liberal goals and I said, "Yes, I have high goals for Stockton."

It was that kind of back-and-forth banter, nothing really substantial, until the question and answer period, when Parsons issued the clinching question to Fargo. "You have been critical of the utility tax as an impediment to attracting new businesses to Stockton. Isn't it true that in 1969 you proposed the utility tax as a way to solve your final, unbalanced, city budget?" Frank retorted that 1969 was the wrong year; it was 1966. "A sewer service charge was considered for the improvement of the waste water treatment plant," he said.

This was my chance. I leaned over to the moderator and said that I wanted to make a statement. "Mr. Fargo," I began with a smile, "to refresh your memory, in January 1969 you left office, having been forced to resign. On November 11, 1969, at your final meeting, your budget was $565,000 out of balance and your expenditure was one half a million over budget. Your remedy was either to borrow from the capital improvement fund or to propose a utility tax or a personal income tax, if it could be approved." Fargo was dumbfounded. *The Record* picked up on my charges and wrote a very damaging article about Fargo that appeared in the paper the next day. Parsons was ecstatic. "Never in my life of politicking, have I seen so clean and so deadly a wound as the one you inflicted on Frank."

In my campaign speeches from then on I used humor and told stories. When I introduced the city manger, Dwane Milnes, to the Rotary Club, I talked a lot about his funny tie collection. "He has a tie with a lot of small turkeys. I asked his assistant, 'When does he wear that tie?' She said, 'Oh, at the regular Monday night meetings, when he is with the council members.'" I found that the more self-effacing the stories were, the more hilariously they were received. At my final goodbye dinner event, given by friends a month after I had left office, I described a highly embarrassing incident at a recent family occasion when I had found myself talking to Bonnie Bensimon, a brunette with dark eyes and hair, who had recently given birth to her third child. She was holding a baby, a light-complexioned redhead whom I mistook for Bonnie's baby when he was actually my own grandson, Guard. As I was remarking to Bonnie for the third time how much her baby looked like Guard, I heard the quiet voice of my son-in-law, Dave. "Joan, I don't think you understand. This is Guard." As everyone burst into laughter, I raised my hand to my head and gasped, "And this is the mind that had the final say on the $200 million city budget for seven years."

I had come a long way from the tight-lipped, serious, gracious little woman who was always on the defensive. That night at the farewell dinner, as I walked back and forth across the stage in my long, slinky dress, microphone in hand, I was a happy, skillful entertainer. I felt like a star. That's what a speech coach can do for you.

The Campaign for Reelection

My second campaign for mayor was far more challenging than the first. This time the tables were turned. My poll showed that the problems—drugs and crime—were still priorities in the minds of Stocktonians, but instead of being the challenger I was now the defender. When residents were asked whether Stockton had gotten better or worse in the past year, 67 percent responded that it was worse; only 15 percent thought it had gotten better. An alarming 91 percent believed that crime was out of control. The image of the council was only slightly better than it had been the first time around. My name identification was higher, but my favorable to unfavorable ratings were down. People had heard of me, but of those who had, only one-third had a favorable impression, not a very impressive showing for an incumbent.

The poll on my job performance found 24 percent who thought I was doing a very good job, 49 percent an average job, and 16 percent a poor job. By election night I had to convince the voters that 1) I was addressing the drugs and crime problem effectively, even though it was not apparent to them, and 2) I was a better choice than my opponent. Again only men, this time four, and no women ran against me in the primary. Frank Fargo, the city manager from 1963 to 1969, and Tom Madden, a former mayor and council member, were my two strongest rivals.

In my first campaign I had minimal consultation from my pollster. The second time I hired Don Parsons, the certified campaign consultant, who was knowledgeable, effective and fun to work with. After the televised debate with Fargo, when I accused him of being fired and raising taxes, Parsons was so delighted that I had at last taken off my white gloves and gotten down to the business of being a politician that he bought me red leather boxing gloves, one labeled, "Taxes" and the other labeled, "Fired." I treasured these tokens of my growing prowess as a fighter.

For the second campaign, my first task was to establish myself as an effective crime fighter. Despite the increased number of police officers and of new programs, polling indicated that the public did not feel there had been any real change. Indeed, it would be years before the average voter felt the city was safer. My pollster advocated that I announce an effective program to fight crime and make sure people knew about it. Milnes, the city manager, had promised a plan, but as late as March of my reelection year, nothing had been announced. Finally, in exasperation, I walked into his office and demanded action. Shortly thereafter we announced "Safe Stockton," an excellent, comprehensive plan that we unveiled with great fanfare in the rotunda of city hall. Dwane Milnes had no stomach for Fargo, the ex-city manager, becoming mayor.

At the time of my reelection campaign, *The Record* had a policy of non-endorsement of mayoral candidates. Nonetheless, the paper tried to put up a candidate against me. The publisher of *The Record* himself paid a visit to a member of my council and, saying that he was a spokesman for the business leadership, especially the Bank of Stockton, urged him to run against me. The council member declined and later told me the story.

Initially, *The Record* staff was no more supportive of me than the paper's leadership. However hard I tried to convince the city news reporter that I had been an effective mayor for two years, he began his pre-election summary on the candidates with "Joan Darrah is Stockton's feel-good mayor—a former public relations person who often seems more interested in handing out commendations and thanking community volunteers than in the nitty-gritty of local government."[1] In the same article, my opponents railed against my lack of effective action. Fargo said he would "bite the bullet." Madden boasted, "Quite frankly I get things done."

The primary did not yield a majority for any one candidate. I got only 33 percent of the vote, which meant that 67 percent of the voters believed someone else could do a better job. That came as a low blow, even though I wore a big smile for the photographers on election night and said that I did not see the primary results as a vote of no confidence in my leadership. All I knew was that I would work like crazy, raise a ton of money, go door to door on Sunday afternoons all summer in 100-plus-degree weather. I was determined to do absolutely everything I could do to beat Fargo in the runoff.

Had Al Bonner not gone after me in my first mayoral campaign, I would have kept my ads free of criticism. It was different in my race against Fargo. I had to bring out the negatives against him. He had been fired, however many times he denied it. There was a report in *The Record* the day after he "resigned" to the effect that six out of nine council members had supported a resign-or-else ultimatum. In fact, two of the members of his final council told me that, practically speaking, he was fired. The city was in a dangerous financial position when Fargo left as well. These facts had to be brought out. He had criticized me during the primary on the utility tax increase, saying that it discouraged business from locating in Stockton, although he himself, at the end of his tenure as city manager, had suggested both a city utility tax and an income tax as possible new sources of revenue. How could I bring these matters out in the open without turning off the male voters of our very conservative community?

In the section "Learning to Speak" above, I described a critical moment in the League of Women Voters debate between Fargo and me. I will continue the story of the debate here. I had been told to hold off until I was attacked before I went on the offensive. For that all-important moment, I had to wait until the question and answer period when my consultant asked a question of Fargo that evoked his criticism of my utility tax proposal. Once criticized, I could defend myself. I noted that Fargo had proposed a utility tax in 1969 to cover his budget shortfall. Then I added that he did not leave the city manager's office voluntarily; he had been pressured to resign. At this, Fargo got angry and defensive. "When you're slandered, you're slandered. It's that simple," was all that Fargo could come up with in reply to my charges.

Jim Nickles, the reporter for *The Record,* who had said that as mayor I was a feel-good PR type, could not have done a better job in picking up on this exchange. He really got it! Later on, it was Nickles' questioning that led Fargo deeper and deeper into trouble. He insisted that he had resigned, but I had brought with me a copy of the 1969 newspaper article which stated that "six out of the nine council members were prepared to fire Fargo if he didn't resign." When Nickles asked Fargo about his proposed tax hikes, Fargo responded petulantly: "That reporter was never a friend of mine." When Nickles questioned him about the budget miscalculations, Fargo acknowledged a mistake. The next day's account of the debate in the paper was headlined: "Fargo Runs for Cover at Debate. Mayor Pulls Record on the Ex-city Manager."[2]

This debate could not have turned out better for our side. I was now free to go on the attack. I put out a blistering brochure, which Parsons designed, with a big, eight- by eleven-inch fold-out, called "The Great Debate." It was the only negative salvo of my campaign, and we sent it to our targeted mailing list. The essence of it was picked up in a later news comparison of Fargo and me. A reporter phoned Lou Arismendi, who had been on the council when Fargo was fired and was one of the two ex-council members I had interviewed, to confirm the firing. Yes, Fargo was fired and he (Arismendi) had been the sixth (and the necessary vote) needed to accomplish this. When asked by the reporter why he had cast that vote, Arismendi replied, "Incompetence. Incompetence in money handling."[3]

Also, during this same interview, when Fargo was questioned about the city's having a $560,000 deficit when he left the city manager's office, he blamed the deficit on a deceased subordinate. He said he hated to befoul a dead man's name, but his finance director was the one who had screwed up. The man's widow was outraged and wrote a very strongly worded letter to the editor condemning Fargo for blaming her husband. She pointed to the twenty-five years of outstanding service her late husband had given the city and the many commendations he had received. "What Fargo did is so reprehensible that I can scarcely find words to describe my feelings. To attempt to shift the blame to someone who cannot defend himself is shameful."[4] Although her letter was received several days earlier, *The Record* chose not to print it until the day after the election.

After the negative blast of "The Great Debate," we sent out three positive mailers. One featured me with the very popular local state senator, Patrick Johnston; another showed me with the former police chief, Jack Calkins, the third summarized my efforts to fight crime. Parsons, a Republican by the way and very active in all Republican contests in our community, got me on the Republican voter's checklist. Fargo, a committed Republican, was furious. I was also on the Democratic Women's checklist, along with Bill Clinton, Barbara Boxer, and Dianne Feinstein. The checklists each cost $1,000, but they were well worth it.

The cost of my first campaign for mayor had seemed exorbitant at $100,000. The second campaign cost a total of $130,000, which I raised in the same way I had always done it. We held very elegant, high-priced events at the lakeside homes of an attorney, a public relations consultant, and a developer, events for which large donors were asked to be sponsors at a ticket price of $500–$1,000.

On one occasion, a South Stockton businessman who said he would make a donation to me called and asked to come to my house. He arrived, we chatted a few minutes, and then he handed me a thick envelope and went on his way. I looked in the envelope and was shocked to see $2,300 in $100 bills. FPPC (Fair Political Practices Commission) regulations prohibit cash donations over ninety-nine dollars from any one source, so I got in the car and went to his place of business and gave him back the envelope and asked for a check for $500, which he gave me. One had to wonder how often such an envelope had been handed to a political candidate and what benefit the donor expected to derive from such a generous, but clandestine contribution.

Of the $130,000 I spent on the second mayoral campaign, $90,000 came from donors outside my family. My mother donated $19,000 to this campaign, and my brothers and my uncle were also generous donors. Jim and I donated $7,000 of our own money and we borrowed another $15,000, a debt that was retired by the subsequent four Women Leading Luncheons. A principle of effective fund-raising is that the one who is asking also has to give. This allows an appeal to fair play. "I have given," says the fund-raiser; "I believe in the cause and this is my pledge that I will work hard to do as I promise. Now it is your turn to give. We are in this together." Or words to that effect!

The largest part of the $130,000, 36 percent, went into printing costs for seven targeted mailings. Unlike most statewide and national campaigns, where the bulk of the money is spent on television ads, we spent only 8 percent on television, all of it on the local cable channel. The audience for the major networks that cover Northern California are residents, for the most part, of other communities and do not vote in Stockton.

Next to mailing came staff expenses. My consultant received $10,000, $14,000 went to the pollsters, and $18,000 went to cover the salaries and benefits of two marvelous women, my campaign coordinator and my volunteer coordinator, who worked every day at my house, which was our campaign headquarters. They recruited volunteers to go door to door with me in the afternoon and on the weekends. They made sure that I had 750 signs on lawns throughout of the city.

We put an additional $6,500 into large outdoor signage. It could have cost a lot more had not Bloom Construction Company, a local business, volunteered to put up my thirty, four-foot by eight-foot outdoor billboards. We spent $4,500 on radio and newspaper ads, $2,600 on candidate statements that went out in the voter statement pamphlet, and $2,000 for the voter checklists. A big difference between the two campaigns was that in the second campaign I employed a highly talented campaign consultant and a paid volunteer coordinator. Both were absolutely vital for my reelection.

In 1995, the receipts and expenditures for my two campaigns were audited. The suggestion at the time was that all of the Stockton candidates were selected in a random statewide sampling. Perhaps that was the case, though I doubt it. After the investigator had met several times with my treasurer of eight years, a friend from Junior Aid, and reviewed literally hundreds of entries listing donations and expenditures and studied our quarterly reports for three years, he gave us a clean bill of health. A member of my council was not that fortunate and ended up losing an election partially because of what the audit exposed and the damaging news article that followed.

On election night, with a recent poll showing me fifteen points ahead of Fargo, I was quite confident of success. As they had been on my first election night, some one hundred supporters and volunteers were at my house, all eager for the results. The first results were bad. I was noticeably behind among the absentees, and that felt dreadful. I remembered that I had been behind from the beginning in my race for the office of supervisor, and it had stayed that way all evening. Dawne Bernhardt, my speech coach, asked me how I was holding up. I squeezed my fist into a knot, held it to my stomach, and said I was sure I was developing an ulcer. But my consultant, God love him, called and told me not to worry. He was monitoring results from the courthouse, and he believed they were going to get much better. When *The Record* called, I was still behind. I said, "I'm worried. I'm very concerned. I've got a knot in my stomach." At about ten o'clock that night, with 54 of 164 precincts counted, Fargo had 50 percent to my 49.5 percent. He went down to the courthouse, where he boasted, "The tight race showed that money doesn't have to be the deciding factor in politics." He had spent just half of what I had.

I stayed home and said goodbye to worried volunteers. My daughter Jeanne, nervous and scared, said there was still hope. Very gradually, the gap closed. By 11:00 I made my final call of the evening to the election office. I was ahead by twenty-four votes. On the basis of all of Parsons' assurances that I would ultimately win, I went to bed. The next morning at 6:00, when I called the election office, I found that I had a secure lead of almost 2,000 votes.

The first edition of *The Record* carried a photo of an ebullient Fargo. The story stressed the anti-incumbent mood of the voters and the closeness of the race. The second edition had the same photo, but a different headline. Instead of "Strong Fargo Showing Leaves Mayor's Race Too Close to Call" it read, "Darrah Heads for Narrow Win Over Fargo for Stockton Mayor." *The Record* even put out a big red and white sign on its newsstands, "DARRAH DEFEATS CHALLENGER," so as to avoid any confusion. The results were not yet final. There were a number of absentee votes that still needed to be counted. One week later, when the count was complete, I had won by 1,313 votes, 51 percent to 49 percent. "Mayor Darrah Hangs On, Defeats Fargo in Squeaker," announced the headline in *The Record*.

That election night was painful for me. "It was such a shock that he was so close," I told *The Record*.[5] It made me grateful for every group and every volunteer that supported me, for every person's contribution, for each lawn sign and every mailing. The tight race made me appreciate all dimensions of this campaign—the staff and the generous volunteers, all the mail, each hour of walking precincts, each person's Wednesday night phone calls. Without any one of those things, I would have lost.

Women Leading Luncheons: Redefining Power

If the story of my training for the debate with Fargo and my eventual killer punch, delivered so that the gents would still vote for me, is the most dramatic moment in my reelection campaign, the story of how I learned to court the women's vote is a much happier tale.

The air is charged with excitement when women gather in a large group to support a woman candidate for public office. I first experienced this in 1991 at a Women of Achievement luncheon that Barbara Boxer put on in San Francisco to reward and celebrate women leaders in preparation for her 1992 U.S. Senate race. I felt it again in Modesto, California, at a 1994 luncheon for Dianne Feinstein's campaign for the Senate. Feinstein greeted me before the event. "But Dianne, there are only women here," I said anxiously. To which she retorted, "Look, Joan, it's women who are getting me elected." I had just had a disappointing showing in the mayoral primary. After Dianne's lunch I decided that I too would put on a women's event. I would call it a Women Leading luncheon. I actually put on four such events from 1992 to 1995. Although they were all meant to raise money, they also contributed to the emergence of a strong female constituency that not only supported me but also, I hope, became a new factor in Stockton politics.

The purpose of the first lunch was to help me get re-elected. I thought bringing together a group of powerful women from different fields and having them feel the same excitement about women holding office as I had felt at Boxer's lunch would invigorate the campaign. I knew my women friends would want to come, but they would be much more likely to do so if the invitation made the event sound fun and different and promised a specific seat for them at a table with their friends. This is what Boxer did at her luncheon for five hundred women in San Francisco, where each one of us was handed a name tag when she entered and was directed to an assigned seat. This created a personal feeling despite the large crowd, and I did the same thing at my luncheon. I contacted several businesses and asked them to purchase tables as donations, which they did. I also asked several friends to get together a table of eight. The red, white and blue invitation card included photos of me with the featured speaker, the two-term mayor of Sacramento, Anne Rudin. We had a marvelous turn-out; more than two hundred women came, including business, social, educational and political notables of the city. The audience also reflected the diversity of our community.

The program was designed to celebrate women. Fran Meredith, a very gracious and popular realtor, was mistress of ceremonies. She was a friend of mine from Junior Aid days, the one with whom we all got together and put on twenty-two annual events to raise money for research to combat ALS (Lou Gehrig's disease), from which her husband Arch had suffered for several years. Fran introduced the elected women in the audience: a supervisor, a superior court judge, two council members, and four members of school boards; she also noted those running for public office and those serving on city commissions.

Fran then introduced the keynote speaker, Anne Rudin, who had been on the Sacramento city council for twenty years and had served as mayor for eight. Anne redefined women's power for the audience. She called it a force that enables us to achieve our goals. Women's power did not need to be the same as male power, which is stereotyped as dominant and aggressive. She told a story about going to lunch with three men who all ordered steak sandwiches; she ordered a chef's salad. "You should order a power lunch," the gents said. Anne replied that she was planning to redefine power.

Like me, Anne had been criticized for a "failure of leadership." "Can she lead?" people asked when she first ran. It sounded like a version of "Can she type?" My opponent, Frank Fargo, took the same tack. He called me a "weak mayor" and promised "vigorous leadership." Anne talked about women bringing civility to city hall, not stridency. She described me as a mayor who accomplished goals through cooperation. She talked about the importance of relationships. She said that leadership was having the moral courage to do what you think is right. In essence, Anne was calling on the women in the room to redefine and expand their own view of leadership. She spoke from experience. Under her tenure as mayor Sacramento achieved national prominence as a prosperous, progressive city.

Anne was followed by an old friend of mine, Judy Chambers, the vice president for student life at the University of the Pacific, who was to introduce me. Judy began by saying that she had read some recent research in the paper that morning which resulted in her throwing out all her prepared material. The research was about how people listen to speeches. Ten minutes into a talk, 31 percent are still listening, 12 percent are thinking about what they will be doing tomorrow, 17 percent are preparing a shopping list, 15 percent are planning a vacation, and 10 percent are sitting there with smiles on their faces because they are engaging in sexual fantasies. This remark brought down the house. She was there, she told the crowd, to talk about a person who was extremely bright, hardworking, dedicated, committed, friendly, well-traveled, sensitive, fun to be around, a proven leader and one of the nicest women anyone would ever want to know. "But enough about me," she said. Her speech was ten minutes in all, six very humorous and four very inspiring and complimentary, indicating that I was a results-oriented mayor who got done what I said I would. "What is important is to give Joan the opportunity to continue doing it," Judy concluded. Of all that happened that day, Judy's intro was what people talked about afterward.

Of no one is it truer than of Judy that she is a hard act to follow. I began my talk with an account of the goals I had set and the accomplishments I had achieved to date, emphasizing the remarkable achievements of women leaders. I cited successes of my administration in fighting crime in neighborhoods where women had taken the initiative in joint strategies with the police to rid their streets of drug sellers. I had invited eight such leaders from high crime areas, one of whom was Mary Delgado from Sixth Street, the founder of the well-known STAND program. When each stood to be recognized, the audience cheered loudly. At the end of my talk, I asked the crowd, "Is this the year for women?" "Yes," they yelled. "Are you willing to vote for me as mayor?" "Yes!" This event showed a profit of just $2,600, but it had a powerful effect on the campaign.

I began my second term with a bank balance of $2,000 and a debt of $15,000. Because so many of those who came to the first luncheon raved about it as a high for women in the community, I decided to make it an annual event, one which would also help to retire the debt. I debated where to have this second luncheon and whom to invite as the keynote speaker. A group of my women friends got together and we decided on Delaine Eastin, then an aspiring candidate for California state superintendent of schools. We scheduled the luncheon at a fashionable new country club in Stockton. It was a sellout. As at the first luncheon, every person had her own table assignment and name tag. My former campaign staff greeted each person and found places for the overflow. Both the mistress of ceremonies, who had been my campaign chairman, and the educator who introduced the guest speaker were prominent women in the city. They brought credibility to the event. They helped communicate the message that Stockton is a community where talented women join to support and promote one another.

Eastin's speech was riveting. She talked about our state's huge average class size, our deteriorating school buildings, the technological deprivation of our students, and our deplorable ranking of forty-seventh in the nation for dollars spent per student. Once again, those present were energized by the power and commitment of a woman in public office. Next came Judy Chambers, and again she brought her remarkable wit and goodwill to my cause. I followed with a rundown of new accomplishments, noting the 11 percent reduction in crime and our efforts at revitalizing the downtown, and I urged the audience to get the news out that progress and change were occurring in Stockton. This second luncheon was successful in every way except its profit, only $2,700, a mere $100 more than the first one. My debt was being retired, but too slowly.

I used the third luncheon to promote my plan for a new Stockton waterfront. The city had a ten-acre parcel of land called Weber Point at the head of our deep-water channel. It was named for the founder of our city, Charles M. Weber, who built his house there in 1848. I had recently taken the problem of this large, valuable, and virtually abandoned site to a conference in San Antonio, Texas, sponsored by the U.S. Conference of Mayors in conjunction with the Institute on City Design. One of the ten resource experts at the conference was Samina Quraeshi, a graduate of the Yale School of Art and Architecture and now the director of the design program at the National Endowment for the Arts. All the experts at San Antonio were excited by the prospect of a piece of undeveloped waterfront property in the heart of a major California city, but none more so than Ms. Quraeshi. I invited her to be the keynote speaker at my third Women Leading luncheon.

While she was in Stockton, I arranged for Samina to talk about design to the city council, to have dinner with an important civic group called Stockton Beautiful, to attend our three museums and the University of the Pacific, and to meet with city staff. *The Record* gave her visit front-page coverage and included a photo of her on Weber Point. The lunch raised $4,100. I only had $8,200 to go before the debt was erased.

Although Senator Barbara Boxer, the featured speaker for my fourth and final luncheon, was a prominent Democrat, I had no problem getting the major Republican business leaders to be honorary cochairs and to buy tables. The bankers, developers, and lawyers must have heard the excitement in my voice when I called to ask for their support. "I know you are not of the same political persuasion as the keynote speaker," I began, "but Senator Barbara Boxer has done a lot for Stockton and will be in a big tent at our waterfront helping me pay off my debt at the fourth annual Women Leading luncheon." How could they refuse! The luncheon had become a major event for women in the city. In addition to nineteen honorary cochairs, seventeen of Stockton's most influential women leaders got together tables for the event. The Hispanic leadership of Stockton, represented by two women who serve on the local community college board, organized a group of twelve. When Senator Boxer arrived, she walked into a big tent where a crowd of three hundred waited unhappily.

Unfortunately, everyone's shoes were wet. The parks and recreation department had failed to turn off the watering system on the lawn under the tent and everyone had had to walk through a swamp to his or her table. Why the water was not turned off, I do not know. The tent had been set up the day before. Someone should have seen the problem, but the sprinklers were on a timer and no one turned them off. A further discomfort was the heat. Summer in Stockton is very hot, and the sides of the tent were down. I stepped to the podium, greeted everyone, and joked about how warm it was. (I didn't mention the lake underneath their tables.) No one laughed. Then came Senator Boxer. Understanding the situation immediately, she said, "Joan, it's too hot. Raise the sides." My husband Jim and my sons John and Peter jumped up and hoisted up the sides. The women sighed, smiled, and applauded. At least they would not suffocate.

Each of the Women Leading Luncheons had its highlight. The first one was Judy's introduction; the second was Delaine Eastin's fiery presentation; the third was the presence of Samina Quraeshi. Though Boxer gave a great speech, as she always does, the highlight of the fourth luncheon was her introduction by Pat Meredith, a speech instructor at our community college, a woman who had been active for many years in local organizations and causes. In 250 words, she captured the essence of Senator Boxer, a fighter for equality for all, especially the most vulnerable. Even her name, Pat pointed out, suggested a degree of pugnacity. Boxer, she said, fights for choice and against sexual harassment and the gun lobbyists and those who would destroy the earth. "We are proud of this woman...who demands that America be what it was born to be, a nation with a soul where all men and women are created equal and where those who are down will be lifted up by those who are in."[1]

Senator Boxer wiped the tears from her eyes as she mounted the podium to make her presentation, which included vivid examples of her efforts in the areas Meredith had mentioned. This was the time of Senator Packwood's resignation over several cases of sexual harassment, which Boxer had pursued aggressively; she noted the large numbers of senators and friends who had urged her to pipe down, ease up, back off. Although she did not give up, she thought it was a lost cause until the Senate went into recess and the members went home. To the surprise of those senators, their constituents asked them what they were doing to get rid of Packwood. The senators came back to Washington and finally joined her in denouncing Packwood. Following Senator Boxer's talk, I gave my update on all the progress we had made in achieving our goals for Stockton.

There is no doubt about it, the presence of Boxer, a woman who stands for causes many women hold dear, made this fourth luncheon the most memorable. And it was a huge financial success. It netted $7,100. With that profit, plus $1,100 from the first term's bank balance of $2,000, the campaign was able to pay off the final $8,200 of the loan. The debt was retired. And much more had been achieved. At four large luncheons, women's leadership had indeed been redefined, as Anne Rudin had promised. Increasingly each year, we sensed our power, our common concerns and the fact that we do things differently. Bring on that chef's salad!

❖ Carlos Rendon was helping his twelve-year-old son fold newspapers for the boy's paper route when I stopped by to solicit his vote for my 1978 county supervisor's campaign—which was doomed to fail.

❖ When the "cupboard was bare" during my supervisor's race, Jim and the kids did the marketing. Jim was always my biggest supporter but some said publicizing the family's need to take on home obligations cost me the election.

❖ Ron Stein, a Stockton attorney, and I wait for results at my house on the night of the primary. He was the first to urge me to run for mayor. *Photo by Clifford Oto.*

❖ The new "genteel" mayor at home. Lessons in hardball were soon to come.

❖ Dwane Milnes, city manager, presides in his office in city hall. A good man for a big job.

❖ Mel Panizza jubilant on the night of his election to the Stockton City Council.

❖ A live interview with KCRA TV reporter Rich Ibarra at election central. It's a heady night.

❖ Senator Dianne Feinstein is a role model and great friend to Stockton and to me.

❖ Conversations with Police Chief Jack Calkins led to my five-star program for community safety.

❖ Ralph Lee White—Stockton councilmember, 1971-1987.

❖ Council member Sylvia Sun Minnick wrote *The Chinese Community of Stockton* for the Images of America book series.

❖ With President Bill Clinton and Vice President Al Gore at a U.S. Conference of Mayors visit to the White House in 1994.

❖ With Mayor Zhong Guangchao of Foshan, Guangdong, People's Republic of China, during a ceremony that created the sister city relationship between Foshan and Stockton. John Wentz, chair of the Sister City organization of Stockton (applauding in the background) led our group to Foshan to establish this relationship. Being Stockton's emissary was one of the perks of the mayor's job.

❖ Thi To Can Nguyen speaks out. *Photo by Calixtro Romias.*

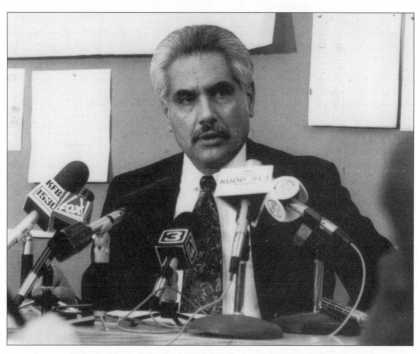

❖ Deputy Chief Edward Chavez announces the tragic shootings of police officer Arthur Parga and home owner Manuel Ramirez. *Photo by Calixtro Romias.*

❖ Pich Saly (left) and Siheang Lim, mother and father of three of the four Cambodian boys who drowned in the rain-swollen Calaveras River, carry a picture of their son Danalee Pich, age eight, after funeral services held for the four boys.

❖ Senator Barbara Boxer spoke at the fourth Women Leading Luncheon in downtown Stockton. She was dynamite.

❖ Weber Point, 1998, after the implementation of recommendations of the RHAA (Royston, Hanamodo, Alley and Abby) study. The historic Hotel Stockton (inset and upper left) was completed and dedicated in 1910. *Photos by Calixtro Romias.*

6

Second Term

Ethnic Politics

Sylvia Sun Minnick: The Race Card

"**S**tockton Council Woman Accuses Darrah of Racism."[1] read the front-page headlines one day during the beginning of my second term. It was the day after I refused to nominate Sylvia Sun Minnick as chairperson of any of the ten standing committees of the city council. Asked by a reporter why she thought she had not been nominated, Minnick responded, "The bottom line—it's racism." I was appalled and denied the accusation vehemently. When it came my turn to speak to the reporter, I explained that my action was in the best interests of the city: "She is not as effective a chair as the other members of the council. Because of her past actions, she does not have as much credibility as other council members have," I told the paper.[2] My words may have been tactless, even cruel, but they told an unfortunate truth. Moreover, Minnick had alienated most if not all of the council; one member had even demanded that she receive no chairmanship. The history of the disaffection between Sylvia and me went back two years, almost to the beginning of my first term.

Sylvia Minnick was elected to the city council in 1990, along with five other new members, including me, and she remained on the council for two terms, until the end of 1994. Born to Chinese parents in Kuala Lumpur, Malaysia, she had come as a child to San Francisco in 1951 to live with her grandmother. Later, she earned bachelor's and master's degrees in history from California State University, Sacramento. At the time she ran for city council, she was the owner of Heritage West Books, a publishing company, and she had recently published *Samfow*, a history of the Chinese in San Joaquin County.

Initially, she supported my goals; she even voted with me for my nominee for vice-mayor, although she had been lobbied by another candidate. She also worked well on the *ad hoc* committee that was studying police funding, the key to our being able to hire new officers. It was her nominee to the committee who came up with the funding concept—an increase in the utility tax over a three-year period—that solved our problem. Sylvia herself helped write the final plan, which was endorsed by whole council. At that point, she was a productive member of an effective council team.

Working on her own, independent of the council, she did not do as well. Her next project concerned blight in the downtown area, the worst ten blocks of which were in her district. It was a part of town where the gutters were ankle-deep in trash and the sidewalks were crowded with drug users and pushers who conducted business on El Dorado Street, a major artery into the city. This street was considered so dangerous that at one notorious intersection motorists did not come to a complete stop at the red light lest they be accosted by pushers. Drug activity at this corner, one block from the police station, defied law enforcement and threatened the surrounding residential and commercial areas. When a cleanup process began, *The Record* called it "Welcome Surgery on a Malignancy."[3]

The trouble was that the "surgery" began suddenly and without council knowledge or participation. It was strictly a two-person show. Working together on their own, Minnick and the city manager, Alan Harvey, had developed a sixty-day pilot project which they suddenly put into effect without any agreement by the council. The presence of law enforcement was increased; parking was banned; streets were repaired and swept; sidewalks were scrubbed; buildings frequented by drug users were closed. Several city departments were involved in this operation. Although meetings had been set up by Minnick to inform the neighborhood of what was to come, the council knew nothing about it. "Sylvia Sun Minnick, the Central Stockton City Council member, deserves particular praise for the cleanup program," the council members read one morning in the newspaper.[4] "This is a declaration of war to bring back the quality of life for people south of the Crosstown Freeway," Sylvia opined.[5] Maybe so, but the council had been completely bypassed, and we were not happy about it.

Considerable resources were directed to this project. Six full-time police officers and a sergeant patrolled the area. In one month, they made 85 felony arrests, 117 misdemeanor arrests and 163 arrests for public intoxication. Shortly after the program had been launched, some people claimed that the drug pushers were gone from the scene. Others said the dealers had simply moved over several blocks and that, even within the ten-block area, one could still buy drugs from a passing car. To the people who lived and worked there the parking restrictions were particularly objectionable, especially the ban on parking from 5 A.M. to 9 A.M., which forced people to park many blocks from their homes and left them vulnerable to attack on the way to their vehicles. When some business owners brought their complaints to the council, Minnick announced that the city would modify the parking program, but would expand the area it covered.

By this time several council members were so upset that they questioned the whole operation. Was this a proper expenditure of city resources? How much had Harvey spent? Had he exceeded the $20,000 limit that the city manager was allowed to spend without obtaining council approval? Although *The Record* ran several stories that praised the project and Sylvia personally, the council was angry about the expense, the non-inclusion, and the parking complaints.

Despite these misgivings, which I shared, when Sylvia requested that a Central Stockton revitalization committee be established, I agreed. I worried at the time that discussion of crucial issues could be preempted by such a committee and come before the council only for final action, but the deputy city manager was strongly in favor, so we went ahead. Naturally, Sylvia wanted to be the chair. Following the procedure for assigning all committee chairmanships, I nominated Sylvia to this position and the council confirmed the appointment. Even more than her sixty-day project with Alan Harvey, Sylvia's leadership of this key committee was what later led to bad feeling between her and the other council members, including me.

The first big issue to come before the new committee was Gold Rush City. This was a $1 billion theme park and resort to be located on a large parcel of land in downtown Stockton. The partnership that wanted to undertake this enormous project included two prominent Stockton developers. There had been vague rumors about such a plan for some time, but neither the council nor I had specific information. It was Sylvia who first spoke about it in public: "This is an exciting project which could have a very positive effect on Stockton," she told *The Record*.[6]

In the same article, she talked about the complexity of the issues, including the acquisition of land by the city, traffic management, and access to the Port of Stockton. She gave this statement to the paper *before* the Central Stockton revitalization committee (later called the downtown revitalization committee) ever met. The conclusion some people drew was that discussions were going on outside of the committee structure. Perhaps commitments were being made, or suggested, on behalf of the city. Once again, we read in the paper that Harvey and Minnick were the sponsors of a dramatic initiative for Stockton, a project that none of the rest of us knew about.

Our fears were more than justified on the day the Gold Rush group of investors had its first meeting with Sylvia's committee. The developers entered the room and, before a stunned committee, stated that they were pulling out of Stockton. They were angry, we learned from *The Record*, at a "unilateral" report by city staffers, particularly a recommendation by the city manager, that the developers put $750,000 in an escrow account to cover the city's costs.[7] How and why Harvey came up with this demand was never known, but allegations of secret meetings and bad faith negotiations ensued. *The Record* reported that "The lack of council involvement in the proposal shrouded it in mystery and embroiled it in controversy."[8] Members of the council reacted in dismay. "I feel like we have fallen down...it has great potential for doing so much for the city," said one council member, voicing the frustration many of us felt.[9] The council sent a letter to the Gold Rush group, trying in vain to reopen negotiations. We soon learned that the developers had taken their project to the nearby city of Lathrop.

Although I am now convinced that Sylvia was as surprised as the rest of us, at the time the council was acutely uneasy with the sense that, once again, as during the downtown cleanup project, she seemed to be working with Harvey behind the scenes. The project had blown up in our faces. Many felt that Stockton had missed a big opportunity. Yet who could know? Following the downtown cleanup project, which had taken the council by surprise and had produced decidedly mixed results, the experience with Gold Rush City further weakened the council's confidence in Sylvia's leadership.

A further episode that undermined Sylvia's credibility for me personally occurred one day when I had asked her to come to my office to discuss some matter. Instead, she insisted that I come out to her office in North Stockton. As I sat across the desk from her, wondering what she might be up to, she played for time. She coyly addressed my issue, then talked about a few other matters. At last she came out with it—she had thought of running against me for mayor in 1992. She implied that, although she had discarded the idea, she might, at a later date, be persuaded to run. It was a tease. Wow! In going to her office, I had gone out of my way to accommodate a colleague; after the meeting, I took my leave of a potential adversary.

The relationship between several members of the council and Ms. Minnick took a decisive turn for the worse over the resignation of the city manager, Alan Harvey. Negotiations over his severance package, which should have been done quietly behind closed doors, were instead publicized when a memo from Harvey indicating that he had been offered the choice of resigning with a lump-sum payment or being fired for misconduct was printed in *The Record*. The paper further reported that "Minnick...said Harvey was forced out by a council majority making a 'power play.'"[10] Sylvia's public attack on the council and her insistence that Harvey had been the victim of a power play while she was the selfless defender of the injured party did nothing to repair her damaged relations with her fellow council members.

Returning now to the issue of committee chairmanships, I should repeat that the mayor's role in this process is to nominate prospective chairs, who must then be confirmed by the council. In early 1991, around the time of the Harvey resignation, when chairs for the council committees were to be reappointed, a person whom I trusted and respected who worked for the city, came to me privately and requested that Sylvia not be appointed chair of the Central Stockton revitalization committee. This person raised questions about Sylvia's ability to work with staff. Since I anticipated that no council member would come to Sylvia's defense and I had an excellent alternative nominee, Councilmember Beverly Fitch McCarthy, I yielded to staff's request. Sylvia was extremely upset and hurt.

Instead of accepting this outcome as I had anticipated she would, Sylvia went on the offensive and attacked the council at its meeting January 28. She alleged that "master manipulators in a major bloc saw committee assignments as a means of rewards or punishment." She did not name names, but it did not take a genius to know that she was referring to Mel Panizza, Loralee McGaughey, Nick Rust, and Floyd Weaver, who often voted as a block. Then Sylvia attacked me for knuckling under: "I question the pragmatic appeasement philosophy of the mayor." Aware that she had alienated a number of people, she protested that "backroom politics played heavily in my not receiving reappointment as the chair of the Central Stockton revitalization committee even though the bulk of the area is in my district." She asked, "What are the motives behind this?" Yes, she admitted, at times she had gone contrary to the council, particularly when she needed to treat Alan Harvey fairly and not yield to political pressure on the Gold Rush issue, but the real question was "Does the color of my eyes or hair play a part in this ostracism?"[11]

At the next council meeting, on February 4, 1991, three supporters spoke on her behalf. Their accolades included the claim that she had created a drug-free community downtown and that she was one of the top three vote getters in the city. They noted that Minnick was the first Asian woman to serve on the city council, and although she was of small of stature, she had tenacity and communicated effectively with her district. This was an issue of fairness, they said.

That was early 1991. By the spring of 1992, when I was campaigning for reelection, though she did not run herself, Minnick worked openly against me. When a reporter for *The Record*, who was doing an article about the election, called council members for comment on my leadership, all were favorable except Minnick, who described me as "gushy and quasi-royalty."[12] These words, too, like my own statement to *The Record* about her incompetence, told an unflattering truth, but this time about me. My efforts to avoid conflict and get along with everyone undoubtedly produced some "gushy" behavior, and my genteel persona— what I thought of as replacing fighting and swearing with civility among council members—could well have come across as snobbish, or what Minnick called "quasi-royalty."

After my reelection, it was again time for me to nominate the committee chairs for the forthcoming council session. There were nine chairmanships: five standing committees, two special committees, and two *ad hoc* committees. Talking to council members about which committee each would like, I worked through the list of which members would chair which committees. I had Sylvia listed to chair the planning and development committee, but the vice mayor, Floyd Weaver, objected. He wanted to chair both the planning and development and the Central Stockton revitalization committees. My conversation with Mel Panizza, my choice as continuing chair of the budget and finance committee, went well because he wanted that job. Frankly, he had power enough to do a lot of damage if I had tried to buck him, but I thought he had handled the committee well and I was comfortable with the reappointment.

At the same time, I told him I would really appreciate his support for Stockton's renewing its lapsed membership in the U.S. Conference of Mayors. The conference had been especially valuable to me in my first term, not least for the way it made each mayor feel important, rather than someone to be manipulated or put down, which the council and the press seemed so to enjoy. The organization also addressed issues that I cared about—crime, hand gun control, affirmative action, jobs—and the women's caucus was a wonderful new group of peers and role models for me. Without Stockton's membership in the U.S. Conference of Mayors, I would not have been invited to the Institute for City Design's conference in San Antonio in June 1994, the event that led to the enormously important waterfront redevelopment plan. Mel conceded that the conference had corrected some dubious accounting procedures, and he agreed to support Stockton's resumption of membership.

Just before I announced the new committee chairs, a council member came to my office and solemnly informed me that several members did not want Sylvia to be chair of either the planning and development committee or the downtown revitalization committee. They felt Sylvia could not be trusted. She not only supported Frank Fargo for mayor, but she had also publicly spoken against me. "She's a Republican," I was reminded. "Look Joan...politics is not Junior Aid. Politics is playing hardball," said this council member. It was also made very clear that the council would oppose renewing our membership in the U.S. Conference of Mayors if I appointed Sylvia chair of any standing committee. This visit suggested that Sylvia had by now forfeited the respect of her council colleagues and that, as a result, her nomination would never be approved. Moreover, without council support, a chair could not effectively perform a job. Because of these attitudes toward Sylvia and my intense desire to rejoin the U.S. Conference of Mayors, I did not appoint Sylvia as chair of one of the five standing committees, nor did I give her one of the four *ad hoc* committees, for various reasons. In consequence, there was no committee chairmanship for Sylvia.

I thought then and do now that it would have been the fair thing to do to make Sylvia the chair of the planning and development committee, as I originally intended. In retrospect, part of me wishes I had told that particular council member to go to hell and threatened at the next council meeting to accuse the group of four of bullying both me and Sylvia. But as I have said often enough, confrontation was not my style. Also, had I challenged the council in public, the press reports might have featured a return to the bad old days of council infighting, creating a long-term detriment to its new prestige, for which I gave myself some credit. Finally, rejoining the U.S. Conference of Mayors meant a lot to me. In the end, I paid heavily for giving in, and I took the rap for the injury to Sylvia.

The day after the council meeting at which the chairmanships were announced, *The Record* carried the headline with which I began this chapter: "Stockton Council Woman Accuses Darrah of Racism." Not only was I insulted by this accusation, I also felt that my actions had been sound and were supported, in fact demanded, by the other council members. The newspaper's editorial page fell short of finding me a racist, but they charged me with "insensitivity," aligning their opinion with Minnick's: "What is obvious is that Darrah should have been more sensitive to the racial and ethnic mix of this city."[13] As she had with the story of the resignation of Alan Harvey, Sylvia used the paper to generate favorable publicity for herself. Once again, she came on as a victim of the council and a defender of the oppressed. Her complaints were "not a form of public balm for a bruised ego," she told *The Record*. Rather, she was just informing the public that both District 5 and the Asian community, 21.4 percent of Stockton, were not being equally represented in city government.[14]

Prior to the next council meeting, Minnick talked with the Asian Pacific advisory committee. Several Japanese, Filipino and Chinese community leaders accused me of prejudice and demanded that I reconsider the committee appointments. "The whole Asian community looks at it as almost an insult," said a board member of the Japanese American Citizens League.[15] I indicated a willingness to reconsider my appointments if any council member was dissatisfied. Gonzales, a newly elected member, was ready for more discussion, but he did not make a motion for reconsideration. All the others agreed with my appointments. Loralee McGaughey went further. Speaking of Minnick, she said, "I believe you have to be able to work with other council members, city staff and business, and I don't think that has always happened in the past."[16] The editorial position the next day was critical of the council for its silence on the issue of reconsideration. Although *The Record* allowed that a person should not be appointed just because she was Asian, nor should a person be appointed who did not have the respect of the council, it restated its sympathy with Minnick's position.

Sylvia subsequently denied that she had ever accused me of racism. Only nineteen days after *The Record*'s headline, at the close of a council meeting, she said that she had listened to all the tapes of recent council meetings and she had not used the word racism about me. She thought that the lack of equal representation was an omission that she had the right to question. "The philosophy of you gotta go along to get along reeks of old boys and elitism," said Sylvia, claiming that it was not her custom to disrupt the tranquility of the council. Flabbergasted, I turned to her and said, "Council Member Minnick, just to set the record straight, *The Record* headlines read, "Stockton Council Woman Accuses Mayor Darrah of Racism." Minnick fired back, "Mayor, I don't write the headlines." I asked her straight out, "So you never accused me of racism? You never said I was a racist?" She stuck with her qualified position, that there were no racist comments in the council minutes, but she did not deny that she had charged me with racism when speaking with the reporter.[17]

This was one too many for Mel Panizza. With his curly red hair framing his full face and his matching red moustache, Mel reminded Minnick that she had raised the issue of racism before. In a previous council meeting, she had asked whether her almond eyes and black hair were the reason for her not getting a chairmanship. Referring to her chairmanship of the downtown revitalization committee, he said there was much concern on the council about where that committee was going. He noted further that he had been bounced from that committee after a year, and he thought his removal was a result of the mayor's best judgment and not because his name was Italian or his hair was red. Visibly angry, he concluded, "I sincerely hope the political gamesmanship can stop."[18]

This remark earned Mel the special wrath of the speakers at the next meeting. One of the three Hispanic speakers at that meeting called him "the strong man." A liberal dentist noted that Panizza himself had three chairmanships. Why could not one go to Minnick? Several speakers pointed to the issue of equity in chairmanships. The president of the Filipino Chamber of Commerce noted that all the other council members had been consulted in advance of the appointments. Minnick had not. He saw this as a conspiracy to maliciously disenfranchise a fellow member. Recalling the intimidating conversation about the chairmanships, I recognized the partial truth of his statement.[19]

Other arguments for reconsideration of the committee chairmanships were put forward that night and at the next council meeting with great fervor and lucidity, arguments we had all heard before. Some of them referred to a statement I had released that set out council goals for the coming term, including greater efforts at affirmative action and cultural sensitivity. My actions had been contrary to these goals, we were told. "Why don't more minorities run for office," queried Nelson Nagai. "Why should they when they don't get appointments, like Sylvia Minnick?"[20] Several residents from Sylvia's District 5, were angry that she had recently been elected for a second term and yet was being deprived of equal representation on the council. Among the speakers that night was a friend of mine, the Reverend Barry Means, a black minister with whom I had served Christmas dinners at the fairgrounds. "A seventy-four-year-old black man of the deep South knows how it is to be passed over. It's far better that you change. How do you think the person feels when she walks among people and they say she is unqualified? Correct this and let the city move forward," he remarked with passion.[21] I was moved by his words.

I had already suggested to Panizza that he give up the building/ space planning committee chairmanship in favor of Minnick. He initially resisted the idea but later agreed. I wanted this council meeting to be the final one on this matter. I reached for reconciliation: "The issue has become a very divisive one for our community and our council and the city will be hampered in meeting our several challenges if this important matter is not resolved. All of us must work together to build a greater Stockton, and this issue certainly is not enabling us to work together. It is separating us."[22]

I noted that Councilman Panizza had given me his formal resignation as chair of the building/space planning committee, and I invited Minnick to accept the chairmanship, which she did, commending Panizza for his generosity. What I learned from the whole tormented process, in addition to another lesson in hardball, was that once the issue becomes one of racial injustice, other considerations are set aside. The anger of the several ethnic constituencies (not only Asian, by the way), who had come to see Sylvia's non-appointment as an affront to themselves, was far more harmful to the functioning of city government than the ineffectiveness of any committee chair could ever be.

Another lesson I should have learned from the chairmanship wars but did not was that I needed to be more aggressive with the press. Sylvia's use of the newspaper to advertise the downtown cleanup project she had launched with Alan Harvey right after she was elected showed that she knew whom to call and what to say at *The Record* in order to present herself and her issues to the best advantage. Later, when her complaints produced the headline that I was a racist, my denials came too late and did very little to improve my image. Her charges succeeded in bringing people to the council chamber to express their outrage at my mistreatment of her. Although I felt very hurt and angry, I did not call *The Record*, nor did I have a surrogate do so, to protest its handling of the story. I still had that old idea that it was the newspaper's job to find the truth, not mine to "curry favor."

Sylvia and I had a rather rocky time of it during her last two years on the city council. More than once, she criticized me for not calling on her to speak in proper order. On the final night of her term on the council, after having received a plaque of appreciation that I had arranged for her, she declared that she could have been far more effective had the mayor not interfered with her actions. "It was unfortunate that during my years on the council I was not given the opportunity to prove my leadership skills because of personality clashes with the mayor," she opined.[23]

A year before Minnick left her council office, in November 1993, she was appointed by Republican Governor Pete Wilson to be assistant director of the California Department of Parks and Recreation. From 1994 to 1996, she served as the Wilson-appointed executive coordinator of the California Sesquicentennial Celebration. Uh-oh, I thought, when I heard of this assignment, the celebration will have problems if she is in charge. Sure enough, the state was embarrassed in January 1998, when the Mother Lode communities felt virtually ignored as the sesquicentennial birthday bash got started. There were financial difficulties too, and staff changes. Although many of these problems were certainly not Sylvia's fault, I know that a celebration on this scale requires complex cooperation among many people and interests, and Sylvia was not a practitioner of teamwork.

By the time these complaints came out in the press, Sylvia was long gone from that position. In 1996, she was the Republican nominee to run for the state assembly seat from San Joaquin County against Assemblyman Mike Machado. When she lost that race, the governor found another spot for her. In October 1997, Sylvia was appointed assistant director of the Department of Aging at $65,100 a year. In June 1998, she was inducted into the International Educators Hall of Fame. She was "recognized for her writing about Chinese culture and heritage in California since the Gold Rush, for starting a small publishing house, and for her achievements as an Asian-American woman."[24]

Sylvia Minnick has received far more press than any other Stockton council member since her departure from office, and almost all of it has been favorable. The only public criticism she has received so far concerned a piece of political symbolism, the renaming of a road, for which she had her facts wrong. Minnick's detractor pointed out that the name Eight Mile Road had been on the city street maps at least twenty years longer than she claimed when she urged that its name be changed to Alex Spanos Parkway. Spanos, we need to remember, was a major supporter of Governor Pete Wilson's presidential nomination as well as an important source of Wilson's campaign funds throughout his political career. During Wilson's administration it seemed to many of us that no one was appointed to a state post in San Joaquin County without Spanos's approval. Although she bungled the street renaming effort, Sylvia can hardly be blamed for wanting to express her gratitude to her political benefactor, the governor, by honoring one of his most loyal supporters.

Charges and counter charges concerning racism have become commonplace in American politics. Certainly, when Sylvia accused me of racism, I was outraged. At the time, I told myself that the issue was teamwork and the credibility and efficiency of council operations. I did not recognize then how much I had been intimidated. Let us remember, too, that I went to a school where all cultures except those of white middle class Protestants and Catholics were invisible, in fact absent. This background was definitely a liability for the mayor of a city which was projected to reach 30 percent Asian and 30 percent Hispanic. In both situations, especially when I was challenged or threatened, I responded with exaggerated gentility; I became polite and aloof, the person in charge.

It is embarrassing but understandable that Sylvia saw me as "quasi-royalty," putting myself above the democratic process. By the same token, she partially validated a caricature of herself too. One of my chief gripes against Sylvia was that she was devious. At the same time, she exploited her identity as an Asian woman to rally support for her cause. The bitterness of our conflict still bothers me, but not as much as the story I will tell in the next section of this chapter.

Parga-Ramirez: Consequences of a Drug Raid

In January 1993, the Stockton Police Department employed SWAT teams that made late night drug raids, a strategy used in many American cities in response to the violence associated with drugs. The police saw such raids as highly dangerous; in fact, the son of the former police chief in Stockton had been shot and killed in a raid a few years earlier.

I feel a lot of anguish as I tell this story, by far the most emotionally charged of any during my seven years as mayor. I think back to the crowds of people who came to the council chamber week after week, asking for justice, and I want to reach out to them. But I did not on that particular night, when, a long seven weeks after the shootings, the matter was finally placed on the council agenda for public discussion. People came to the council chamber to express their horror at what had been done to the Manuel Ramirez family: The father had been shot and killed, his pregnant daughter and retarded son had been brutally treated by the police. People demanded answers from the city government.

Arthur Parga, the coordinator of the raid, was a thirty-one-year-old police officer. An Hispanic like Ramirez, he was also mortally wounded that night. Parga had a wife, Lisa, who was pregnant with their second child, and a five-year-old son, Arthur. The day after the shooting *The Record* described Ed Chavez, then our deputy chief of police, as "holding back tears, his eyes red and watery," as he spoke of Parga, saying, "Art was a very professional officer, well liked by everyone who knew him. The potential he had in the department was limitless."[1]

Thirty-eight California police agencies sent representatives to Arthur Parga's funeral. Two hundred police officers drove from Stockton to Merced to attend the services. Outside the packed church there were scores of black-and-white cars and officers in full dress uniform standing at attention. I shared their admiration for the courage of one who had died in the line of duty. I felt that all of these men and women, as well as Parga, deserved the respect of the mayor.

The raid was part of a coordinated drug response procedure between San Joaquin County and its several cities, including Stockton. In any instance where sufficient evidence suggested that drugs were being used or sold, a CRAC-NET team could obtain a warrant to enter the house from the night judge on call. On the afternoon before the night of the raid, Stockton police had arrested two men who were carrying several pounds of marijuana. One gave as his address a street number on Pemberton Court that turned out to be the home of the Ramirez family.

The police obtained the required night warrant to raid this address and that night, Friday, January 22, 1993, at 2 A.M., several officers went to the door of the Pemberton Court address. They later claimed they knocked three separate times and announced their presence in English and Spanish. They reported that a curtain was hastily drawn back, a figure looked out and then dropped behind the curtain. No one came to door. The police broke it down and rushed in. As Maria Ramirez and her younger brother Juan were being handcuffed, Officer Parga rushed into the back room. There, waiting in the closet with a shotgun, was Manuel Ramirez, age sixty-three, the father of Maria and Juan. Whoever shot first was never determined, but both were found seconds later with wounds in their chests. An ambulance took Parga to nearby Saint Joseph's Hospital, where he died. A second ambulance took Ramirez to the more distant San Joaquin General Hospital, where he also died. The raid took place on a Friday night. On the following Monday, January 25, the council chamber was packed.

I came in from the right rear door, my customary entrance, stepped up two stairs to the dais, and walked to my place in the middle, flanked on each side by three council members. Looking out at the audience of some one hundred persons, I saw Maria Ramirez, her friends and supporters, and many leaders of the Hispanic community seated on the left side of the chamber. On the right side of the chamber were members of several other ethnic groups who had come to contest a different issue, namely my not nominating Sylvia Sun Minnick to a committee chairmanship. Arguments over this issue had been going on for several weeks. The disastrous drug raid, coming at the same time, made for heightened indignation and outrage among many minorities over perceived abuses and neglect by those in power. I looked out at the people in the council chamber that night and knew that, in their eyes, I had a lot to answer for.

More than anything, I wanted to show proper respect for Maria. I thought it heroic of her to be there that night, only three days after her dad had been killed and she herself had been severely mistreated by the police. I called on her to speak first. Curiously, I, who wanted to be so respectful, addressed her as Mrs. Ramirez, which was probably offensive to her. She was the deceased man's daughter, not his wife, but she was also pregnant and I was flustered.

A soft-spoken, attractive woman of thirty-one with dark brown, curly hair pulled back from her face, Maria walked quietly to the podium. "Good evening," she said as she took a deep breath and in a quiet voice read her prepared statement: "I want to ask if there could be a more thorough investigation because I am disappointed and devastated by how the police handled the situation. We were treated like criminals, thrown in handcuffs for hours without any knowledge of why we were handcuffed and why the police busted into our house. I also had no information of where my dad [was] or how he was. Mr. Richard Lopez [a well-known Latino leader in Stockton] recommended for the city council, and I am asking you as well, to call a federal investigation." Feeling intense empathy for this woman, but also feeling the need for caution since no one knew the complete circumstances of the raid, I responded, "Thank you Mrs. Ramirez."[2]

I knew many people in the audience that night. Jose Correa was the leader of a Mexican-American coalition of several organizations. Frank Orozco was a longtime school board member whom I had supported and worked with for many years, and Susan Casillas, another person I knew well enough to consider as a friend, was a counselor at the Family Service Agency. They were all extremely respectful in their requests for an outside investigation. Decrying the tragedy that had resulted in the deaths of two men and objecting to the treatment of a pregnant woman and her brother, they wanted a review of these highly dangerous nighttime drug raids. As they pointed out, many people give out their addresses. Could they, too, become the victims of a 2:00 A.M. attack by the SWAT team?

The tone of people's comments at this first meeting was remarkably controlled and thoughtful, despite a moment when Richard Lopez stepped to the podium in his familiar broad-brimmed, gold, cowboy hat and criticized me soundly for taking sides in favor of the police in the first news reports. "I have had at least thirty-five people call me and ask why I supported this lady," he said as he held up a sign that read: "Justicia para todos." "Justice for all," he translated, and tore it up. He got a big hand from the crowd. Other speakers, not only Hispanics but also many Asians and African-Americans, called for a halt to day and night raids and demanded a federal investigation. The president of the NAACP told the council, "My organization stands with them shoulder to shoulder in this matter."[3]

The following week two hundred and fifty persons held a forum to express their dismay over the raid and its consequences. At the council meeting of February 1, a spokesman for the Hispanic community, an attorney and a former county supervisor, presented fourteen questions for which he demanded answers. At each subsequent council meeting more people spoke out, their voices becoming more strident as the weeks went by, and still there were neither explanations for the raid from the city government nor any changes in policy. The crowds became angry and wrought up. They carried signs, stood in the back of the room, and booed and clapped for speakers. More and more, they demanded that a civilian police review board be established. Finally, following a motion by the Hispanic member of the council that was seconded by the member of Chinese descent, the matter was placed on the agenda for the council meeting of March 15, seven weeks after the raid. The motion was to discuss a civilian review board. The day before this meeting, *The Record* advocated that the city council itself act as the civilian review board: "If the current council chooses to ignore its responsibilities, it should be recalled and replaced by one that will honor its responsibilities."[4] This editorial also noted that no drug dealer and no drugs had been found at the Ramirez house.

On that March day when the council was at last prepared to discuss the raid, to listen to speakers and to answer questions, I met with the senior city staff as usual during the morning. We knew that there would be a large number of angry residents, as there had been at all the meetings since the raid. Many people could talk a long, long time, and the meeting could well go into the early hours of the morning. The signs and booing and clapping that had gone on for six weeks had made the council chamber seem unruly and disorderly, not exactly out of control, but poorly managed. In the interest of order and decorum, I decided to set some restrictions. The city attorney indicated I could limit signs and boisterous responses as long as I treated everyone equally. The council could limit speakers to five minutes each, as we had been doing in our efforts to restrain the weekly tirades of Mrs. Nguyen. The problem with the five-minute rule is that it must apply to all the speakers from the audience on the same issue—five minutes for one, five for everyone.

In addition to the possible length of the meeting, I was concerned about safety. Could there be a riot? I was afraid that there could be. The city manager assured me that there would be a sufficient police presence to handle any problem. I felt reassured on the one hand, yet concerned that excessive police could offend the speakers. I was warned that a representative from the ACLU had been invited who was expected to advocate the establishment of a civilian police review board. I was convinced that there would be serious problems with instituting such a board in Stockton.

My opposition to the civilian review board grew out of my sympathy with the Stockton Police Department. No police department likes such boards and ours was no exception. Another factor was that Stockton, at least in its dominant voices, was a conservative community. Berkeley has such a board, but Stockton is not Berkeley. To prepare, I telephoned the mayor of Berkeley, whom I knew, and asked her about Berkeley's experience with the police review board. I also read about the experiences of other communities and learned that the budget of such a board, especially if it carried out its own investigations, could be several hundred thousand dollars. Further, a board's recommendations for punishing an abusing police officer were rarely put into effect. Finally, the Stockton police department itself seemed to have quite a good system for disciplining its own officers. In short, I came to the meeting with an anti-review board mentality. I had also developed a compromise package because I knew that the cry for the review board would be intense. I was glad *The Record* had made the case that the council should take on this responsibility.

That evening I took special care with my appearance. I was wearing my red suit with a royal blue, red, and gold silk blouse. My gold earrings matched my gold ring. A heavy, gold bracelet hung from my right wrist. Large, fashionable, multicolored glasses framed my eyes. My hair, colored strawberry blond, had a combed, but not a set look. My face was fully made up—moisturizing cream, foundation, bisque, neck tanning cream, blush, lipstick, eyebrow pencil, eye shadow, eyeliner, mascara—ten products in all. The clothes, jewelry, and cosmetics helped me feel that I would be "respected" and "in charge." Control was a big item for me that night.

The council chamber was filled to its maximum of 100 people, the lobby outside the chamber was full, and there were chairs set up on the first and second floors of city hall to accommodate the overflow. A week after the raid, I had addressed those assembled in a quiet, hesitating tone, but this night, as I read my prepared statement, I wanted to sound forceful. I indicated that I had reviewed the fire regulations and only 100 persons were allowed inside the room. No one could be standing; everyone must be seated. "There can be no signs," I said, "no signs on sticks, no signs at all. They represent a distraction and a fire hazard. With respect to decorum [I cleared my throat], it is hard for some to realize that it is frightening and intimidating for some to speak before the city council. Tonight we need to provide a forum so every person feels respected and listened to and this will not be possible if any person calls out during someone else's presentation or if there is any booing or clapping or [I groped for another word] cheering before or after presentations. So, in conclusion [wrapping it up], the rule tonight is no interruptions during presentations and no showing of approval or disapproval after a presentation is made." I then explained the time schedule for speaking. We would gather the number of cards of speakers, count them, and then divide them into the allotted time frame. There turned out to be thirty cards, so at five minutes per person, this would amount to two and a half hours of testimony. It all seemed very tidy. I declared a ten-minute break. "Do you agree with the ruling of the mayor?" shouted Leonard DeVera, a Filipino attorney who had become the major spokesperson of the opposition. "Say, yes or no," he screamed. "No," the hundreds shouted back.[5]

After the break, I resumed the meeting and soon had to remind the officer that I did not want any signs in the council chamber. Then Leonard, without being recognized, stood up holding a sign that read, "Freedom of Speech." "She is taking away the only right we have," Leonard yelled, and the crowd whistled and shouted its approval.[6]

Chagrined by this outburst and knowing there was no stopping the angered crowd, I gave up on the rule of no clapping, booing, or shouting. I would have had to adjourn the meeting had I insisted on it. No one wanted that, but no one in the audience was going to succumb to the mayor's demands. Maintaining my composure, I described the work the council and I had done in preparation for this meeting, reviewing the tremendous number of documents we had received from California cities, the library articles, the whole packet of material a proponent of police review boards had sent us, and numerous letters. I cited phone conversations with three people from Berkeley, including the mayor, and the mayor of Sacramento. In short, I implied, I had done my homework. So had Ed Chavez, who had consulted a great deal of material. Before the citizen presentations began, Chavez would give a fair review of the issue of police review commissions.

Chavez asserted that nationally, in jurisdictions that had police review boards, an average of 10 percent of complaints against police officers were sustained, whereas in Stockton the rate was 25 percent. He described the high standards the city manager maintained for all departments. He talked about the council's support of community-oriented policing which had fostered more respectful relations between the community and the police. He spoke of the high cost of external investigations, compared to internal investigations. After his speech, I encouraged him to give statistics for SWAT and nighttime raids. In the past several years there had been 274 raids, with only fifteen undertaken at night, and only one injury resulting from all 274 raids. Chavez spoke for thirty-five minutes.

I had already told the crowd that everyone else, including the major spokesperson for a civilian review board—the ACLU man who had driven the eighty miles over from San Francisco to attend this meeting—could speak for only five minutes. This ruling infuriated the crowd. At one point, they threatened to boycott the meeting but then changed their minds. I asked if the ACLU attorney wished to speak first, but the head of the Human Rights Task Force, Louis Gonzales, indicated that Leonard DeVera would speak first.

In an angry voice, gesticulating and looking around the council chamber, Leonard shouted, "Today, March 15, 1993, is a day that will go down in infamy, for it is on this day that the first amendment right of the citizens of Stockton was viciously and treacherously attacked by the very representatives that have been elected to this city council." Everyone clapped and cheered. He held up another sign which read: "Who Will Be Next?" He asked if the prohibition against clapping applied to the hundred or so persons in the lobby and on the first floor. Cheers from outside the council chamber erupted in response.

Following DeVera's lead, Louis Gonzales castigated the council for its treatment of those assembled. "If you went back fifty years there would never be a time when the citizens were treated worse," he declared. He referred to the four SWAT cars and three motorcycles that he had seen circling city hall as people came into the building that evening, a sign of police and council hysteria because, "We are minorities, we are Hispanics." Everyone clapped.[7]

The next speaker, a man about age forty, who had an athletic build and was dressed in a gray suit with a well-trimmed beard and moustache, came to the podium and introduced himself as John Crew, staff attorney and director of the police practices project for the Northern California ACLU. "I share deep concern about the status of free speech in the city of Stockton," he began. He endorsed the police review process, saying that he was absolutely convinced that it worked and that the council needed to read a great deal more unbiased material and speak to authorities in this area before it came to a decision. He held up several documents. "Please read them and make an informed decision," he pleaded. At this moment, I realized that we should have allowed John Crew the same amount of time that we had given Chavez, but it seemed impossible to change the "rules" now.

Todd Summers, president of the local chapter of the NAACP, echoed the outrage of earlier speakers over the procedures: "I cannot recall a single council meeting of the old or the new council that restricted people's ability to speak." He said our conduct was "condescending and borderline." He asserted, "You work for all the people of Stockton, not just the police department." Todd is a hardworking and very well-meaning man and not quickly driven to anger. I was impressed with his remarks. I had known him for a long time; I considered him a friend and he had always been a supporter.

I felt the same way about the next two speakers, who also opposed my procedures. One was Richard Oliver, an attorney for the California Rural Legal Assistance. He spoke particularly to the existing complaint procedure, saying that it was intimidating and far too long. I knew that he had a lot more he would have liked to say that night, but he had to stop after five minutes like the rest. He came back to council meetings weekly for the next several months, recounting five minutes at a time the contradictions and inequities of the case. For example, he noted that Officer Parga's ride to Saint Joseph's Hospital took ten minutes, whereas Manuel Ramirez's trip to the county hospital took thirty minutes.

Finally, Robert Green spoke. He is a big man, with a booming voice, a Unitarian minister and an attorney, and like Richard Oliver, he speaks frequently and forcefully on issues of the disadvantaged. This evening he was enraged. In a piercing voice, he stated, "Mayor, in all the years I have appeared before this city council, I have never experienced the kind of restrictions that have been placed on the freedom of speech, the freedom of assembly, the freedom to redress grievances as I have tonight." Cheers and clapping resounded. Then he got to the nut of the matter. He said that the council's confidence in the police department was not shared by the people in this room. "We do not get the deference and respect from line police officers that the police chief does. We experience them as intimidating people who impose fear upon us." Loud cheering repeatedly interrupted his words. What is appalling to me even today as I write these words is how much my concern was focused on keeping the meeting short—to not let it go on until two in the morning. I wanted to avoid disorder! I shake my head in dismay when I think of this.

My other task, as I saw it that night, was to keep a lid on the public anger. Looking back, I see that anger as directed more toward me and the council for suppressing discussion than toward the police for the raid. In fact, my effort to control public outrage significantly increased it.

At the end of the meeting, when no one else asked to speak, I turned to the subject of the civilian review board and made my five-part motion, the text of which I had distributed to the members of the council before the meeting. It set up the council as the review board with the responsibility to review complaints and depositions and to develop a procedure that would make it easier to make complaints. With limited discussion, the council approved these recommendations by a 5 to 2 vote, the Hispanic and Chinese members voting in the negative. The meeting was over at 9:30, and I am now mortified to recall feeling proud of myself that the issue had been handled so efficiently!

For the next four months, at every council meeting, twenty to forty people came to speak, during the time period allotted for citizens' comments, about the injustice of the raid. The protesters brought signs and held them up in the crowded council chamber. I continued to rule that no signs could be brought into council meetings. They were outraged at that ruling. What was wrong with a sign? Did it interfere with a person's right to speak? At first the signs were very big—three feet by four feet—and they blocked the view. In response to complaints about these signs, and at the recommendation of the city attorney, I said that a one-foot by one-foot sign could be held in a person's lap. I was never successful at keeping members of the audience from clapping, which they did even more loudly as time progressed.

The Human Rights Task Force, as the organization of protesters called themselves, met regularly to discuss strategy for the subsequent council meetings and to stimulate a large turnout for every meeting. Every week, regular council business was delayed for at least an hour until the statements of all the angry people had been made. Mr. Oliver did extensive research on the circumstances of the raid itself, and every Monday night he began: "Because I have only five minutes to present, I shall carry forth with the next episode in the continuing saga of the Parga-Ramirez incident."

During this time, the issue of the raid itself remained unresolved. The police department, worried and on the defensive, was not forthcoming with the facts. The county district attorney's office continued to review the circumstances of the raid to see if any prosecution was in order. The F.B.I. offices in both Sacramento and Washington were also conducting reviews. All of this was further complicated by my not having appointed Councilwoman Sylvia Sun Minnick to a committee chairmanship, an action that incensed many people, not only Asians in Stockton but others as well. As time passed, everyone—the Ramirez family sympathizers and the Sylvia Sun Minnick agitators—became angrier. Week after week, council sessions were dominated by the outcry of residents who felt that, as ethnic minorities, they had been denied justice by an oppressive white majority in city government.

Predictably, a legal case was eventually brought against the city of Stockton for its actions in the drug raid. The civil rights suit was filed by Ramirez's survivors, his wife Griselda, his daughter Maria, and his son Juan. U.S. District Court Judge Lawrence T. Carlton ruled that there had been misstatements and omissions in the paperwork used to justify the police request for a warrant to search Ramirez's house. He also ruled that police wrongfully held Maria and Juan for seventeen hours following the shooting. I will never forget the 1996 closed session when the council was given the final figure required by the Ramirez family to settle the case. It was $650,000 to be paid to the family of Manuel Ramirez, with $450,000 coming from the city of Stockton, $75,000 each from the county and the state, and $50,000 from the city of Lodi.

Our choice was to accept this figure or go to court. I voted for settlement because we were given confidential information about a weakness in the city's case that made me believe a jury could award more than the Ramirez family was requesting. In short, I opted for the cheapest way out. In defense of the large payout and the city's actions, Assistant City Attorney Cynthia Neely said that this was not an admission of any liability. This was simply an assessment of benefits and risks of litigation. I hoped that the money would in some small measure right the wrongs done to the family, but my role was not to assuage their pain with money. It was to get the best financial outcome for the taxpayers of Stockton.

Five years later, and after I had left office, my friend Carmen Fernandez told me I had come a long way in my understanding of Latinos. I still felt that I had a long way to go! At that first council meeting, Maria Ramirez had tears of humiliation and anger in her eyes when she asked me "Why are there so many police officers outside city hall? We are not violent people. We are people who are here for help, who came to our council for help." She also told me that "there would have been many more in these chambers tonight but they were terrified by the police cars, motorcycles and officers outside the steps of city hall."

The Record columnist, Michael Fitzgerald, wrote a thoughtful article that appeared two days after the March 15 meeting in which he found the council's crowd-management restrictions and the ban on speech deplorable.[8] At the same time, he praised the council's deliberate and well-informed handling of the review board issue. I have to agree with his objections. It would have been far better that night if we had listened to everybody, however long it took. Each person had his right to speak, and we had the responsibility to listen. It was outrageous that John Crew from the ACLU in San Francisco was not allowed to make his presentation in favor of the civilian review board. He should have had at least as much time as Chief Chavez took to cite evidence opposed to such a board. As it was, the council heard only a drastically abbreviated presentation of the other side. Basically, we heard only the negatives, and not nearly enough about the benefits of a civilian board.

I also think that, unlike the power structure of the city, those conservative business people whom I was certain would disapprove of a review board, a large part of the city's population, might have welcomed an external review. Fortunately for us at this time, we had an enlightened police chief under whose leadership the police significantly changed their procedures following the Parga-Ramirez affair. The stated aim of the changes was to ensure an equal concern about the well being of the residents, not just police officers, in any future conflict. After this there were fewer, if any, night raids. A new brochure was designed which described how to make a police complaint and, through continued pressure from civilians, this form is now easily available at the police department as well as at the public library.

As for myself, I learned one of the fundamental principles of governance: People absolutely have to be listened to. This is their right and this is a leader's obligation. After this experience, when an issue came before the council that we expected to draw a large crowd, I moved the meeting to the civic auditorium, which seats a thousand people. And lastly, there is now no more five-minute rule. Even if efficiency were the only goal, which it ought never to be, it would have been infinitely more efficient to spend another four hours at that March 15 meeting than to sit through the months of wrangling at subsequent meetings. A lot of the anger was provoked by the council's behavior that night, as much or more as by the raid itself. I did not see at the time that the issue had become justice and respect for every citizen, or the lack of it, on the part of the mayor and the city government.

The name of our central library is now the Cesar Estrada Chavez Library. This is a surprising name for a county where the shots have been called for so long by big agribusiness interests who do not exactly revere the name of that famous advocate for farmworkers' rights. But when Chavez died, those same Latinos who were so articulate during the Parga-Ramirez hearings came before the city council, and, one after another, they fervently requested that we name the library in his honor. Having listened to these people through the spring of 1993, I had come to know them better. I knew they would not give up. I also knew that Floyd Weaver, the vice mayor, wanted the support of Hispanics and been recently criticized by them. On my left was Ted Gonzalez, who would surely be favorable to the new name. After some forty speeches had extolled the leadership of Cesar Chavez, his historical importance, and his love of books, and knowing that those in the audience expected us to refer this matter to a committee, I turned to Floyd and said, "If you'll make the motion to name our central library for Cesar Chavez, I'll second it." He made the motion, I seconded, and the motion passed five to two. People in the audience were surprised and delighted.

One final point. If we had not named the library for Chavez, there might have been intense pressure to name a street after him, and changing a street name is a great big hassle. Although we moved on, I felt that there was no really uplifting end to the story. We were back to politics as usual.

Consensus For Change Luncheons: Reaching Out

In the context of the preceding two stories, readers may be struck by the irony of the fact that, after I had seen city government from the inside during my first term, one of my personal goals after my reelection was to was reach out to the several ethnic groups of the city. Stockton is expected to be a prototype of the average California city by the year 2020 when we are projected to have the ethnic mix that most cities will not arrive at until well into the twenty-first century—30 percent Asian, 30 percent Hispanic, 10 percent black, and 30 percent white.[1]

Stockton has had citizens of Asian descent since its beginning, and many of their families, now among the longest established in the city, are descendants of mid- and later nineteenth-century mining and railroad workers. In addition, since the 1970s and 1980s, large numbers of people from Southeast Asia have come to Stockton. Hispanic people, too, have been here from the city's founding, many as farm laborers, yet this population now also includes many recent arrivals, especially from Mexico and Central America. After three years in city hall I felt that their voices needed to be heard and that the interests of these groups should be appreciated more fully than they had been in the previous deliberations of municipal government.

I had been successful in putting on luncheons as part of my public relations business in the eight years before I became mayor, so I decided to invite leaders of several ethnic organizations to city hall for lunch. I arranged lunch meetings with interest groups as well, such as the media, the rental property association, the physically and mentally disabled, business, labor, seniors, environmental groups, education, culture and the arts, and social justice organizations. Since such a thing had never been done and there was no provision for it in the city budget, I got in touch with friends of mine at the three big banks in town and asked each bank for $500 to underwrite the cost of these events. The checks arrived forthwith.

My only intention when I planned these lunches was to explore ways that city government could be more inclusive; in other words, these were a series of fishing trips. City hall was frequented by the few people who had business with the city—anything from payment of a monthly water bill to a business item before a Monday night city council meeting. I wanted to make city hall friendlier, so that all Stockton residents would feel welcome to come there to express their concerns and to seek solutions to their problems. At the very least, they should know where city hall was located and that there existed an elected mayor and city council whose job it was to assure the well being of all city residents. Because of my school counseling background and three decades of community volunteer leadership, I knew how to create a productive and receptive group environment.

Over an eighteen-month period, I hosted twenty-three lunches with eleven ethnic groups and twelve interest groups. We usually met in the Round Room, right off the council chamber, and the menu was informal—sandwiches, salads, and sodas. Occasionally, as I did with Continental Cablevision and Kaiser Permanente, I went out to businesses to give these luncheons rather than asking their employees to travel to city hall. I always included at each lunch several city administrators from whom I thought the group might like to hear, such as the city manager, the deputy city manager, the police chief, or members of the council whose interests coincided with those of the group. Following introductions and some time to eat, the format of the meeting was simple: opening remarks by me in which I set forth the goals of the city government—reduction of crime, more jobs, downtown revitalization—and then a discussion of the group's concerns. At the end of an hour and a half, I passed out questionnaires that asked participants to evaluate the meeting.

In my letter of invitation I said, "In the long run, I hope these luncheons will increase communication and build partnerships." The blandness of this statement is remarkable given the chronology of events in the first three months of my second term. The new council was sworn in at its first meeting of the new year, January 4, 1993. The Parga/Ramirez drug raid occurred on January 23. The lunch invitations were sent out on March 8. The big public meeting to discuss the raid was March 15, and the first of the Consensus for Change lunches, the one with Hispanics, as luck would have it, had been scheduled for March 30.

People were angry and the turnout was low: Out of fourteen invited, only six showed up. One person demanded that all documents concerning the raid be made available to the public. Another, a city employee and leader of an Hispanic organization, threatened that the Human Rights Commission would file suit and pursue this. The facts of the shooting had still not been made public. Police Chief Ed Chavez, who came to the lunch, explained that the U.S. Department of Justice and the F.B.I. would be reviewing the case; their reports needed to be received before facts could be presented to the public.

Somewhat mollified by the chief's words, the participants went on to discuss community needs: jobs and activities for young people, volunteer programs in the neighborhoods, safe places for youngsters to hang out. I took notes during the lunch. Evaluations showed a surprising result: Two checked that the meeting had been excellent, and four more thought it "might be of some help." Asked what could what be done to improve future meetings, the respondents indicated that they wanted more meetings of longer duration.

The topics covered at subsequent lunches ranged all over the map. The African-American group focused on economic issues. I had invited sixteen people, and eighteen showed up. The main issues were jobs, fair employment, affirmative action, and the recording of data and statistics involving these matters. The group was also concerned about what was being done to get rid of the higher-level drug dealers. They felt that there were still too many on the streets, particularly in the areas where they lived. The city manager talked about drug prevention in the Safe Schools program, as well as in recreation programs and parenting classes. Mary Flenoy-Kelley, the vice principal of one of Stockton's high schools, described a program she had instituted called the African-American Leadership Male Academy. Later on, I called this same woman for advice more than once, and she contacted me periodically for particular needs for her academy and requested my attendance at events. I believe that this sort of personal connection was a benefit of these luncheons.

I continued to meet with a subgroup from the African-American lunch. At an August 1994 meeting, Bobby Bivens, a management consultant, proposed a twelve-point plan for the African-American community's economic recovery. He wanted the city to set targets for the number of minority- and women-owned businesses the city contracted with. At the time, the city had set goals to have at least 15 percent of its contracts with minority business enterprises (MBEs) and 5 percent with women's business enterprises (WBEs), but our records did not show the breakdown by ethnicity of the "minority" or the "women" because our computer program did not provide that information. Indignant, Margaret Burroughs, the president of the Black Chamber of Commerce, demanded that the software be changed. She got what she wanted. The city required HTE (Harwood Technological Enterprises), our computer provider, to change our software to include the breakdown by ethnicity within the "minority" category; this change was available not only to Stockton but to all other cities that requested it.

A further issue raised by the African-American consensus group was whether the city directory, used by the primary vendors as their source of business contracts, listed all the businesses owned by women and minorities. Were we leaving some out, ones that would consequently never get a contract with the city? The finance department sent out a request for information about MBEs and WBEs in the business license bill. As a result, more were identified and listed. Primary vendors were reminded of the city's targeted goals. These two results, the reprogramming and the increased listing, represented important outcomes for the African-American Consensus for Change luncheons.

The Japanese group, on the other hand, spoke from the perspective of economic advantage. The leadership of this community consists of established businessmen who have lived in Stockton for many years. I sent an invitation to nineteen people. Fourteen attended. Kate Komure from the Calvary Presbyterian Church was a native Californian who had been in nursing for forty years. George Matsimoto started the very successful Red Wing shoe store and is a member of the sheriff's volunteer police organization STARS. Kenji Takeuchi has been here since 1948. Kuniko Yagi volunteers for the Japanese newspaper. Barry Saiki was born in Stockton and describes himself as "the oldest Stocktonian here." He is a constant advocate for downtown revitalization, and he remembers the Stockton from the old days as crowded and full of vitality. All of these participants wanted a stronger business environment downtown, supported by more police involvement.

Twenty-three were invited to the luncheon for the Vietnamese and thirteen came. Again, City Manager Dwane Milnes and Deputy Police Chief Ken Wilbon were there. Crime was a major concern for this group. They wanted expanded city programs for young people. During these luncheons, an intense distress was expressed by many of the Asian groups—Filipino, Hmong, Vietnamese—over the loss of control over their children. Their ability to successfully discipline them seemed to have broken down. Beating their children was a common practice for parents at home in Laos, but in the United States these same parents were put in jail for child abuse. The fears they expressed—that their children were getting into violent gangs—led directly to several components in the design of the Safe Youth program that came out of city hall soon thereafter.

Another group that continued to work together after the initial lunch included people from the various organizations that were trying to mitigate gang violence. They worked hard, though ultimately unsuccessfully, to fashion a single, coordinated program. The handicapped talked to us about curb cuts, and the social justice organizations spoke about their powerlessness in city government. The senior citizens brought up a big list of issues, so many, in fact, that they asked for more time and discussion. And so it went. What started as a familiar idea—putting on a luncheon for a particular constituency—ended up a freewheeling experiment in participatory democracy. Looking through my boxes of evaluations from the luncheons, by far the most frequent comment is that people wanted more time, more meetings, and more discussion.

The original intention of the Consensus luncheons—greater participation for ethnic groups in city government—was swiftly overtaken by two large, ongoing events: the public uproar over Sylvia Minnick's chairmanships and the explosive consequences of the Parga-Ramirez drug raid. Nonetheless, several useful conclusions can be drawn from the Consensus project.

First, there was a real need for communication. People were glad to come and talk to us, and many of the points they raised led directly to positive results, such as the design of the Safe Youth program and the promotion of the city's contracting with businesses owned by women and minorities. It is unlikely that Sylvia Minnick could have raised such a hue and cry from Asian and other groups had there not already been a perception of prejudice and unfair treatment by city government of ethnic groups.

Second, there was a sense of tokenism about the lunches—that they were only a gesture toward inclusion rather than the substance of it. This existed because of the lack of follow-up, which itself resulted from the fact that no structure in city government—no committee, no staff person—was organized to continue the job. An individual, the mayor in this case, can take the initiative and get the ball rolling, but that individual can not sustain the work alone. STAND is a case in point. There again I started off on my own, going to see Mary Delgado, working with her to arrange a first meeting. Within short order, however, people from the community had organized and taken over the project, the police were brought in, and the mayor was politely sent on her way.

In the very brief story that follows, I again acted alone. And although again there was no long-term benefit to interethnic understanding, something personally important to those involved was accomplished.

The Drowning of the Cambodian Children: An Immigrant's Story

The following events took place almost two years before the Parga-Ramirez raid, but I include the story here as a final reflection on the relations between the several ethnic groups that make up Stockton. I have suggested that the demographic mix in Stockton is becoming a paradigm for many other American cities. The story of the Cambodian children is one small and quite different piece of that complex social puzzle.

On Wednesday evening, March 27, 1991, I was leaving an event at the University of the Pacific when I heard the engine and saw the bright red and white lights of a huge helicopter directly overhead. It seemed to be combing the landscape just beyond. "What's going on?" I asked. "Some kids drowned in the river," someone told me.

The next day the story dominated the front page.[1] Four Cambodian children, who lived in the nearby Kentfield apartments along the edge of the Calaveras River, had drowned in its raging waters. That year's spring rains had been torrential, causing the river to run at twelve feet rather than the customary one foot or less. The children, who normally walked out in the dry riverbed to play on a small island, did not understand at all about the power of the river when it was high and moving fast. Not one of the four could swim. They held hands, but to no avail. They were immediately sucked up by the river. One boy, who also went in with them, was saved by a passerby who threw out a plastic strip and pulled him in. This fifth child could swim. The three Pich brothers, age seven, eight, and nine, were the sons of Siheang Lim and her husband Pich Saly, a Cambodian refugee family that had moved to Stockton in 1983.[2] The boys were visiting their cousins, the Soun family, who lived in the Kentfield apartments. Vanna Soun, age ten, was the fourth victim, and his brother Sitha was the child who was saved.

When I arrived the next day at the river's edge, Mrs. Lim was there. A thirty-one-year-old woman of moderate stature, she appeared frail, bewildered, and heartbroken. She kept saying, "They were hardly gone from my sight, only a minute." When the newspaperman asked for my comments, I said, feeling defensive on Mrs. Lim's behalf, "Like all mothers, she blames herself. The boys were outside playing. Then all of a sudden they were gone. Like any mother, she wishes that she had been watching them every moment." There were TV cameras everywhere and people were standing on the levee. A special diving unit with several divers in wet suits was trying to locate the children and bring them up. Police and fire department vehicles were all around. Mrs. Lim was kneeling on a blanket in the mud on the river's edge, and there was a Buddhist priest with her who was trying to induce the evil spirits to release the boys' bodies. The priest chanted prayers and poured liquid over a roasted duck. He threw chunks of the duck into the river in symbolic exchange for the boys. After a while Mrs. Lim gave up and went to sit in the car of the victim witness advocate. I sat in there with her for more than an hour, with my arm around her, trying to give comfort.

By Friday, three bodies had been found, but Mrs. Lim was desperate to find the body of her third son, Herbert. An elaborate feast of fruit, roast pork, chicken, rice, bottles of soda, and brandy was prepared in the belief that the food would attract the spirit and thus bring up the final body. Friends and family lit incense and built a small fire, then knelt and chanted in a ceremony just above the river, on almost the exact spot where the four boys had disappeared. At the height of the ceremony, word passed through the crowd that the fourth and final body had been found very near that spot. The small gathering broke out into applause. The sense of relief was palpable. The paper reported the next day that the veteran police officers hovering nearby had looked at each other in amazement.[3]

On Saturday, I attended a special ceremony in the Park Village apartment complex, where Mrs. Lim lived. She sat in the center of a group of sixty people who were led in prayer by three Buddhist monks. As always with the many immigrant groups in Stockton, those present were pleased to see the mayor of the city at their service.

The police department contacted Mrs. Lim's husband, Pich Saly, who had been on a thirty-day trip to Cambodia. He returned home immediately and was extremely distraught. He was met by two officers at the airport, one a Cambodian community service officer in the police department, who remembered him as upset and angry with his wife. "He was so wild," said the officer, but he was able to calm Pich Saly down and to counsel him about the psychological benefit of not casting blame onto his wife. It is important to have police officers who represent the diverse members of your community, especially at crisis times like this.

Next, I contacted the Cambodian Community Center and arranged a meeting with several Cambodian leaders and also Raj Ramaya, the executive director of the American Friends in Stockton. As we tried to figure out what we could do, a consensus developed around raising money for the families. A local mortuary had donated the funeral services. A cemetery in Manteca donated burial plots, but we knew there would be a need for more money for the children's caskets, clothes, food, and other expenses related to religious observances. Then in a hundred days there would be another feast and this time a celebration. Buddhists believe that a person's spirit roams on earth for a hundred days before being born into a new body, and that is the time for food, which is an expense to the family. We decided to set up the "Help the Cambodian Families Fund" to cover the expenses for the funeral and the ceremonies which would follow. I cochaired this project with Savan Koy, the executive director of the Cambodian Community of Stockton.

Carrying sticks of incense and bunches of red carnations, some two hundred people solemnly gathered at the funeral to pay their respects to the dead. Each boy, dressed in a white shirt and black pants, had been placed in a separate, open casket, lined in white, that had above it his portrait framed in hundreds of white carnations. Mrs. Lim, herself in white, went up to the caskets, touched each boy for the last time and cried. I went up and stood beside her, providing what comfort I could. I also brought condolences from the city of Stockton. After the service, Mrs. Lim and her husband Pich Saly carried three-foot by four-foot portraits of their sons out of the chapel to the waiting hearses. While carrying out the third portrait of their youngest son, Mrs. Lim, who was five months pregnant with her sixth child, staggered and nearly fell. The bodies of the boys were taken to the Park View Cemetery, where they were buried.

A community services liaison, who worked for a county organization that provided help to immigrant families, was especially helpful during this crisis. He was our main link to the Lim and Soun families. He called to tell me that Mrs. Lim was distraught over a $600 phone bill she had received from AT&T. She thought her children had made the calls before the drowning. I asked if it had in fact been the father, her husband, but she said, "No," that the calls were made during the day and her husband worked during the day. I believed that this bereaved woman should not be burdened with this gross expense, so I called the company and asked that it be dropped. Many supervisors told me that this was impossible, since the cost would have to be assumed by AT&T. I was insistent, and I hope threatening, noting that I was the mayor of the city where these children had drowned. Finally the company agreed to retract the charges.

Three hundred and forty people from Stockton, San Joaquin County and the Bay Area contributed more than fifteen thousand dollars to the "Help the Cambodian Families Fund." As we allocated this money, I constantly relied on the advice of the county liaison and the Cambodian leaders, who met with Savan Koy and me regularly to decide on who should receive checks. The flowers for the funeral were $538. Our liaison advised us to pay out $4,200 to local Cambodian markets to cover the cost of food for the several services. Then he indicated that the Pich/Lim family had borrowed $3,000 from a local Buddhist monk for expenses related to the drownings. We voted to cover this debt. We purchased monuments for the boys' gravesites and had them engraved with the boys' names. This gave much solace to the families. That cost was $1,500. Eleven months later all donors had been personally thanked, and the funds had been spent, including $1,200 for a swim instruction program at the YMCA.

This experience brought me close to Stockton's Cambodian community of nearly eleven thousand—hardly a small number of people. On several occasions I attended their events where I was always celebrated. In my own speeches I often referred to this terrible drowning and mentioned the departed children with reverence. I had a replica of a head from Ankor Wat in my office. A professor who ran a school to teach Cambodian language and history came to my office several times and urged me to visit Cambodia; she tried to set up a sister city relationship as well. Whenever any dignitary from Cambodia came to Stockton, I was present. During my tenure the Park Village Apartments, which housed several hundred Cambodian families, worked out with HUD and the State of California a program of self-ownership. The nonprofit corporation for Park Village, ASPARA, honored me at my final council meeting. Of all the Southeast Asian groups—Hmong, Laotian, Vietnamese—I felt a special rapport with the Cambodians. One young man, a translator for Cambodians in the courts, went door to door with me in my reelection campaign. He got me more than a few votes.

I would like to think that Stockton, whose already large population of Asian immigrants is rapidly increasing, learned something lasting from this experience, that it helped our citizens to see each other in more human ways. One can point to the $15,000 fund, a large sum, which was donated in immediate response to the crisis. That is a sign of generosity for one's fellow man, and it certainly helped the families in their need. In the long run, however, it is hard to know what it all meant to the people of the city. Even as the two searches for the boys' bodies went forward together—the big American machines and the ancient Buddhist ritual—so perhaps did the minds of the older residents and the newly arrived Cambodians move in parallel paths, aware of each other, but confined within separate cultures.

The Power Game

The General Plan of 1990 and the Loophole of 1993

Suburban sprawl is one term for it; uncontrolled development is another. Issues of new building, expansion, and growth are on people's minds and on city council agendas in many parts of the country, and they have been for much of the fifty-year post-World War II period. During this time California has experienced more than its share of population growth, real estate development, and the familiar consequences—traffic congestion, water pollution, crowded schools, loss of natural habitat. Stockton sometimes feels like the epicenter of this movement. In the past thirty years especially, and really going back to the end of World War II, we have felt the effects of rampant expansion. One of the most controversial of these effects is the political and economic influence of developers, including the whole nexus of development-related interests—bankers, builders, investors, and lawyers. In Stockton this influence has come to dominate the life of the city. It is a phenomenon that has not gone unnoticed or unopposed.

In order to give the reader a feel for the way this influence gets put into practice, I want to describe a particular council meeting where twenty-one advocates in three-piece suits and twenty-one opponents in a range of folksy attire battled for six hours over the term "approaching buildout." This particular meeting was itself only one in a series of encounters in Stockton's stormy debate over development and its ramifications. At times my account of the arguments of both the developers and the slow-growth advocates gets quite technical, but political motives and strategies are not hard to discern behind the legal formalities. The final clash of the two sides before the council and the denouement that followed are instructive in the way the power game is played in Stockton, and I suspect elsewhere as well.[1]

California requires every city to have a General Plan, a reasonable blueprint for orderly expansion. In Stockton, the plan is formulated by the city staff, reviewed by the City Planning Commission, and then brought before the city council for approval. A key element in many plans, including ours, is the "Urban Service Area," a designated area within which the city provides the necessary services for residential development— parks, sewers, water, roads, traffic controls, police and fire protection. The General Plan must be reviewed and updated every ten to twenty years.

Formal city planning began in Stockton in 1929, with the establishment of the City Planning Commission. The first master plan and zoning ordinance were approved by the city council in March 1934. After that, with the Depression and the war, the General Plan was not revised until 1957, and then not again until 1970. Following the explosive residential development of the mid-1970s, the debate between developers and advocates of controlled growth became much more contentious. In 1978, the city council adopted a revised General Plan that tried to offer something to both sides: boundaries on development, especially in the area of North Stockton, but also large areas beyond these boundaries (some fifteen thousand acres) called the Municipal Land Reserve (MLR) where, with voter approval, development could take place in parcels of fifty acres or more.

After the adoption of the General Plan of 1978, with its mixed message of setting boundaries and providing conditions for development beyond them, both sides geared up for further action. Slow-growth forces drafted a petition which reaffirmed the boundaries in North Stockton and elsewhere within the city limits (the Urban Service Area) and also restricted development in the Municipal Land Reserve (beyond the Urban Service Area). The petition stated that for ten years the fifteen thousand acres of land in the MLR could not be planned, annexed or developed without the approval of the voters. This provision would change the process by which developers got their plans approved, by taking planning authority away from the city planning commission and the city council and giving it to the voters.

The petition had enough signatures to put the developers and their council majority of supporters in a bind: Either the restrictive provisions of the petition had to be submitted to the voters on the next ballot, or else they had to be adopted by the council and enacted into law. Rather than risk putting the petition's provisions to a popular vote, the council took the alternative route which was to adopt it. It did so by enacting Ordinance 3142 in December 1978. At the same time, in order to accommodate the developers' wishes, the council decided to place Measure A, which repealed Ordinance 3142, on the ballot for the following fall. This developer-friendly scheme failed when the voters defeated Measure A, and the growth-control provisions of the Ordinance 3142 remained in effect.

Since voter approval was now required for expansion, the developers turned their attention for the next two years to an ambitious public relations campaign. So successful was this effort that they got voter approval for six major developments in North Stockton and one in South Stockton. Five of these were residential. They provided 20,700 units of housing for 50,000 persons, enough for the projected growth for all of metropolitan Stockton until the year 2000. In 1988, ten years after its passage, Ordinance 3142 was nullified when the new city attorney declared it contrary to the city charter. This ruling put the city planning commission back in business in time for it to prepare for the revision and update of the General Plan in 1990.

The major developers wanted the 1990 General Plan passed. A lawsuit had been brought against the city by the responsible-growth advocates in 1989 for not having an updated, approved General Plan. In the absence of a new General Plan, the five major residential developments, which had been approved by the voters in 1986, could be stymied. Alex Spanos and Fritz Grupe, the developers with the two biggest projects, each paid $300,000 to the plaintiffs to settle the case.

Additional developers wanted their own projects included in the General Plan, but this would necessitate an expansion of the Urban Service Area, a move that could have stopped passage of the plan. Wishing to avoid this outcome, all the developers agreed to support the 1990 plan with the understanding that their group, the Building Industry Association (BIA), would also support a greatly expanded area for development, known as the Special Planning Area Study (SPAS) when it came up for a vote before the city planning commission in 1993. This way all of the developers could have a piece of the pie.

On January 22, 1990, five weeks before I took office, the old city council passed the 1990 General Plan. It provided for a 65 percent increase in planned housing units, from the 89,338 already existing to 150,431, an increase of 61,093 units. Interestingly, no designated time in the future by which these units were expected to be built was indicated in the General Plan. The General Plan also addressed a crucial question: When could building take place outside of the Urban Service Area? Policy 2 of the Housing Element of the General Plan stated the answer: "The Urban Service Area shall be expanded only when land within the existing Urban Service Area is approaching buildout and it can be demonstrated that the existing services and networks can safely and efficiently be expanded to accommodate additional growth."[2] The term "approaching buildout" became the key language.

At the same meeting, in response to last minute demands by the developers, the old council allocated $350,000 for the Special Planning Area Study (SPAS).[3] In 1992, my council, also in deference to the developers' wishes, allocated an additional $350,000 to continue the study. The completed study proposed an expansion of the Urban Service Area by some twenty-one square miles, and it doubled the number of housing units provided in the 1990 General Plan. Instead of 61,093 additional units, the SPAS allocated 128,884 units. It is worth noting here that members of both councils had benefitted from generous contributions by the developers to their election campaigns.

The environmental reports in the SPAS suggested that expansion on this scale would bring consequences that were overwhelmingly negative—traffic congestion, air pollution, inadequate water supply, sewer plant needs, and degradation of prime agricultural land. As expected, the presentation of the SPAS before the city planning commission brought forth a fearsome outcry from the proponents of responsible growth. Yet in spite of the reports and the public anger, the city planning commission barely turned down the SPAS plan. The swing vote was Commissioner Dr. Richard Nickerson. He could not accept the major designer's recommendation that the only way to mitigate traffic congestion was to build a beltway through the Delta, prime agricultural land where the friable soil was not suitable for highway construction. Only one developer, Alex Spanos, opposed the SPAS. All the others were adamantly in favor of it. Nickerson told me that Bill Filios, Spanos's man, spoke to him several times and asked him point-blank, "Are you really going to vote for a beltway, Nick?"[4] In the end, Nickerson concluded that the beltway was untenable. On June 29, 1993, at the final meeting on this volatile issue, Nickerson voted "No." The SPAS failed on a 4 to 3 vote by the city planning commission. The developers decided not to appeal the rejection.

Why was Spanos against the SPAS? Perhaps for reasons of competition with the major developer, Howard Arnaiz, who was promoting it, but perhaps also for reasons of good government. Anyone could see that it would have disastrous effects on the city. Arnaiz and his attorney owned an 825-acre parcel of land (A & M Farms) in the expanded Urban Service Area of the SPAS that they planned to develop into a residential area with a golf course and an equestrian rink close to a Spanos-owned golf course and residential development project. I was told later that when Arnaiz lost the SPAS vote he turned to one of the planning commissioners who voted against it and said, "You just cost me a million dollars."

The engineering designs and environmental reports for the SPAS, protracted over a three-year period, cost the city $750,000. This amount is being repaid to the city treasury at the rate of $100,000 per year by a fee on every new building permit issued by the city. The fee is assessed on all permits, not just those for new houses; thus, a central Stockton homeowner who decides to add a bedroom has to do his part to pay off the SPAS debt.

After the defeat of the SPAS, the Building Industry Association retaliated with another strategy. The BIA members proposed to change Policy 2 of the 1990 General Plan by striking the words "approaching buildout" as a condition for expansion beyond the Urban Service Area. The change was approved on a 4 to 3 vote by the city planning commission. This time Nickerson, again the swing vote, went the other way and supported the developers' "loophole." On December 5, 1993, the proposed change in language came before the city council.

I knew the responsible-growth advocates would be out in force at this meeting, so I moved it to the civic auditorium to provide space for the several hundred people who would be sure to be present. The speakers on both sides, forty-two in all and evenly split—half for and half against—made a striking picture. Those in favor—the attorneys for the developers, the bankers, the owners of real estate companies—wore blue and gray suits and white shirts and red and blue ties. Those against— the environmentalist, the bicyclist, the pacifist/orthodontist, the liberal dentist, the impassioned minister/lawyer, the downtown developer— wore a variety of dress and spoke with many voices. Those in favor were visibly more prosperous than those opposed, as one of the latter pointed out: "The proponents are being paid for being here tonight. We are not."

The awkward part of this story for me is that the proponents in business suits were my friends and campaign supporters. They had given money, put on events, and enthusiastically endorsed me in both campaigns. They were also in many cases personal friends. Many of us had been on the same boards together, worked in the United Way and, after my election, on projects for the city. The opponents, though I respected them, were not friends of mine and none had been political supporters or donors to my campaigns. Yet I was strongly opposed to the change in language that would allow a loophole through which uncontrolled, non-contiguous, and unneeded development could go forward.

The proponents led off with a prominent banker who argued that "approaching buildout" was vague language and therefore should be deleted. A second speaker, the spokesperson from the Stockton Christian Life Ministries, said he represented five thousand persons in the several Christian ministries in Stockton and that they were all in favor of this change. The truth was that the Christian Life Center was also a big developer, including residential development. The pastor of this church was a longtime friend of Arnaiz; both supported my candidacies for mayor. This was also the minister who helped me during my reelection campaign when I was being attacked over the gay pride march.

Four attorneys, all my good friends and supporters, followed. The proposed change does not really gut anything, said one. Instead, "What we have done is surgically taken the laser to the part that doesn't work, 'approaching buildout.'" "This is simply an issue of good government," said another. "The current policy creates inflexibility and the proposed change puts the decision back into the hands of the elected officials. It's the democratic process," he declared.

Other proponents argued that the change would allow the planning process to proceed in a more streamlined, less cumbersome way. One of the attorneys threatened that "This policy is an invitation to litigation." Builders appealed to the issue of prosperity; since 1993, the building industry had been in recession: "With the proposed change, Stockton retains its ability to participate in the prosperity. It provides jobs, much needed revenue, and is a catalyst for downtown development." A labor leader cited the 40 to 70 percent unemployment among the members of the Building Trades Council. The senior vice-president for CB Commercial Real Estate, a clean-cut young man, talked about the need to be as flexible as possible in bringing companies and more jobs to the area.

Then came others who advocated for their own special interests, like the big burly owner of land on Bishops Tract and the soft spoken former city manager who happened to be Arnaiz's partner and Matt Arnaiz, Howard's son and also a partner. Twenty-one well-dressed and well-heeled people urged the council to adopt the change and allow the loophole.[5]

Speakers who opposed the change in language put forth, with much earnestness and eloquence, the predictable arguments. "Keep 'approaching buildout'; it meant that there was a 'definitive, calculable guideline,' for when the city could expand." Opponents also claimed that the city's current General Plan had enough room for houses for thirty to fifty years. "This proposal, plain and simple, is not about need, it's about greed," said one. The conservation chair of the San Joaquin Audubon Society noted that there were literally thousands of acres already zoned for commercial/industrial development that were lying vacant: "This is not about jobs; it's about more houses." One environmental activist argued that those in charge should promote the highest good for the greatest number of people: "If [this decision] is for the purpose of more housing, then tell us how that can possibly benefit us when we have...enough for thirty years."[6]

Of course the developers were objects of the opponents' wrath. "The developers orchestrate the city's development. The city council is in the pockets of the developers," we were told. This last point had been voiced for a long time, and considering campaign contributions to council members, it was highly plausible. Six months before this particular council meeting, *The Record* had done a review of contributions to council campaigns and found that a significant amount came from development and real estate interests, in four races more than 40 percent: 48 percent of Weaver's, 70 percent of Rust's, 42 percent of Minnick's, and 50 percent of Panizza's contributions. *The Record* went on to report that I had the largest single amount contributed by the developers, $41,296. Though it was only 28 percent of my total campaign fund, it was a hefty amount of money and I needed every dime of it. McGaughey's take was 32 percent, including the highest amount given by organized labor to any candidate. Gonzales raised only $1,200, none of which was from either developers or organized labor.

All of these council members flatly denied that there was any correlation between their vote and their donors. "I think it's ridiculous to think that the average person is going to sell their soul for $1,000. Because you donate $100 or $1,000, you don't buy a vote," said McGaughey.

Minnick said it a little more practically: "The money is needed to get the candidates' messages out. You can walk and walk, but you still have to buy yard signs and mailers. We need the money. But we also have to maintain our integrity and philosophy."[7]

The testimony for and against the proposal to delete "approaching buildout" went on for six hours. Finally the last speaker wrapped up and it was time for the council to make its decision. Weaver, Gonzales and Rust spoke quickly and vehemently in favor of the change. Rust argued that developers were simply residents, taxpayers, citizens, and employers who have their personal interests, yet "They're vilified; they're terrible people...they build homes and they make profits. Give me a break," said Rust, his voice heavy with sarcasm.

I spoke next. I had just spent the weekend at Landmark Education Forum, a consciousness-raising group that urges participants to figure out what they think is right and go for it. I spoke against the change. There was enough land in the Urban Service Area to provide for residential growth for at least twenty years and maybe forty, I said. Regarding commercial growth (and jobs), if a company came to Stockton and wanted land outside the Urban Service Area, I believed the council would undoubtedly accommodate the industrial developer with or without the change in wording. The change was in fact a violation of the General Plan that had taken months of discussion in 1990 and a reversal of the SPAS outcome several months earlier.

The next three council members, McGaughey, Minnick, and Panizza, saw the wording change as a benefit for future planning. Be pragmatic, use common sense, they advocated. The vote was called. The proposal to delete "approaching buildout" as a criterion for building outside the Urban Service Area was passed by a vote of 6 to 1. My "No" vote cost me the support of Howard Arnaiz. "I will always be friends with you and Jim," he said, "but I will not support you politically." At the time, I rather brushed off his words. I could not run again for mayor because of term limits, and if I ran for higher office, I would run as a Democrat. Howard, and all the rest of these men who had supported me as a nonpartisan candidate for mayor, were staunch Republicans. But I may have been fooling myself. A Democrat from our district in the state legislature once told me that there is no way Democrats in San Joaquin County can get elected to state office without strong support from the business community, i.e., Republicans. Arnaiz supported my reelection with substantial financial assistance from himself and several friends. Regardless of what I may have told myself at the time, withdrawal of support of this kind was a real threat.

My vote got me great press. *The Record*, then still under the more liberal Gannett management, editorialized the next day, "Mayor Joan Darrah, the lone dissenter in the council vote, correctly identified the problem. She was blunt. 'I think the truth of the matter is what we are talking about here is residential growth. We have enough houses now...I see it as contradictory to the concept of the General Plan, which should be comprehensive development.'"[8] The paper added that Stockton had "within its General Plan enough land zoned and planned—some 30,000 buildable lots by most calculations—to last for fifteen years at even the most optimistic Stockton growth rates." Two weeks later, columnist Mike Fitzgerald applauded my participation in the Forum and noted that, "although the development community largely financed Darrah's campaign, the mayor courageously voted her conscience."[9]

By 2002, no developer had chosen to build outside the Urban Service Area, even though that option exists, so long as the services can be provided. In the mid-1970s, building occurred at 3,000 houses per year, but in the 1980s, population growth slowed and houses went up at an annual rate of approximately 1,100. In the five years since I left office at the end of 1996, Stockton has grown at a slightly slower rate (924 homes per year) than the previous five years (1,021 per year). A lot more houses per person are going up in Tracy than in Stockton. Tracy is just west of Stockton, and a half hour closer to the Bay Area. The main reason for Stockton's slower growth seems to be lower demand. Fourteen residential developments with 29,819 proposed units are already approved. At about a thousand per year, this is enough for several decades. Second, building outside the Urban Service Area is much more expensive than construction within it. Lastly, given their response to my vote, the press might be expected to join the public outcry that a proposal for expansion would elicit.

Looking back on this episode of my time as mayor, I can see the way the developers' influence worked in this case. Having scored a partial victory in the General Plan of 1978, they were then set back by the restrictive Ordinance 3142, sponsored by advocates of controlled growth. Following the failure of their effort to get the ordinance repealed, they devoted their energies and resources to a public relations campaign which was so successful that it secured voter approval for twenty-two years worth of residential expansion. They supported the General Plan of 1990 (to oppose it would have held up several projects) despite the distress of some of their number, who were placated by the SPAS proposal. When that proved too extreme for Spanos, a key player, it lost. This loss was repaired by the loophole, the deletion of "approaching buildout" as a condition for expansion beyond the Urban Service Area.

Yet even with this victory through the auspices of a compliant city council, the developers did not let up the pressure. When my friend Arnaiz promised retribution for my disloyalty, he probably spoke what several others were thinking. I still savor my small moral victory that night, but I have to admit that I might have regretted it had I decided to run for higher office. One of the hardest tasks of practical politics is to choose those issues on which principle needs to yield to expediency if the politician is to remain viable and live to fight another day.

Although Spanos' opposition to the SPAS was signifcant at the time, the developers were united throughout this long-running battle. Later, in the debate over the proposal to bring a big casino to Stockton, where Spanos comes in on a different side from the others, the power players are divided and the final outcome is harder to predict. With the casino story too, the difference between making their case to a committee in closed session, the method they prefer, and contesting its merits at the ballot box can be critical to the result. The developers can not always count on popular support. Too often, in the city council, they can expect to prevail.

The Debate Over a Stockton Casino: Cash Cow or Skid Row

I first heard of the possibility of a casino in Stockton by chance. I was in Joe Barkett's office in August 1994, where I was fund-raising for the gubernatorial campaign of Kathleen Brown against Pete Wilson. Barkett had been a longtime supporter of Governor Jerry Brown and his father, Governor Edmund G. Brown. Barkett was an enormously successful man, a physician, a major business leader, and a formidable political insider. In fact, a year later, when the city staff and I needed meetings in Washington with top White House staff personnel and U.S. senators, it was Joe Barkett who arranged the meetings. This kind of power was the result of his very significant political contributions, especially to the Democratic campaign committees and candidates.

I liked his location, the old Elks building in downtown Stockton, which he and his son-in-law had recently purchased and were now renovating. He welcomed me into his modest office, newly occupied and furnished with only the basics: a desk, a bookshelf, and a couple of chairs. We chatted a little about the importance of family and passing along your resources to your children at an early stage so that all family members could benefit.

We talked about the usefulness of politics to business and business to politics. He believed his understanding of that important relationship had been the key to his success.

"Joe," I said, "I know you are a longtime friend of the Brown family. I am fund-raising for Kathleen's campaign for governor. I would like to respectfully ask you for a check for a thousand dollars for her campaign." He could not have been more amenable. He took his checkbook from the drawer, filled out the check for the requested amount, paid to the order of Kathleen Brown for Governor, and handed it to me. It was almost as if he had anticipated my coming and had planned the scenario that followed.

There was another matter he wanted to discuss with me, he said. Some very close friends of his were involved with Hollywood Park, a major California gaming corporation that had a racetrack and casino in Inglewood. Joe had spent considerable time and effort to have Stockton selected as the location for a major card room. There would soon be a casino here very like the one in Hollywood Park. It would be a great boon to our city as it would bring us hundreds of jobs and millions of dollars in tax revenue.

Without any apology or explanation, I looked him in the eye and said, "I am death on gambling." Suddenly, I felt it was time for me to go. He walked me to the elevator. As I was entering he said, "It is all right for you to be against it, but you won't oppose it, will you?" I did not answer. It may not have mattered; I think he would have proceeded with the project anyway. Besides I had his check in my purse. There were other folks in the elevator. Why start a fight?

I should say at the outset that, in addition to the several major concerns about the potential impact of a large card room in Stockton that led to my opposition to the casino, there is a part of my hostility to gambling that is personal. My grandfather gambled, and my father was so upset about it that he went into a violent diatribe against gambling of any kind whenever the subject arose. Given this background, there is no way I could have agreed to Barkett's request that day in his office or welcomed Mike Hakeem's letter of May 3, 1995.

If you have a difficult or sensitive item you want passed by the Stockton City Council, the man to hire is Mike Hakeem. He works for several of the major developers in Stockton and gets excellent results. Joe Barkett could not have selected a better spokesperson for a delicate job.

The letter from Hakeem to the mayor and council was hand-delivered.[1] It laid the groundwork for a momentous proposal in the most mild and reasonable terms. Hakeem was writing on behalf of Mr. Joseph Barkett and Hollywood Park, the letter began. Barkett would be filing an application for a conditional use permit to accommodate an upscale card room and restaurant at Highway 99 and Arch Road. The projected facility would have 100,000 square feet and employ 500 people. Hakeem spoke of the economic benefit of such an enterprise to our city. With Stockton's unemployment rate hovering at 13 percent, the promise of 500 jobs was not to be taken lightly.

Second, the letter informed us that Stockton needed an updated card room ordinance that would make its gambling business economically competitive. The current ordinance, which had not been reviewed for ten years, allowed for only eight tables per card room, with a 2 A.M. shutdown time. At that time, we had four card rooms in the city that were quiet operations. Hakeem's letter concluded with the request that this agenda item be placed under "written communications" and be referred to the appropriate committee. I knew that if the matter were handled this way, it might not be discussed at all by the full council in open session. Rather, it would be quietly referred to a council committee where it would be reviewed and acted upon with relative anonymity. It would then be sent forward to the full council as an item on the "consent calendar," a designation that implied that discussion was unnecessary and therefore approval was virtually automatic.

Immediately I insisted that this item be put on the regular agenda so that it could be discussed as any new and controversial item would be. Second, I faxed Hakeem's letter to Paul Feist at the city desk of *The Record*. I was determined that this issue was not going to be hidden. The public had the right to know, and it was up to me to make that happen.

"Making Room for Cards" was the title, two days later, of the front-page article in *The Record* that proclaimed the benefits of a card casino, including 500 new jobs and 3.5 million dollars in new tax revenue for the city. The paper quoted Hakeem: "Facilities for horse track wagering, card rooms and other forms of betting are already sprouting in cities around California. Why shouldn't they do that here? Why shouldn't Stockton have the same type of facility?" As a whole, the council was favorable to the casino, but I was not and the paper said so.[2]

One reason for my opposition was that, at least in California, gambling was often targeted to and uniquely affected the Asian population. My concern for Asians as a group—that they were vulnerable to the lure and the destructive consequences of gambling—had been heightened by a recent article in the *San Francisco Chronicle* which discussed the special problems of Asians at the San Jose Bay 101 card club.[3] Asian Americans, the paper said, were the solid majority at the club, even though they made up only 17 percent of Santa Clara County's population. Gambling problems had exploded in the Asian community, plunging people into debt overnight and destroying vulnerable immigrant families. Stockton would be 30 percent Asian by 2000. Any injury to these people, I felt, would be a significant injury to the welfare of Stockton as a whole. When a reporter for *The Record* questioned one of my council colleagues about my concern over targeting gambling to an Asian market, the answer was: "It kind of smacks of father knows best.... That sounds like a tinge of racism. It sounds like big brother and government planning. It reminds me of stories about people of Italian descent smelling of garlic."[4]

The Record's editorial page picked up on this idea. "Darrah's faulty assumptions about its potential clientele...border on racist," it said. *The Record* suggested that I should recuse myself from all further discussion because I had made a public comment on the proposal: "Her two-pronged attack on the card room proposal—that it is immoral for the city to profit from gambling, and that the card room would prey on Southeast Asians— is astonishing for its naïveté and its racial overtones. There isn't an iota of evidence—anecdotes, yes; facts, no—to support a claim that legalized gambling attracts one ethnic/racial group more than another."[5] This editorial trumpeted the benefits of the proposed card room and condemned my position even to the outrageous extent of saying that I had no right to discuss the matter in public or to vote on it. The newspaper insisted that the issue here was a land-use question only.

That kind of public blast is very unsettling, but it can also be quite useful. Although I myself did not respond to these insulting editorials, others did. I recall receiving a copy of a letter sent to *The Record* from Gerald A. Sperry, a prominent lawyer who had once been city attorney and whose firm represented Alex Spanos, a Stockton resident and the top rental unit developer in the county.[6] On my behalf, Sperry stated that *The Record's* card room editorial was "a clear, shameful attempt to silence those who might express opposition.... An elected official not only has a right but an obligation to discuss issues of vital concern with constituents and to state views on matters of public importance." This, Sperry continued, was the position of the Supreme Court of the state of California. His letter concluded that the newspaper should "encourage public participation in all future discussions of the card room proposal and publicly apologize to Darrah."[7] I kept looking for Sperry's letter in "Letters to the editor." When it did not appear, I called the editorial page editor who said he had not seen it. I sent him a copy, which he published on June 1, 1995.

I also asked for a ruling from the city's legal department on the issue of my participation in debate after I had taken a public stand on an issue. On May 23, I received a memorandum stating that I could of course participate. I sent this memorandum to *The Record,* together with a letter in which I cited the Bay 101's experience with Asians and a copy of the March 3 article from the *San Francisco Chronicle*. There was never any response or any apology.

Nonetheless, the publicity had begun to do its work. *The Record* put the community on notice that large-scale gambling was heading for Stockton and that anybody who was against it needed to speak out now, loud and clear. The first and most vehement voice was that of Dr. Martin Edwards, a local chiropractor and director of Community Concerns for Stockton, an umbrella group for community-wide religious interests. From the moment he saw *The Record's* editorial attack on me, Edwards became the major opponent of the casino in Stockton. In his first call to me, immediately after the publication of *The Record* article, he completely agreed with my position. He had 300-plus pages of research regarding gambling and the very negative impact it had on cities, and he wanted to share this material with me.

Other calls followed, often indicating 100 percent support. One call was from an old friend of mine from the United Way, Bill Perry, the mayor of Manteca, a city adjacent to Stockton. He had kept gambling out of Manteca and wanted to advise me on how to do the same in Stockton.

Naturally, the mail brought mixed messages. One was a postcard from a Stockton resident who wrote: "The proposed card room at 99 and Arch sounds good to me, but I have noticed that every time something worthwhile is proposed for Stockton, you oppose it. YOU'RE BAD FOR STOCKTON!"

Meanwhile, there was a factor of urgency working behind the scenes, which partly explains the efforts of Hakeem and the casino sponsors to forestall the full-scale, painstaking review that a city government usually requires before making major changes. On August 3, 1994 (only days before my visit to Joe Barkett's office when he first mentioned a casino to me), Governor Pete Wilson had signed a bill that put a three-year moratorium on the expansion of gambling in California. After January 1, 1996, no new card rooms could be built. Hence, there was a rush for casino construction in several California cities, Stockton included. There were also legislative initiatives to control card room gambling. Assemblyman Phil Eisenberg and Attorney General Dan Lungren had introduced an assembly bill that required a city to obtain a two-thirds vote of the electorate before it could initiate or expand card rooms. Even the most needed library and school construction bonds could not get two-thirds in California.

On May 15, 1995, the change in ordinance came before the council, which voted 6 to 1 (Darrah in opposition) to send it to the legislation and environment committee, as requested by Hakeem. *The Record* was again favorable to the card room and critical of my position[8] but now there was an aroused public for the gambling proponents to reckon with as well. A deluge of information on gambling began arriving in my office, some of it positive, much of it negative. At my request, the public library researched and forwarded recent articles on card rooms. The religious community, specifically Dr. Martin Edwards, brought in a whole stack of memos and articles and papers—many from other states—that emphasized the most negative effects of gambling.

The city hall staff kept their opinions about the casino to themselves and stuck to business. The legal department obtained ordinances from other communities. The city manager's office gathered information when asked. One administrator did tell me that the first question asked by card room developers was, "How many Asians live in your community?" The large number of Asians in Stockton was seen as vital to its being considered for a card room. The planning staff indicated that, contrary to *The Record's* argument, site location was really not the issue—existing zoning law permitted a card room in that location. There would need to be an environmental review, but that would take only a matter of a few months. There would be traffic problems, but they could certainly be worked out, given the huge profits that such an enterprise would generate. The police chief too was circumspect, not only because the issue was so very political but also because no convincing evidence of increased crime in a Northern California city where a card room was located had been discovered. That was to come later.

As information accumulated in my office, I developed a package that condensed my opposition into four major points. The first was that card rooms bring greater crime. I quoted Dan Lungren: "Card rooms are a major draw for criminal elements, from the potential of takeover by organized crime to offenses reported to this office that include extortion, murder-for-hire schemes, kidnaping, loan sharking, armed robbery, follow-home robberies, credit card fraud, forgery, tax evasion and embezzlement."[9] I cited a chamber of commerce report that stated that one particular type of crime that comes with the establishment of major card rooms is the bribery and corruption of city officials.[10]

Second, my package argued, a new and bigger card room would lead to full-scale, Nevada-type gambling. My best piece of evidence for this was the case of Hollywood Park. When it was built, the owners put into the new structure a network of ducts that ran just beneath the surface of the gaming room floor even though they were unnecessary for playing Texas Hold 'Em and Asian Pai Gow. "It's cheaper that way," said Hollywood Park Board Chairman R. D. Hubbard. "When the casino wheels in the slots to replace the poker tables, we won't have to tear up the whole floor."[11]

My third argument, and the one most important in the eyes of many people, was the economic impact of gambling. Rather than providing the incredible job gain promised by its sponsors, we would actually lose jobs with the casino in Stockton, I argued. The evidence showed that businesses would not locate in our city because card casinos are seen as attracting illegal activity and mafia-type organized crime. Certain types of companies, particularly office-users and high-tech manufacturing, were unlikely to be attracted to areas with this image. That very year (1995), the Business Council of San Joaquin County produced an economic report entitled "Vision 2000 Relook," which said that crime was the main liability to the business climate in San Joaquin County and particularly in Stockton. Casinos would only reinforce that negative image. In making this point, I found *The Kiplinger Washington Letter* of May 5, 1995 extremely useful. It noted that patrons of river boat and Indian casinos tended to come from the local area, unlike those who traveled to Las Vegas and Atlantic City from all over the country. Casino gamblers, *Kiplinger* found, spent money that would otherwise have gone towards entertainment, food, recreation, cars, clothes, even debt repayment. The result was that casinos had a particularly damaging effect on leisure businesses in the local area.[12]

Fourth, I talked about the social costs of gambling, especially those associated with the small but significant percentage that become pathological gamblers. Howard Shaffer, then director of the Zinberg Center for Addiction Studies at Harvard University, reported that 3.5 to 5 percent of those exposed to gambling can be expected to develop into pathological gamblers. The percentage is higher for high school and college graduates.[13] I sent this packet of material to the council members, to the top city staff members, and to *The Record*. I took it to the governmental relations committee of the chamber of commerce and argued for that organization to take a stand against the casino.

It is interesting to note here that Stockton historian Olive Davis had written a recent letter to the editor of *The Record* wherein she described Stockton's skid row becoming the largest in the United States in the 1930s.[14] At that time it was common knowledge up and down the state that Stockton was a "wide-open town" because of the available gambling and prostitution. She urged the city to stand firmly against casinos. A similar picture of Stockton's past is found in the book *China Men*, where the celebrated writer Maxine Hong Kingston describes the Stockton she knew growing up here in the thirties: "We were getting the gambling house ready. Tonight the gamblers would come here from the towns and the fields; they would sail from San Francisco all the way up the river through the Delta to Stockton, which had more gambling than any city on the coast. It would be a party tonight. The gamblers would eat free food and drink free whiskey...." Kingston knew what she was talking about. Her father was the gambling house manager. Kingston continued: "According to MaMa, the gambling house belonged to the most powerful Chinese American in Stockton. He paid my father to manage it and to pretend to be the owner. BaBa took the blame for the real owner. When the cop on the beat walked in, BaBa gave him a plate of food, a carton of cigarettes, and a bottle of whiskey. Once a month the police raided with a paddy wagon, and it was also part of my father's job to be arrested."[15] If Stockton were to build a Hollywood Park-type casino, it would be celebrated on billboards all the way up and down the state—on Highway 99, on Interstate 5, in Los Angeles and San Francisco—as having the largest card room in California. Its notorious past would be surpassed by an even more excessive present.

Over the summer of 1995, the legislation and environment committee held several meetings to discuss the proposed change in the city ordinance. On June 2, the opponents, led by Dr. Edwards, as usual, cited government and university studies that showed increases in crime, suicides, and other problems in cities where casinos had opened. Mike Hakeem, ever present, countered Edwards, saying that his fears were not based on card rooms in California. At the committee meeting of July 12, the proponents' claim regarding numbers of jobs to be created by the proposed casino had increased 60 percent, from 500 to 850. On the opposition side, other significant local religious leaders had joined the fight against the card room. New people entered the debate with followers and fresh considerations, and the continual presentation of new studies meant that action on the proposal was delayed.

Another cause for delay was the decision of council members to visit several card rooms in San Jose, Inglewood, and Jackson. One council member said that he would get his own information and vowed to talk to the police chief and city manager in Inglewood, the home of Hollywood Park. *The Record* reporter, too, called officials in Inglewood and was told that the city had seen no significant increase in crime. The Inglewood police captain found the people who went to the card room to be a very nice crowd, and the Inglewood city manager stated that during the club's first year of operation the city had received $4.6 million in direct revenue and that 1,500 jobs had been created.[16] All in all, on their visits to these card rooms, council members liked what they saw. The places seemed clean, well monitored, and safe. Without announcing my plans to local officials in advance, I went to Inglewood with my brother, Peter Van den Akker, to visit Hollywood Park and the Bicycle Club in Bell Gardens.

The Hollywood Park casino is built right next to the racetrack, and it is huge. It has six stories, 315,000 square feet, and sports a glitzy facade that looks very Hollywood. As we entered, my brother and I were struck by how new, clean, well lighted, and attractive the facility was and how well protected it was by the many security personnel and overhead monitors. The two card rooms are both on the first floor: the "California" side, with the Asian card games of Pai Gow and Suer Pan 9, an the "Nevada" side, all poker, with some seventy tables of ten persons per table. Contiguous to the card rooms is a large bar and a pari-mutuel betting area. Peter and I had lunch in one of two attractive restaurants. It served an extensive buffet (thirteen salads, blackened salmon, roast beef, chicken, and six desserts) for only $6.95, a remarkably low price that supported the *Kiplinger* finding that local restaurants were undercut by casino food. This restaurant also served Chinese, Korean, Thai, and Vietnamese specialties, catering to the significant Asian population we saw there.

We explored the upper six floors. On the second was a fitness center and massage club that were rather small in size. The remaining five floors had facilities related to the racetrack: boxes and special seating for the racetrack, pari-mutuel betting windows, private suites for viewing the races, and special rooms for karaoke. I wondered how much of the $4.6 million in revenue that came to the city of Inglewood from the casino in one year was produced by the racetrack betting and the entertainment rather than the card tables alone. Since just the card tables had been proposed for Stockton, the case for economic advantage might have been significantly overstated.

The Bicycle Club in Bell Gardens is a much older facility and it has a history of legal violations. At one point, the federal Department of Justice almost closed it down. The day Peter and I were there, however, the Bicycle Club was in full swing. Like Hollywood Park, there was one very large room that offered poker only; some eight hundred people were playing. In a second, smaller room, there were two hundred fifty people, almost all Asian, playing Pai Gow and Super Pan 9. In two, even smaller, high-stakes rooms, decorated with Chinese red and golden dragons, a group of about twenty-five Asians at each of two tables were betting excitedly and furiously, faster than your eye could follow, using big bills. Many thousands of dollars were being won and lost in a matter of minutes. It was a frightening scene. I came back to Stockton and wrote a summary of my visits and passed it out to council members.

During the summer of 1995, I continued to receive letters and phone calls from organizations and individuals who shared my position. The pastor of Bible Baptist Church wrote to express the gratitude of his church of four hundred members for my stand against this "social evil." Stockton Metro Ministry, a coalition of churches, took a strong stand against the change in ordinance that would allow the card room. A number of people wrote personal testimonies, citing the devastation caused in their own families by gambling addiction.

My friend and campaign coordinator, Don Parsons, called me with great news. He was going to join me in opposition to the casino. He also said that the developer Alex Spanos was against the project and felt it was terrible for the image of Stockton. Spanos's opposition meant, among other things, that there would be significant funding for our side from this point on. These men were distressed, as I was, at the prospect of so much power concentrated in the hands of the very few casino principals, especially in light of the large-scale bribing of local officials that was documented in the Bicycle Club experience of the late 1980s.

As they say, "politics make strange bedfellows." The Mi-wuk Indian Casino group from Jackson, a town fifty miles away, now entered the fray to thwart competition against their own interests. They were ready to contribute legal advice, money, and people-power to the defeat of the Stockton card casino. In South San Francisco, Artichoke Joe's, an Indian casino, had helped defeat the location of a Hollywood Park casino there. The same dynamic would come into play in Stockton.

In spite of this mounting organized opposition, the sponsors of the casino were making their case successfully to the public. *The Record*'s poll of July 19, 1995 found that Stockton residents backed the twenty-four-hour gambling proposal by a margin of 45.8 percent to 39.6 percent. Only 14.6 percent had a mixed opinion or no opinion at all.[17] However, there had been no public testimony in the newspaper about California card rooms causing increased criminal behavior. Few Stocktonians had read the *San Jose Mercury News*'s article of May 30, 1995, with its grim stories of pathological gambling, careers ruined, and families disintegrating among the 90,000 Vietnamese immigrants in Santa Clara County.[18]

On September 6, following four months of investigation, visits, the reading of similar ordinances, and hours of testimony, the council committee of three announced their decision. As requested by Mike Hakeem and the casino supporters, the committee approved the proposed changes to the city's gambling ordinance. The revised ordinance would set a maximum on the number of tables for the whole city at 200. This meant that the city could keep intact its four card rooms with eight tables each, allow the Hollywood Park casino with 160 tables, and still be under the limit of 200 total tables. The card room would be authorized to operate twenty-four hours a day. The proposal also contained a requirement of $850,000 for an annual license fee to cover direct, immediate, policing costs, and a tax on card room revenues to be figured on a sliding scale, from 7.5 percent to 15.5 percent: the higher the monthly revenue, the greater the percentage of tax. The city of Stockton could receive annually at least $840,000 and up to $11.7 million in the event that monthly revenues reached as high as $7.5 million. This was the proposal that the committee would bring to the full city council for its consideration.

The public hearing and vote of the full council was scheduled for October 2, less than a month away. Casino opponents worked diligently to mobilize the religious community and, in the event that the ordinance change was adopted, to carry petitions to get the matter placed before the electorate. The casino's sponsors, in anticipation of the council vote, sought two critical endorsements. The first was from the board of directors of the San Joaquin Partnership. The partnership board is composed of private sector business leaders whose organizations have contributed at least $20,000 per year to the partnership and of elected officials from the county and selected city governments within the county. I was on the board as the representative of the city of Stockton. The stated purpose of the organization is to bring jobs to San Joaquin County. This group represented the power structure of San Joaquin County: present that day were three major developers, three bank presidents, two business leaders, the publisher of *The Record*, the president of the University of the Pacific, the CEOs of the Port of Stockton and the Greater Stockton Chamber of Commerce, and four elected officials from the cities of the county.

The businessmen on the partnership board are unaccustomed to operating in the public view. They prefer to make major decisions away from the public eye. Knowing this, I felt particularly courageous when I called the city editor at *The Record* and asked that he send a reporter and a photographer to the meeting at which the partnership's endorsement of the card room would be discussed. This action on my part was both legitimate and fitting, inasmuch as the city of Stockton contributes $75,000 annually toward the operation of the partnership. I believed that the public had the right to know what was going on in a quasi-public body that was partially funded by public dollars.

When I entered the partnership meeting room that morning, September 29, 1995, I knew that considerable work had been done to get all the players there. Rarely was the attendance as high as it was that day. I am sure that the expectation that morning was that the endorsement would be a slam-dunk. Joe Barkett, who was to control 15 percent of the partnership which was proposing the card club, had probably contacted every person at the table. Certainly the developers and the bankers had heard from him.

As a woman, I felt uncomfortable in this men's group at this moment. I could not help asking myself, what is really going on here? Why would all the men at the table be so willing to join Joe in this endeavor? Was it that they really believed the casino would be good for Stockton and that, in fact, it would bring jobs and revenue to the city? Or was it that they wanted to support Barkett's project, especially since he had mentioned that the Bank of Stockton was favorable to the project? Had anyone asked about the downside of gambling? Was it simple greed that was the major motivation, dressed up as a proposal for jobs and revenue? And what about someone like Howard Arnaiz, who had property interests around the intersection of Arch Road and Highway 99, the proposed casino site?

It would have been easy for me to vote with the majority of the partnership at this meeting. Many of these men had been contributors to my political campaigns and were personal friends. Anything that I would hope to achieve in this city would be more easily accomplished with their blessing. On the other hand, unlike all of them, my economic well-being was not dependent on their success or their favors. In that sense I had more independence than they had.

Joe Barkett, who now predicted a job gain for the Stockton area of up to two thousand, was, of course, the major spokesman for the card room. Bank of Stockton president Doug Eberhardt noted that, "Our job is to encourage jobs in this county." I responded that Stockton was already battling an image problem and acquiring a reputation as a gambling Mecca would not help job creation. A new partnership board member, the president of the University of the Pacific, Donald DeRosa, concurred that a less than favorable image is a threat to long-term development.

The board of directors of the San Joaquin Partnership, having deliberated the merits of the proposal, concluded their discussion. The motion was made. The vote was taken. The outcome was 11 to 2 in favor of endorsement of the casino project. The publisher of the paper and the CEO of the Greater Stockton Chamber of Commerce abstained. Dr. DeRosa had to leave the meeting early and did not vote. I was joined in opposition by the member from the city council of Manteca.

Under normal operating procedure, that would have been the end of it, but on this occasion, as a result of my having arranged for a reporter from *The Record* to be present at the meeting, the votes of all present were listed in an article in the paper the next day. The major promoters of the project became front-page news. An adjacent article included a discussion that explained how the card room could go to the voters in a referendum. It noted that of the twenty-three casino proposals put to public votes in California since 1992, eighteen had been defeated, and those that passed had done so with slim margins. These articles came out on September 29, three days before the public hearing before the city council.[19]

On September 30, *The Record* carried an article discussing the pastors' stand against the ordinance and noting that thirty Stockton churches were waging a last-minute grass roots campaign against the new law.[20] In the same issue, however, the paper continued its support of the casino with a comprehensive and laudatory article about Joe Barkett—his Lebanese background, his early childhood, his education, his Navy career, and his medical and professional background.[21]

Sometime after the partnership meeting, I saw Joe Barkett at an event at a local country club. "Hello, Joe," I said, as if some amicable relationship was possible, which in retrospect was ridiculous. He made a retort. Then with his thumb and forefinger he gripped the skin under my chin and gave me a quick, painful pinch. Later, at the close of another partnership meeting, he gripped my shoulders and shook me, and again it was quick but painful. "That hurts, Joe," I said. He apologized.

The other group whose endorsement was sought by the casino's advocates was another business group, the Greater Stockton Chamber of

Commerce. They did take a public position on the card room, but a somewhat surprising one. They chose neutrality. After a thorough review of the material on both sides, the members of the local government committee of the chamber found themselves split on the issue. The chamber likes consensus before the body takes a stand, and on this issue there was no consensus.

As the debate drew to its climax, another factor in people's minds was the experience of South San Francisco. Hollywood Park was trying to set up a casino there too, and although they spent $1.5 million in support of the campaign, or sixteen dollars per voter, the casino was defeated by 56 percent to 44 percent. This outcome was gratifying to the opponents of the Stockton casino. In the period before the public hearing and vote, I received numerous very thoughtful letters. Almost all opposed the casino.

While this turmoil was happening locally in the days leading up to the public hearing and council vote, on the state level the idea of a gambling commission for California, promoted by Attorney General Lungren, folded. Senator Bill Lockyer killed it in committee. On the national level, Representative Frank Wolf, R-Virginia, advocated the establishment of a federal commission to study the impact of gambling. Wolf's proposal was endorsed by the *San Jose Mercury News*, which noted that "Mississippi and Louisiana both are disillusioned with their growing gaming industries, which are siphoning billions—not millions, but billions—of dollars into wagering while other types of businesses withered away."[22]

A couple of nights before the big meeting, I met with the leaders of the opposition to formulate a coherent presentation. Others were lining up Vietnamese social workers to make presentations, and the lawyer for the Mi-wuk Indian group was contacted to get the precise language for the petition in the event the matter needed to be brought to referendum. The petitions could not be circulated that night, but signatures could be gathered starting the next day.

Of the six hundred and fifty people who crowded into the Stockton Civic Auditorium on the evening of October 2, approximately fifty were in favor and six hundred were against the casino. After city staff briefly explained the ordinance changes, Hakeem held forth for an hour on the benefits of the casino. He had brought with him a high-powered delegation that included R. D. Hubbard, the CEO of Hollywood Park, Mark Rivers from the De Bartolo Entertainment Company in San Francisco which then owned the San Francisco Forty-niners, and Roger Craig, a former player with the Forty-niners. Hakeem wanted all of them to follow him to the speaker's platform, but I made them wait, as I had said I would at the beginning of the meeting, in order to let the leader of the opposition, Martin Edwards, present his "Position Paper Against the Delta Park Casino Proposal."[23] Edwards called the casino "a hundred and fifty-seven thousand square feet of absolute misery." Hakeem's supporters had their say as well, of course. In all, there were ninety-six speakers, thirty-two in favor and sixty-four against. The meeting started at 5:30 in the evening and lasted for seven hours.[24]

Although I cannot describe or even summarize seven hours of testimony, a few speakers were especially memorable. To me, the most impressive were two Vietnamese social workers from San Jose, Tuan Tran and Hieu Tran, who had experienced the devastation of the Bay 101 Casino. Tuan Tran was a supervisor of social workers from Child Welfare Services in Santa Clara County. He spoke of the significant increase in child abuse cases directly related to gambling. He cited case studies: A mother and father left their two small children locked in their car while they gambled; a husband demanded money from his wife to pay his gambling debts and then beat her and his children; a single mother on welfare lost all of her four children because of her gambling addiction. She herself became homeless.

Compelling testimonies were presented by members of families that had been irreparably harmed by a gambling addiction. One woman spoke of her father, who had died twenty-two months ago that evening. He started out having fun weekends at Tahoe and Reno. He would take an occasional quick trip to Las Vegas. Then he became addicted and lost his job. Her mother, who was also addicted, would telephone and describe their destitution and the long, long hours spent in card rooms. "She worked as a card dealer to pay off the loan sharks." The speaker had lost all contact with her mother, father, and brother. All of them were in denial about their addictions. "The pain is too deep to express in words at this moment how this affected my life and my children's lives," she concluded. A local physician and acupuncturist described gambling as a chronic disease. The addiction progresses very slowly, and the process of rehabilitation is also exceedingly slow. It is hard to treat.

Often at a meeting of this kind, persuasive speakers come forth whom one has never seen before. Such a person was Ronald Teal, an economist with the state of California. He noted that high-tech industries are not locating in areas where there is gambling. "They understand the importance of the environment that their workers are put into," he said. "The decision of where companies are located is made by executives who consider where they want their families to live. Not," said Mr. Teal, "in communities like Inglewood and Gardena and Reno."

Many highly respected Stocktonians spoke in favor of the casino. One of the most eloquent was the president of Stockton Savings and Loan, Bob Kavanaugh, a city resident for fifty years, who argued that the casino would be an economic boon to the city. He knew Joe Barkett well and believed he cared strongly about Stockton: "I don't know anybody who cares more about the city of Stockton than Dr. Barkett."

The speeches concluded. Every person who wanted to speak and who stayed until the end had his or her say. The council members had their say as well. At one o'clock in the morning the ordinance was adopted by a vote of 5 to 2. Councilman Victor Mow, a hospital facilities planner of Chinese descent, joined me in opposition. Although the meeting ended in a loss for the opponents, there were gains for us as well. First, the televised council meeting clearly presented the very real negative impacts of card rooms to the local Monday night television audience. Second, the meeting became a venue where Don Parsons could pass out the yellow card asking people two questions: Would they pass a petition against the ordinance change? and Would they gather signatures to put the matter on the ballot? He gathered hundreds of yellow cards that evening.

The opponents now had one final opportunity to defeat the casino, to get enough signatures objecting to the ordinance to take the matter to the voters in a ballot referendum, but they had to move swiftly. A total of 9,485 valid signatures, or 10 percent of the registered voters in the city, had to be obtained within thirty days of the adoption of the ordinance, or by November 1, 1996. An immediate rush to get petitions out and signed ensued. Don Parsons worked frantically with the religious groups to have their members obtain signatures. These petitioners sat at tables in major retail locations throughout the city. The church volunteers paid for their own petitions. The church coalition, or someone among the anti-casino volunteers, provided precinct lists for the signature gatherers. Parsons worked separately with paid petition gatherers financed by the Mi-wuk Indians. Although the church members and the paid workers had the same goal, they did not want to be associated with each other. Fifty thousand dollars, provided mostly by three American Indian casinos, was spent on the petition drive. I have no doubt that Alex Spanos contributed to the endeavor as well.

It is a well-known fact that people who sign petitions are sometimes not registered voters in the district in question. This happens for a variety of reasons, including simple mistakes, and is not to be taken as evidence of foul play, but it does mean that many more than the required number of signatures must be obtained. On November 1, using his hand truck, Don Parsons delivered boxes upon boxes of petitions to the elections office, 14,139 signatures in all. It had been an incredible organizational effort for him, with the assistance of the church leadership as well as the paid people. Would this be enough? The elections office did a partial count of the returns and found that there were not enough valid signatures to qualify the petition automatically for referendum. Every single signature had to be examined.

In the end, the long-awaited announcement came. To our immense relief, 9,976 valid signatures had been obtained, 401 more than needed. At its subsequent meeting the city council voted to put the referendum on the March 26 ballot. Although the council could have repealed the ordinance, it was decided that the community should have the final say.

Fortunately for our side, *The Record* published new information about the impact of card rooms. Bert Eljera, a staff reporter, did a piece on October 22 called "Compulsive Gamblers in an Unlucky Grip."[25] He discussed the growing number of people becoming addicted to gambling, from 1.7 percent of the population in Iowa in 1989 to 5.4 percent in 1995. On December 3, 1995, the paper featured another anti-card room article, "Cards 'N' Crime—Stockton Can Learn from San Jose," which reported an increase in criminality in San Jose since the opening of its card room.[26] On February 11, 1996, *The Record* released the results of a poll taken in Stockton that showed that 63.9 percent would vote "No" on Measure Q, an ordinance change that would allow the large card room; only 26.4 percent responded in favor. The front-page headline read, "Casino's Voter Support Is Folding."[27] In spite of these articles, the paper's editorial position remained supportive to the end.

Don Parsons coordinated the mailing of three very slick and effective brochures. One quoted Attorney General Dan Lungren, another the San Jose police chief, Louis Covarrubiaz, who said that large-scale card clubs are a magnet to crime. The final brochure printed the *San Francisco Chronicle*'s February 15 article on "Gaming's Violent Price," which talked about a San Francisco mother and children being terrorized after the husband and father won money at gambling.[28] It was a large slick red brochure, with a picture of a gun on the front, that read, "First they beat her. Then they beat her children." Contrary to the South San Francisco experience, where the Hollywood Park interests spent $1.5 million to win the election, no money was spent by Hollywood Park and its interests in Stockton. They knew failure was imminent, and indeed it was. On March 26, election day, about ninety thousand votes were cast, approximately thirty thousand in favor of the card room and sixty thousand against.

The backers had started with all the cards. Most of the business power structure of the city supported Barkett and the casino. The gaming proponents had not only money and connections, but also the help of many well-known and influential people in the community. The paper was behind them all the way. Yet it was the public exposure in *The Record*, particularly the early exaggerated attacks on me, that ultimately worked toward the casino's defeat by getting the debate out into the open. The power game is most often and most successfully played behind closed doors. By involving the churches and community, holding the huge meeting at the civic auditorium, and getting the referendum on the ballot, the opposition deprived the backers of the advantage of secrecy. In so doing, it prevented them from establishing a casino that would have enriched the few at the expense of the many, an outcome that was feared and finally defeated by a majority of the citizens of Stockton.

World Wildlife Museum: Educational Opportunity or Tax Write-off

At a Monday night council meeting in September 1992, my vice mayor leaned over and whispered to me that I had to see an amazing collection of stuffed wild animals that was stored in an East Stockton warehouse. "It's the biggest collection in the world, Joan. There are grizzly bears, mountain lions, a jaguar, tule elk, hundreds of animals, many stuffed and standing." With my husband Jim and our son Peter, both curious to see an exhibit none of us had ever heard of, I went to the small warehouse where these wonders were housed. It was jam-packed with stuffed animal bodies standing in crowds, and many, many heads covered the walls—deer, elk, bison and others many times over. Two enormous brown bears were posed fighting over a fish, and a pair of lions crouched in attack position. The dioramas of animals in their natural habitats that I had enjoyed as a child at the Los Angeles Museum of Natural History never looked so vicious.

Jack Perry, the head of the World Wildlife Museum, the entity that owned the collection, was a tall, thin, graying man of about sixty. He spoke in a dominating, demeaning way, practically ordering me to admire his two thousand stuffed animals. Pointing to the head of a narwhal, an arctic mammal with a seven-foot tusk, he demanded: "Isn't that fabulous?" (Where was the body? I thought.) He insisted that a cabinet filled with eggs, some 1,759 of them, was an irresistible attraction. "Wouldn't this be a terrific asset for the city?" he queried. I was not about to agree. He sounded as if he wanted some form of assistance—funding or land—from the city.

Perry made the mistake of addressing all his attention to Jim; he hardly spoke to me, the mayor. Evidently, he believed that only a man could understand how important this stuff was. I wanted to get out of there. In the meantime, however, Peter was being taken around by another principal of the outfit who boasted that what this museum was all about was a tax write-off for wealthy hunters. They shoot their prey, get it skinned, donate the pelt to the World Wildlife Museum and take a tax write-off for their costs. In 1994, the multimillionaire Ken Behring, former owner of the Seattle Seahawks, donated an African bull elephant hide to the museum for which he took a $150,000 write-off that included the cost of the trip to South Africa, a $30,000 fee to shoot the elephant (which went to local schools and anti-poaching programs), and the cost of the taxidermy job, $25,000.[1]

It takes a lot of money to properly display large animals. While I was on the board of regents of the University of the Pacific, one regent's family contributed over one hundred thousand dollars to the California Academy of Sciences to create one diorama. Fifteen years later, dioramas at the academy were estimated to cost over two hundred thousand dollars. Given Perry's objectionable personality, I did not believe the WWM would ever be able to raise the kind of money necessary to create a viable museum with adequate display space. According to some people, what Perry wanted from the beginning was a donation of free land from the city. What I wanted, if we went ahead with this project, was a museum that was financially sound and could recruit a board of directors that could raise the museum's operating expenses.

Perry himself was a good hunter. He bagged *The Record* columnist Mike Fitzgerald early on. For the next two years, Fitzgerald, who likes to turn issues into causes, consistently proclaimed the virtues of the museum and took swipes at the politicians, mainly me, who thought otherwise. To my mind, it would have been irresponsible for a mayor to endorse a project that had no financial backing and whose sponsors wanted gifts from the city. Fitzgerald imagined that the museum could be a major tourist attraction, even a catalyst for waterfront development. He called city officials visionless. He quoted me as saying that there were a lot of projects the city would like to put together but it just did not have the finances to do so. "Typically tepid is Mayor Joan Darrah."[2] Fitzgerald and Perry fomented competition with other cities, warning that at any moment Stockton could lose this fabulous collection.

Eureka! That is, Eureka, California. All of a sudden there seemed to be a real live offer. This Northern California city "rolled out the red carpet," according to Perry.[3] The Eureka City Council had voted to approve the museum as part of a fifty-acre waterfront project. The whole mass of stuffed heads and bodies, the shells, the skulls, the fish, and the 1,759 eggs would soon be on a bus traveling 350 miles north. "Stockton Blew It: the World Wildlife Museum Is Leaving," cried Fitzgerald in a subsequent headline.[4] Unabashed, I was quoted as saying, "Those who really enjoy animals should go out and enjoy the lemur exhibit at Micke Grove."[5] Speaking of this comment, Fitzgerald lamented, "You could just scream."

For several months, I had been asking city staff members to provide the council with financial data about the museum, such as five years of audits and this year's financial reports. I also wanted a list of the museum's board members. This was basic information that all nonprofits I had ever worked with were asked to supply when they requested significant public or private help. This information was not forthcoming. By August, Perry had announced that he wanted a two- to three-million-dollar piece of city property. In return, he claimed, his organization would finance a wildlife museum/aquarium in Stockton as a satellite operation to the main one in Eureka. *The Record's* editorial position, though not Fitzgerald's, was circumspect, noting that the city needed to be wary.[6]

As quickly as Eureka came onto the radar screen, it vanished. It seems that when its council promised Perry fifteen acres of waterfront land, it had acted on the mistaken understanding that the museum had a collection already mounted and displayed as well as the money to build the new facility, which it did not. But Perry had a powerful ally in the Bank of Stockton's president, Robert M. Eberhardt, himself a hunter and a generous philanthropist, who told Fitzgerald, "I think it's important as hell. It would be...a great attribute to our downtown."[7] Typically, Eberhardt put his money where his mouth was and offered the bank's empty 15,000-square-foot Coors distribution warehouse to Perry to house his collection. So Perry never loaded up the ark for Eureka. Instead he stayed in Stockton. After all, he had three things going for him here: a place for the collection, a popular columnist's advocacy, and the support of the business leadership. Whatever Eberhardt advocated, big business supported; once that happened, small business and the chamber of commerce often fell into line.

The World Wildlife Museum took steps to increase its public support and visibility. It provided the Stockton's Children's Museum with an exhibit of 279 mounted animals. It opened a gift shop in the mall, called "Wild Things," which lasted for two years. It also put on fund-raising events at its warehouse location and invited the Business Council and San Joaquin Partnership to hold a reception there. Eberhardt helped the museum prepare a thick report outlining its goals for the future. It envisioned a $63 million complex set on 9.8 acres of waterfront land, with a natural history museum of 98,328 square feet featuring the animals, birds, reptiles, insects ("beasties" as Fitzgerald called them) of the seven continents in their natural settings. The plan also included a 38,000-square-foot aquarium, a 5,000-square-foot Delta Hall, an otter pool, a dock, interpretive trails, and a butterfly house. It anticipated an annual attendance of 885,000 visitors, visitors who would stay in our hotels and motels, eat at our city's restaurants, and bring millions of dollars in new revenue to the city. These seemed to be quite ambitious goals for an organization that in two years had never produced a shred of financial information.

The museum did not ask for free land outright. Instead, it requested exclusive negotiating rights for eight months on ten acres of waterfront land along the south shore of the channel. In return the museum would complete the necessary improvements to the warehouse, make plans for the permanent facility, and devise a strategy to raise the $63 million. This proposition was approved by the redevelopment commission and then brought to the city council for its approval.

On the morning of the day when the council was to discuss this proposal, December 5, 1994, *The Record* headlines read: "Mayor, Museum Backers Clash." I was quoted as saying that I "felt compelled to speak out because...museum backers don't have the money or expertise to complete their plans. We would be tying up 9.2 acres of the most valuable land in San Joaquin County for what appears to me to be an impossible dream." I admitted that a majority of the council favored the project. Panizza told the reporter that I opposed the museum because of my dislike of mounted animals. I denied this, saying that the problem was the financial viability of the organization.[8]

The executive director of the Business Council led off the discussion at the council meeting that evening.[9] Tall, clean-cut, well spoken, Ron Addington is always a smooth presenter. A good friend of all of us, he said, had asked him to become involved (no doubt Bob Eberhardt, I thought). Item number one of the agreement, the improvement of the temporary facility to meet fire standards and Americans with Disabilities Act requirements, was well underway, with donated labor and materials. Many had been asked to volunteer, and many had stepped forward. The project had the approval of the Business Council. Had the Business Council voted on it, I asked. "No," he responded, adding that "there are times when you just know, when the chairman, Fritz (Grupe), just knows there is universal agreement and no vote is necessary." How comfortable, I thought. Here is the business leadership of the community falling into line behind Eberhardt and Grupe with nary a question about the real financial viability of the project. The president of the chamber of commerce, who was also Grupe's general counsel, came next. He said that the board of the chamber was 100 percent behind developing downtown Stockton. The city should give the Wildlife Museum backers eight months to get their numbers in line. I thought the board of the chamber had not taken a formal vote either.

The major presenter for the evening was the newly elected treasurer of the WWM, Joe Zeiter, an ophthalmologist, a prominent businessman, and a hunter. As he approached the podium, a picture flashed into my mind of his office when I had visited it last. Its walls were covered with the heads of animals he had shot: a ram, a water buck, a red stag, a fallow deer, an impala, a mule deer, a chamois, a Stein buck. He also displayed a king salmon and pairs of drake mallards and pheasants that were mounted on the wall behind his desk. "Quite a few stuffed birds and animals, Joe," I ventured, trying to sound appreciative. "Mounted, Joan, not stuffed."

That night, standing before the council, very sincere and committed in his presentation, Zeiter reported that the treasury had received $5,000 in donations from banks and another $5,000 from his firm. He said how important the museum was, that not many children would be able to see a polar bear in their lives. I wanted to suggest to him that there were live polar bears in the Sacramento Zoo, only one hour away, where the animals could be viewed in a situation that was quite different from the rearing, angry specimens at the WWM. Zeiter stuck up for Perry, saying that he had invested a quarter of a million dollars of his own money in this project. However, he had no response to the request for financial data. He told us the first he had heard of my request for financial information was this morning, and it had just been too late to obtain it.

The issue this evening, I contended, was that the city was being asked to place a ten-acre, two- to three-million dollar piece of property in a negotiating rights agreement whereby no other party interested in the land could be given consideration. This project would succeed only if the organization was financially strong. I did not have before me any data on its financial position, its expenses, income, or assets, even though I had been asking for this material for more than a year. "As keeper of the city's trust, its land trust, I feel that I must have this information." I said, concluding my statement with vehemence: "You're coming back (in eight months) and wanting a gift of the land—I am dead against that." Perry was present at the council meeting that night but apparently he was told not to speak. When I asked him directly if he any financial information, he did not even respond. The discussion closed and the matter went to the council.

Once again, the council complied with the wishes of their benefactors in the business community. As I had anticipated, the other six members were all in favor of granting the request for the eight-month option on the city's land. Panizza was even in favor of giving the land to Perry, then and there. I made only one short statement: "I am not going to vote for this. There is no evidence that this organization has any of the wherewithal to make this project a reality. Let's just say that the mayor of the city of Stockton is raising a red flag." I called for the vote. The proposal passed, 6 to 1. The museum had the land for the next eight months, until October 15, 1995, and maybe longer, since these options are often renewed.

About halfway through the eight-month period another party, Griffin Foundation of San Jose, got very interested in this same piece of property. It wanted to build a sports complex similar to a successful one it had built in San Jose. Councilman Panizza and the deputy city manager had met with the principals of the Griffin Foundation and were excited about the possibilities of a volleyball complex, ice skating rink, and sports bar in this location. So was *The Record*. So was the council. But what to do about two competing entities that wanted the same property? The choice was made easier by the fact that the WWM had not met the conditions of its option. It had not yet opened its "temporary" headquarters in the Coors warehouse, nor had it provided plans for the permanent facility and a fund-raising strategy for its construction. It had also failed to seek an extension of the October 15 deadline.

I finally received a financial statement from Perry, dated December 31, 1994, which I sent to *The Record*. It showed that the museum had $32,495 in the bank, $42,000 in pledges, $32,550 in loans, an art collection valued by the art dealer who donated it at $1.5 million and a collection of zoological specimens it claimed was worth $31 million. The museum also had a debt to Perry of $244,650.

Perry was enraged when he heard that the option for negotiating rights might not be extended. *The Record* reported "outrageous threats" by Perry to file suit and tie up the land in court for years. It advocated granting the option to Griffin Foundation, "a much surer thing than the Wildlife Museum" in its view.[10] The council voted unanimously to grant the Griffin Foundation the option and directed staff to attempt to find another location for the museum. Before the vote, I took a final shot at the museum. "Was there ever any real evidence that the World Wildlife Museum had amassed or, in fact, could amass the kind of support that would enable it to build a museum on that piece of property? I see very little evidence of that. At the same time, I see a big debt to one of their chief executive officers." I repeated my favorite point, that the museum was no more than a write-off for rich hunters.[11]

The Griffin Foundation's project never materialized, and the World Wildlife Museum opened in the Bank of Stockton's warehouse in February 1996. In the spring of 1999, the Bank of Stockton sent a letter to the museum saying that the bank had a buyer for the warehouse and the museum had until May 10 to purchase it for the same amount, $575,000. At one point it looked as if a backer would save the building for the exhibit, but he pulled out. Then another man, John Dentoni, a Bank of Stockton vice president and a friend of Perry's, stepped forward to save Perry's hide. "The deal is all but done," he told *The Record*.[12] In fact, there was no such deal.

I made periodic visits to the museum, one in the summer of 1998 and another in June 1999. There was no doubt that it held a large number of animals from all over the world, a very large number. They were grouped according to regions, with the indigenous animals in the first room, along with the North American animals and the Sheep Mount, a collection of sixty sheep from all over the world. Animals, birds, reptiles from Africa, Asia, East India, Australia, South America and many other areas were arranged in the second room, a single huge space where the stuffed and mounted animals were so numerous there was little room to walk around and look at them.

I went down to the museum, pad and pencil in hand, intent on getting the facts. It was a warm summer afternoon, and the atmosphere in the building was heavy. Two small fans were all that kept the air in one of the warehouse's two large rooms circulating, and faintly, at that. The museum could not afford to light the interior effectively. The quiet was pierced by the shrieks of a caged cockatoo. This dreary environment may have been the reason that during the ninety minutes I was in the facility there were only five other visitors: one woman with two young children and two teenage boys. The museum claimed to be educational, and yet two-thirds of the specimens were not even identified. This may have been because the animals were so crowded that more labels would only have added to the clutter. On the railing that divided the specimens from the walkway, there were only eleven one-page "educational statements." Although the museum certainly housed many specimens, it appeared to have overstated its holdings. At the time of my visit, the brochure claimed there were 2,000 mounted species, but I counted no more than six hundred, and I counted all I saw. I wrote them down on my pad, group by group, and then I added them up. I had the museum by the tail, by God!

The museum never did find a benefactor who would make possible the $63 million complex. In August 1999, for lack of funds to purchase the warehouse, the museum was forced to leave, and the animals (*The Record* used the figure 5,000) were put into storage.[13]

Jack Perry died suddenly a year later, at the end of June 2000. The obituary article in *The Record* informed us that Perry had sold most of the collection to the Rolling Hills Refuge, a zoo just outside of Salina, Kansas, which had plans to build a 64,000-square-foot structure that would house the animals in natural dioramas.[14] At the time of the sale, six months earlier, *The Record* described the sidewalk scene in Stockton during the packing of the collection: Children oohed and aahed as large animals were carried out to the trucks and a warehouse wall was dismantled to allow an elephant to pass through in a specially built crate on its way to a specially built flat-bed trailer. The reporter waxed nostalgic, quoting a Stockton resident who lamented the "real nice museum" that might have been there for his grandchildren.[15]

Had such a thing ever been possible, had Perry been able to put together a first rate museum of natural history, Stockton might have benefitted. But even with five years of support by wealthy friends in high places, the "modern-day Noah" could not make that happen. "For all its missteps," wrote Mike Fitzgerald in his valedictory to the departing collection, "the city of Stockton has given Jack Perry a pretty fair chance. As much chance as you get when you want others to finance your dreams."[16]

Concealed Weapons: Gun Control or Armed Citizenry

At the U.S. Conference of Mayors Women's Caucus meeting in 1994, while listening to Mayor Rita Mullins of Palatine, Illinois, describe the gruesome murder of seven employees at a fast food restaurant, I was moved by memories of the awful Cleveland School shootings of 1989. I eagerly signed on to the caucus's advocacy of national gun control, and I was happy to be one of the mayors that year who stood on the steps of the capitol building with Sarah and James Brady in support of the Brady Bill.

Back in Stockton, I wanted the city council to take some of the same steps toward gun control that were being discussed and adopted in other cities at this time. Citing a one-hour television program on CBS about kids killing kids, I recommended that the council gather information on such matters as the number of gun dealers licensed and unlicensed in our city. I suggested we look at our police department's policy on confiscated guns. Ultimately I wanted the council to consider stiffer ordinances that would reduce the number of guns available.

Councilman Nick Rust, a member of the NRA, objected immediately. He suggested we set up a ten-person task force, to be composed of gun shop owners and representatives from the NRA, to review gun control measures. Rust told the newspaper that such a task force "would come up with less biased proposals for coping with gun violence."[1] I was not able to persuade the council to reject this idea altogether, but I did manage to modify it. By a 4 to 3 vote, the council set up a seven-member group to be composed of one person appointed by each council member. I chose Judge Sandra Butler Smith, a tough judge with a prosecutorial background and an enlightened mind. The council gave the task force two months to come up with its recommendations.

The Record was fully on my side in this matter. Virgil Smith, the publisher, had just concluded a Guns for Exchange program that resulted in 153 rifles, shotguns and handguns being taken off Stockton streets. In September, the editorial page advocated federal legislation in five areas to get and keep guns out of the wrong hands. The paper treated Rust's proposal with scorn.

With the task force already established and functioning, we were all very surprised when, in October 1994, Councilman Rust proposed a piece of legislation, which he called the Public Safety Ordinance, by which all law-abiding Stocktonians would acquire the right to carry a hidden weapon outside of their homes. That translated into the possibility of 130,000 adults in the city going about their day-to-day business with a gun in their purse or their glove compartment or in a shoulder or leg holster. Why did Rust want Stockton to be the first city in America to have such an ordinance? "My ultimate goal is to make Stockton a safer place for people to live," he told the *Los Angeles Times*, when the paper did a full-page article on his proposal.[2] I thought Rust's ordinance was preposterous. As I said to *The Record*, "I think it is absolutely ridiculous and absurd," and I added a threat: "If this council were to pass it, I would bring it up immediately for review when the new council meets."[3] Police Chief Chavez also opposed handing out permits to carry concealed weapons to anyone who might qualify for a license. No other of the 456 cities in California had such an ordinance. The procedure on the books was that anyone who wanted to carry a concealed weapon had to obtain permission to do so from the chief of police. Only 207 permits had been issued, one for every 1,111 persons in the city. To my amazement and chagrin, four council members voted to place Nick's proposal on the agenda for November 14.

The Record's editorial writer had a field day mocking Rust. Tongue in cheek, the paper implied that if all council members did not go along with Rust, *The Record* would replace them for incompetence: "They've got a chance to turn Stockton into a real armed camp and make the city the subject of national press and TV coverage the way we were after the Cleveland School shootings."[4] This, of course, was a really damaging aspect of the proposal—the extraordinarily negative press it attracted that pictured Stockton as returning to the glory days of the Wild West. After we had taxed ourselves in order to increase our police force by 130 officers, instituted community policing, and were just beginning to see reductions in our crime rate after a decade of increases, this publicity would be both painful and terribly unfair.

In an editorial published the day before the matter was to come before the council, *The Record* called the Rust ordinance "a cockamamie proposal" that shouldn't go anywhere. It also pointed out that it was against state law, since it took away from police chiefs and sheriffs the sole discretion to determine who gets such permits. The editorial concluded by urging the council to dispose of the proposal quickly and decisively. "The last thing Stockton needs is more guns—legal or illegal—on the streets."[5]

On November 14, 1994, the council chamber was crowded with speakers, observers and television cameras. After all, if it passed, Stockton would be the first city in the nation to advance the notion that a safer city would be one where almost every person who owned a gun or was legally entitled to buy one could carry that gun in a concealed manner. Already we had had major negative press in the *Los Angeles Times*, the *Orange County Register*, and the *Sacramento Bee*. Television networks covered the issue in nightly newscasts. That morning, Rust appeared on "Good Morning America" in opposition to Patrick Murphy, former police commissioner of New York City and director of the Police Policy Board for the U.S. Conference of Mayors, a man whom I had recruited to challenge Rust in my stead.

One of the key elements of the meeting that night was that the business leadership of the city came out unanimously opposed to the Rust proposal. This was the principal reason that the three members of the council who had been responsible for putting it on the agenda ended up voting against it. Representatives from the Business Council and the San Joaquin Partnership said that the ordinance was likely to have a negative effect on their efforts to attract industry and jobs. It would reinforce the old image of Stockton as an unsafe community. The head of the Stockton Convention and Visitor's Bureau testified that people were calling to say that they would not hold conventions in Stockton if the law passed. The head of admissions at the University of the Pacific, noting the potential impact on student recruitment, deplored Rust's "horrible" timing. Prospective students and their parents repeatedly asked the question, "Why does the city council want to arm everybody?"[6] Police Chief Chavez warned that to process some additional 10,000 licenses would cost his department more than $430,000 a year. Finally, the city attorney said it was probably illegal.

The meeting was continued for one week to permit the council to hear the final eleven speakers. In all, fifty speakers addressed the council, twenty-seven in favor of the Rust ordinance and twenty-three against. The final speaker, a California Rural Legal Assistance attorney, recalled a group of angry, impulsive hotheads who had shaken their fists at the TV monitor while Judge Smith was speaking to the council the previous week. "No one's safety would be enhanced by issuing them gun permits," he concluded. A motion was made to reject the Public Safety Ordinance by Councilwoman McGaughey, a consistent antigun crusader whose son had died from a gunshot wound at a young age. It was seconded by the vice mayor and then passed by the council, 6 to 1, with Rust alone opposed. Knowing that this outcome would be carried nationwide, I crowed, "This is a victory for Stockton."[7]

That same evening the Gun Task Force presented its recommendations: 1) education for kids on firearms and conflict resolution programs in the schools from K-12, and 2) police tracking of guns, leading to a crackdown on illegal sources and appropriate criminal charges against violators. The council also refused, though only by a 4 to 3 vote, to review existing procedures by the police chief for issuing concealed weapons permits. *The Record* applauded the council for all of these actions. "Mayor Darrah and the council didn't follow. They led."[8] I would have to add to that comment that once again the council members "led" in the direction the business leadership wanted them to go. This time, happily, that was the right direction. It must be admitted, however, that Rust's ordinance and the ensuing debate had the effect of preempting my intended proposals for increased gun controls in Stockton.

Final Two Years: Getting More Done

Graffiti, Blight, Code Enforcement

However much we may maintain that issues matter, and they do, there is no denying that the temperaments and idiosyncrasies of individual people make a tremendous difference to what does and does not get done on a city council. For the last two years of my second term as mayor, three of the other six members of the council were new; three former council members—Nick Rust, Loralee McGaughey, and Sylvia Minnick—were no longer members. The new combination of people, as well as the particular attitudes of the three new members, made for a very different council.

Looking back, I would have to say that without this change in personnel, my last two years would have produced very different results. A good example of what I am talking about was the way Stockton went about dealing with its graffiti problem. One woman, Ann Johnston, a new council member, a small business owner, and a charismatic committee chairwoman, made all the difference.

In the early 1990s, approaching Stockton from the north on Interstate 5 and glancing to the left, you could see fencing located about a hundred feet from the road, fencing that was remarkable for its ugliness. Slats had been ripped out leaving open spaces through which trash, weeds, and garbage were visible. What fence boards remained were smeared with graffiti. The houses in the area, primarily owned by absentee landlords, were dilapidated, and broken down cars and trucks sat on the bare dirt outside. Debris littered the driveways and collected in street gutters. Young kids hung around aimlessly in small groups. Because this scene, known as Kelley Drive, stood between the highway and several new middle-class developments, all you could see of Stockton as you passed by was wreckage.

Were you headed for the city hall, you would take the Fremont Street exit and drive down a two-lane street with small businesses on both sides. Several had been there for decades. Every morning as I drove to the mayor's office, the large, distorted spray-painted letters almost jumped out from the side wall of a clothing designer's shop, the brick wall of the retail appliance distributor or the long granite wall of an electrical company. Many of the business owners along Fremont Street were friends of mine. Two of the store owners lived in my neighborhood. I was a customer at several of these places, and one of them had donated the use of sound equipment to my fund-raising events.

In August 1993, graffiti seemed to explode everywhere in Stockton, and especially on Fremont Street. Everyone could see the change. One day one of the Fremont Street store owners phoned me at city hall and requested that I attend an evening meeting he had organized and that I bring along police officers and code enforcers. Tension permeated the meeting room as I entered. Twelve area store owners told us how angry it made them to see gross writing on their walls and how expensive it was to clean up. What was the police department doing to stop this offensive activity? "We do what we can," the officers answered, "but it is hard to catch taggers when their work is done mostly at night and very quickly." The code enforcement officers concurred: "With such a small staff, our hands are tied." Turning to me, the owners asked, "What is the city going to do to help us?" My response was that the city's lean budget prevented us from doing this job; cleanup was the owner's responsibility. City codes required them to keep their own buildings clean. If they did not, we would send someone to clean them and they would be charged for the service.

The owners could not accept these answers. They wanted the taggers caught and ordered to clean up the graffiti: "Let those little punks know what we have to go through to clean up their slime." I promised to write a letter to the judiciary, which I did. "On behalf of this group (West Fremont Improvement Association), I am writing to request that you make the removal of graffiti the public service requirement for the abusers and fine them the maximum amount allowable by law."[1] The county district attorney's office phoned back to say that there was no mechanism for supervising the vandals while they were performing this activity. He did not say that he would try to create one. His indifference was typical of local officials.

Next a jewelry store owner wrote a letter to me repeating in very strong language the demands of the Fremont Street group. She had recently paid approximately two thousand dollars to have her store repainted after four major graffiti hits in the past five weeks. By holding property owners responsible for cleanup, the city victimized taxpaying citizens, while taking no steps to protect them from this assault. She ran a respectable business that was being violated. She was informing her elected official of a crime committed against her, and it was the responsibility of police and judges to protect her building and manage the cleanup. She was doing her job, bringing products and job opportunities to Stockton. Others should be doing theirs. She strongly objected to an article in *The Record* that described the taggers as "artists" and argued that property owners should make wall space available for the work of the taggers. I wrote her back suggesting a nonprofit corporation that did volunteer graffiti removal and urged her to invite other business owners in her area to a meeting. She ignored these suggestions. The chamber of commerce weighed in with a letter to the city demanding that maximum penalties under the city penal code be imposed on graffiti offenders and that both the penalties and the names of those receiving them be publicized. They also did a check of stores selling markers and spray-paint cans and found most of them in violation of city and state codes.

The rage in these letters and in the voices of speakers at the Fremont Street meeting surprised me. Previously, I had thought of graffiti as the expressions of troubled youth. I liked the one-day mural program set up by a local organization. But any soft-hearted thoughts of a rehabilitation program was greeted with scorn by the store owners and business people, and I soon came to see the problem through their eyes. It was not harmless; by God, it was criminal.

Searching for answers, I met with a friend who cleaned off graffiti every morning from his building because, he said, twenty-four-hour removal denied the vandal recognition, which was the purpose of the graffiti. I thought that this was a good idea and I put out a memo that I entitled, "The Graffiti Scourge," which urged immediate removal of graffiti and explained how to do it. I even recommended particular products for removal and protection, and I urged people to report stores that sold spray cans or markers to persons less than eighteen years of age. I also spoke with the city manager, only to be told that graffiti was one of the oldest acts of mankind. He said that graffiti could be found on ancient edifices built thousands of years ago. It had always existed and always would. Graffiti removal was nowhere on his priority list, nor was there a council majority that cared about it.

The police department must have felt some pressure, because they began a crackdown that would continue indefinitely. Using unmarked cars and stakeouts, they arrested five adults and four juveniles in five separate incidents and gave the adults' names to the paper. All but one was charged with malicious mischief. The police set up a graffiti hot line and gave rewards to persons who reported offenders. They also obtained a grant for $239,000 from the State Office of Criminal Justice Planning for a program they called "Operation Zero Tag," where officers supervised convicted taggers as they painted over graffiti. Helpful as this initiative was, the grant for the new police program was for one year only and it operated only two days a week. It was not big enough to take care of our problem.

Sensing by this time that graffiti had to be addressed by city government, I referred the issue to the drugs and crime subcommittee of the city council, which I chaired. We met for three months and heard several proposals from nonprofit agencies for graffiti removal. The most expensive program, the one that would paint out graffiti in twenty-four to forty-eight hours, would cost $131,195. The city manager pronounced this amount too much for our budget; he averred that hard-working, well-supervised young people who worked for the California Conservation Corps could be hired at a cheap rate. They could spend their summer with an Americorps Summer of Safety program and paint out graffiti at the minimal cost of $15,000. The council went for this instead of the experienced but more costly programs run by the nonprofits. Thus, almost one year into the issue of graffiti control, little had been accomplished. We had had angry outbursts from business, excuses from city staff, denial from the judges and the district attorney's office, and minimal city funding, except for a few thousand dollars for a summer program to do cleanup and a state grant that would last only one year. Things had to change.

In the first three months of the hot line's operation, 359 calls came in. The hot line was obviously needed, but it had to be kept before the public eye. I appointed an *ad hoc* committee and called it the Graffiti Abatement Task Force, which initially I chaired. At the very first meeting, we were startled to learn of recent changes in state laws. Punishment for graffiti vandalism had become much stricter, the maximum penalties being $5,000 in fines, damages up to $25,000, loss of driver's license for one year, a requirement for offenders (and their parents) to remove the graffiti, and up to one year in jail or six months for possessing graffiti tools. Immediately, the business people on the committee wanted to publicize the new laws by poster and billboard. A gifted graphic artist designed a poster for us: "Graffiti Artist Wanted." ("Artist" was later changed to "Vandal" at the behest of the business representatives.) Penalties were cited on the poster. I wanted to publicize the hot line and I knew a local labeling company that would donate decals with the hot line number and the penalties, using the same design as the poster.

The smartest thing I did at this point was to ask Councilwoman Ann Johnston, the owner of a business that was a frequent site of graffiti attacks, to take over the chairmanship of the graffiti abatement task force. Under her leadership, our efforts escalated into a full-fledged war on graffiti. She enlarged the committee to include three council members, six people from the business sector, two from graffiti abatement groups, six from Safe Neighborhood groups, a representative from the county supervisor's office, one from a nonprofit agency, and three from the schools, including a student. Because graffiti removal now had the force and sanction of city government, there were always between five and eight staff members present at the committee meetings: the deputy city manager, three representatives from the police department, including the police chief himself, the code enforcement supervisor, and the city attorney. More people were added as new issues arose. Faster conviction of vandals brought in representatives from the district attorney's office and probation department. There were always twenty-five to thirty people at the monthly meeting. Ann welcomed and stimulated everyone who came.

The newly expanded committee held a kickoff, at which it displayed a new poster design, a billboard design, and a decal. We had secured funds enough to print 6,000 posters, half in English and half in Spanish, and the downtown label maker donated 160,000 decals that were distributed to residents in their monthly utility bills. The decal itself was bright yellow, with bold black print, listing the penalties; it had red graffiti down the side and the hot line phone number printed on a removable label that could be affixed to any surface. I stuck mine to the dash of my car so that I could phone in violations as I saw them.

Ann's next big event was a "graffiti wipe-out day." More than six hundred people signed up to participate. *The Record* gave it extensive coverage in two major editorials, the first noting that the day reflected a remarkable public-private sector partnership. Following the wipe-out day, an appreciation dinner drew three hundred volunteers. Ann acknowledged each person by name, and I handed him or her a certificate of recognition. Forty-three businesses were also recognized. Another wipe-out day was planned for a few months later. These events served to publicize the activities of the committee, the effectiveness of the hot line, and the further steps necessary for a comprehensive abatement program. It also involved teenagers. Those who came to the task force meetings organized large activities at the wipe-out days. Whole groups or clubs from specific high schools painted out one long wall or one particularly difficult site.

Without the commitment of the justice system to render effective punishment, no amount of participation would have solved our problem. Ann Johnston set up a law enforcement committee that included the district attorney, a probation officer, a police lieutenant, and herself to consider more rapid disposition of cases. She visited with the juvenile court judge, who urged that punishment be given more publicity. *The Record* was only too eager to quote the judge when he sentenced four teens, ages fourteen to seventeen: "All I can see is a bunch of non-caring, selfish little punks...destroying people's property."[2] He ordered that they spend sixty days in Juvenile Hall, followed by thirty days of weekend and vacation work as restitution to damaged businesses, and suffer a suspension or delay of their driver's licenses. He also ordered the vandals' parents to accompany their children to school, keep them in the house from 10 P.M. to 6 A.M. and pay the county's court costs. The editorial pointed out that these kids were responsible for tens of thousands of dollars of damage in the northwest Stockton area. In addition to spraying stores, fences, mailboxes, sidewalks, and trash bins, they had etched windows in an office building, to the tune of $22,000.

A beautiful example of cooperation between citizens and city government was the work of a local volunteer, Ginny Kafka, who had followed these four teenage taggers with a camera as they made their rounds and took photos of the work they left behind. Then she called the police, who pulled the youths out of school and got them to confess. A branch of the Bank of Stockton in Ginny's area had advertised that the bank would give a reward of $500 for each arrest and conviction of a graffiti vandal. They sent Ginny a check for $2,500. The Homeowners Association also won a $700 judgment against the taggers' parents in small claims court to cover cleanup costs.

Once you mobilize the volunteers from the public at large, as Ann Johnston did, you have a momentum that the police, the judiciary, and the politicians can join. The combined force of judicial sentencing and aggressive volunteers resulted in many more arrests being made, and of those picked up, many changed their ways after punishment. Of 136 tagging arrests in 1994, 83 were re-offenders. In 1995, there were 132 arrests, involving 91 re-offenders. But in 1996, there were some 212 arrests, with only 23 re-offenders. A former tagger who had been ordered to clean up graffiti and litter testified to the task force that her punishment had a definite impact on her. She had not tagged since then.

Another outcome of the graffiti committee's work was that the city brought its ordinance into alignment with the new state laws. Now liens could be levied against the property of parents of minors who committed acts of vandalism, and the city could pay rewards for information leading to an arrest, even if there was no conviction. When it was found that spray-paint and wide-tip marking pens could be purchased in some of the commercial pockets of the city that were in the county, the committee requested that the county change its laws to conform to the city's. The county did so and, in return, county residents could use the city's hot line to report businesses that were selling markers and spray paint to minors.

As graffiti was associated with the late night hours, there developed a greater interest in controlling the nighttime activities of young people. In 1995, a curfew center was established. In a short, three-month period, approximately three hundred juveniles were picked up and transported to the police curfew center where their parents had to pick them up between the hours of 11 P.M. and 6 A.M. There were very few repeat offenders. Likewise, a truancy center was established for the daytime detention of young people out on the streets and not in school, and schools were asked to close their campuses during the lunch period. All these changes helped reduce juvenile crime in general, above and beyond the reduction in tagging.

One of Johnston's committee's most successful projects was the paint trailer. Often called the best weapon against graffiti, it was a faster and cheaper means of getting rid of graffiti than hand painting, and the color came out an exact match to the paint that had been vandalized. Essentially a paint store on wheels, the trailer could use four spray-painting lines at one time, mix paint colors on site, change colors in seconds, and cover over twenty-two thousand square feet of wall space in a day. The cost of the operation was five cents per square foot compared to seventy-five cents for a person using a brush.[3] Moreover, the trailer allowed the city to get rid of graffiti within twenty-four hours. When I heard about its effectiveness, I immediately advocated a fund-raising effort to purchase a paint trailer, but city staff upstaged me. The chief of police decided to use "asset seizure funds" for this purpose, and the next thing you knew Stockton had a paint trailer. We held a contest to name the paint wagon; JAWS, the Graffiti Eater, was the winning design, invented by a college student from Stockton. This trailer was so often used and so well received that funds were raised privately to purchase a second one. We may have to thank a long trailer with big shark jaws on the sides for the yearly decreases in calls to the hot line.

Inspired by the success of the graffiti wars, the deputy city manager asked me to appoint a committee to address another component of Stockton's urban blight, neglected buildings. At this time the great obstacle to renovation was the process prescribed by city codes themselves. Property owners were given a month to make repairs; appeals could be filed over another month or two. If the owner did not comply with the city's demand, the city attorney would write a letter to the owner, who could then appeal to the city's board of appeals, which would delay action another thirty to sixty days. The city could take a misdemeanor criminal case to court. One or two cases were filed each month. The whole process took at least six months and often longer.

The task force replaced this procedure with a new system of citations for violations under which landlords or tenants were given a specified time to make property repairs. If repairs were not made satisfactorily, the city could follow up with a fine of up to one hundred dollars for each day the violation continued. The fine could go as high as five hundred dollars per day after three or more offenses. The new system also prevented appeals from going to court. Instead, recipients of citations had to appeal to an administrative hearing officer.

One of the first successes of the new procedure is now visible on Kelley Drive, that derelict area on the north side of the city that one sees when approaching Stockton on the freeway. In one day code enforcement officers checked each of the 167 homes along Kelley Drive and handed out ninety citations to landlords for structural problems, such as broken windows and faulty wiring, and to tenants for junk cars and piles of trash. While this was going on, the graffiti trailer worked the street, spraying new paint over graffiti scrawled on fences and lampposts.

Along the backside of Kelley Drive was the broken fence area that was such an eyesore to motorists traveling along I-5. The assistant city manager, Gary Ingraham, took it upon himself to demand that the homeowners along the highway do their own fence construction and repair as required, or the city would do the work and charge them for it. He required redwood or cedar fencing plus steel flashing secured by lag bolts. No one would steal this fencing for timber! The city hired the Conservation Corps to do the work and then charged the homeowners. Ingraham arranged to have oleanders donated for the site and worked out an irrigation plan. Today the entrance to Stockton from the north is a fine sight—solid fences behind a colorful array of pink, white, and red oleanders. I never drive by without a feeling of excitement at the fantastic change and gratitude to the fellow who made it happen.

The cleanup by code enforcement has become more intense as the number of officers assigned to this job has increased. By 1997, the city had instituted a "strike team," a group of code enforcement officers who obtain search warrants to enter buildings that have a history of violations, such as overcrowding, unsanitary conditions, or crime problems.[4] In 1996, my last year in office, the council passed an ordinance allowing code enforcers to post "slum signs" on buildings with a history of problems and code violations. "Stockton is one of only a few cities across the country to take such a measure," said *The Record*, with justifiable pride.[5]

The moral of this tale, as it was with STAND, is that collaboration between city and county officials and private citizens produce far more substantial results than either group could accomplish alone. The fact is that individuals such as Ann Johnston or Mary Delgado, in the case of STAND, are what make institutions work. In turning to my next subject, the crisis over the FEMA flood plain map, I am reminded of how much particular people matter. We had the right city manager in Dwane Milnes, who orchestrated the whole effort, we had two splendid senators in Washington, Dianne Feinstein and Barbara Boxer, and we had another new member of the council, Duane Isetti, who came along with the group that pled our case before the federal bureaucracy. I hate to think what would have happened in this matter without them.

Senator Feinstein and Senator Boxer: Role Models and Key Players in Stockton's Battle with FEMA

In March 1989, after nine highly successful years as mayor of San Francisco and several months before she became the Democratic nominee for governor of California, Dianne Feinstein agreed to be the keynote speaker at the Women's Center luncheon in Stockton. Thirteen hundred people, mostly women, came to hear her, the largest turnout in the twenty-five year history of this annual affair. I sold one hundred tickets and had one hundred guests at one immense table.

Before the luncheon began, Feinstein met with local leaders to ask us what issues were most important to us. This was the first time I had been in a room with Dianne, and I was impressed with the careful attention she gave to everyone—from the city's biggest developer who talked about child care to a black activist who ran a halfway house for cocaine users. She was a doer as well as a listener, a woman who not only advocated mentoring but also met weekly with a junior high school student in San Francisco. At the end of her keynote speech, she advised me briefly on some ideas for women to consider in practical politics: Do our homework, be team players, and never cry in public. "Save the tears for the shower."

As a Democrat and mayoral candidate in the summer and fall of 1990, I was selected to introduce Feinstein when she returned to Stockton for visits during her gubernatorial campaign. I always knew what I wanted to say in these introductions—that Dianne was a woman of wisdom and strength. In November 1978, after the murders of Mayor George Moscone and Supervisor Harvey Milk by Dan White, it fell to Dianne, as president of the board of supervisors of San Francisco and acting mayor, to speak to the city at that terrible moment: "Though we feel sorrow, we must avoid the spirit of bitterness and recrimination; remorse must not beget revenge. Let us join together in a spirit of unity and reconciliation."[1] When she stopped in Stockton on a campaign train trip through the Central Valley, I introduced her again, this time to a big downtown crowd. After the rally was over, she asked to see the Children's Museum, our memorial to the children killed at Cleveland School. Later, when she was traveling the country in support of a ban on assault weapons, Dianne referred to the Stockton experience as a key point in her arguments for the weapons ban.

On the night of Tuesday, November 5, 1990, in the final hour of her campaign for governor, I waited with the others for the returns in the Grand Ballroom of the Fairmont Hotel in San Francisco. At about 11:00 we filed out, downhearted and despondent. Dianne Feinstein would have made a splendid chief officer of the state of California.

A politician needs to be personal. She intends to recall everyone's name and personally sign every thank you letter for a contribution. This is the least she can do for all that donors and volunteers do for her. Yet the reality is that the tremendous demands on a politician's time allow most of us no chance to be personal. This, however, is not true with Dianne Feinstein. Imagine how many big checks she received in her campaign for governor. Yet when I sent her $100, I received a letter that appeared to be composed for me alone and that ended with her signature and the handwritten words: "Please stay close."

Again, when I coordinated a fund-raising event for her in 1994 during her successful senatorial campaign, I received a letter in her handwriting, "Joan, my day in Stockton, thanks to you, was wonderful. Please know that you are my friend. Also, I will help Stockton however I can. Best love, D." When my daughter and I were invited to her home in San Francisco along with many other politically active women, it happened to be my birthday. As we were leaving Jeanne said, "Senator Feinstein, my mother wouldn't want me to tell you this, but it is her birthday today." Dianne left the line, went upstairs, and returned with two current, nonfiction books personally autographed by her. She invariably added a personal note to her response when I wrote her a request from city hall.

In the early 1990s, when I was first mayor and when Dianne Feinstein had been a highly visible and successful politician for over twenty years, Barbara Boxer was a total stranger, at least to me. Then one day in the spring of 1992, Congresswoman Boxer asked to meet with me at the Hilton in Stockton. I showed up and met an attractive, talkative congresswoman who wanted to tell me that she intended to be elected to the U.S. Senate from California in November, an outcome I thought unlikely. And yet she was compelling. For about half an hour, we spoke about issues she cared most about and hoped to promote as senator. They were issues I cared about too: health care, abortion rights, child care, and gun control. She had energy, charisma, and brains. I was impressed, and I came away willing to support her. A few months later, I was asked to help on a fund-raising event for her in Stockton. It was to be cocktails and heavy hors d'oeuvres at thirty-five dollars per person. Boxer arrived early. What I remember most clearly about the evening is that short period of time when people were still arriving. There was no one talking to her at all. She checked out the bookshelves, smiled at a few guests, chewed on a carrot, and waited. That was then. Now hundreds pay $500 apiece to grab a stand-up snack and have a quick moment with two-term Senator Boxer.

In late 1994, the Federal Emergency Management Agency (FEMA) announced that it was about to publish maps of Northern California that showed areas that were prone to flooding. These maps located Stockton and its surrounding towns in the flood plain. News of the forthcoming FEMA maps caused a frantic response in city hall. Flood plain designation meant that any new building would have to be raised by as much as a foot or two above the flood plain floor. By making construction far more costly, this regulation would make it next to impossible for Stockton to recruit new business.

At the time Stockton suffered from double-digit unemployment, and the business community and local government had set aggressive goals of creating several hundred new jobs per year. Flood plain designation would stop us cold. Moreover, less business would mean less tax revenue for enhanced city services, such as increased police presence. Early estimates of the impact of the FEMA flood plain maps projected losses of 2,750 jobs, $145 million in construction contracts and $40 million in uncollected taxes. Worse still in some ways, it would force residents to purchase flood insurance at $600 to $1,000 per household.

It was the city manager, Dwane Milnes, who alerted us to this crisis. He knew whose heads would roll when local residents had to start picking up the bill for sewer lines and a water conveyance system. These were being built mainly to serve anticipated new development, which was expected to pay for them. The FEMA maps, by forestalling this development, would shift the cost of the new infrastructure to city residents. Milnes convinced me and the council that the FEMA maps had to be stopped or at least delayed. The alternative, which Milnes advocated, was for Stockton and its surrounding county area to raise their levees to meet FEMA's demands. It would be far cheaper for our residents to fix the flood problem themselves by raising the levees with funds obtained through a bond issue than it would be to pay for personal flood insurance. But could a mid-sized city force a huge federal agency to back down?

Pleading with FEMA was our first tactic. Milnes, Vice Mayor Floyd Weaver, newly elected Councilman Duane Isetti, and I went to Washington. We contacted the offices of senators Feinstein and Boxer and asked for meetings with them as well as with the top FEMA personnel. Senator

Feinstein could not see us, but she set up a meeting for us with FEMA officers, including the director, James Lee Witt. Before some fourteen high-level bureaucrats, senatorial aides, and an aide to Congressman Richard Pombo from our district, the four of us from Stockton argued that there were legitimate reasons to delay the maps. They were incomplete, we asserted, because they lacked a flood depth study and because there were serious shortcomings in the flood plain survey's technical information. They wanted to know how many residences in the affected area had flood insurance. When we responded that the figure was 423 out of more than 100,000 households, they were surprised and concerned. "How do you know it's not going to flood next year?" they wanted to know.

Senator Boxer saw us in person. When we arrived at her office her staff member, Rob Alexander, escorted us to the Capitol and let Boxer know we were there. She came off the Senate floor to meet with us. Characteristically, she knew all about our situation. In fact, she had already written a letter for us objecting to FEMA's requirement that only federal funds be used for levee reconstruction. Such a law prevented Stockton's funding its own levee improvements, for which we had already set up a city/county agency. Boxer promised she would call Witt and make a plea to delay the flood maps. She gave us an extra boost when she said, "If FEMA will not bend its rules, we will need Congress to rescue the city with special legislation." This statement proved prophetic. The next day Milnes met with the second in command at FEMA and, just as he had expected, the agency refused to give an inch. After this rebuff, we turned to a second tactic, all out political pressure on our elected representatives to effect the result that FEMA had denied.

Back in Stockton, Milnes and his staff managed to generate a kind of frenzy over the issue. The newspaper railed against FEMA. "Don't let the feds destroy Stockton," warned the publisher.[2] He called on all taxpayers and voters to "flood" the offices of elected federal officials with mail, telephone calls, and faxes denouncing FEMA's action. Congressman Pombo received hundreds of letters, calls, and faxes. Witt became the villain, the insensitive bureaucrat, the target of the paper's frustration. In my report to the city council, I noted that it took pressure from someone at the While House (a contact we had through local businessman Joe Barkett), our senators and representatives, and a personal request from California Lieutenant Governor Gray Davis to even get an appointment with Witt. In a succeeding editorial, *The Record* asked angrily why it took "White House intervention to get an appointment with a bureaucrat like Witt? That just adds to our suspicion that FEMA's brass is totally out of touch and out of control."[3]

Seventeen members of Congress from California signed a letter to Witt urging delay of the implementation of the new flood plain maps, but there had been no statement of support from Senator Feinstein. Milnes was concerned about this and hinted to me that she was about to receive very negative press in *The Record*. I wrote to Feinstein saying that there was a growing belief in Stockton that she was not going to bat for us on the flood plain issue. I quoted the publisher of *The Record* and two top business leaders: "It seems Feinstein is the major holdup." I always wanted to defend her, I said, but it was now the case that Boxer had met with us personally and promised to call Witt on our behalf, and seventeen members of Congress had signed a letter to Witt, "yet nothing strong and definitive has come from your office." I suggested that negative press could have a deleterious effect on the 1996 presidential campaign.

Almost immediately Feinstein called me at city hall to express support for FEMA's position that Stockton residents be required to carry flood insurance. She told me that while she was mayor of San Francisco the public works director had pointed out the need for earthquake repairs for Candlestick Park. She had had those improvements made and, as a result, twenty thousand persons were saved from death and injury during an ensuing earthquake. She believed that the protection of their constituents from disaster was a significant responsibility of all elected officials. She added that she had spoken to Mr. Witt's assistant, Martha Braddock, who said Stockton should "relax," that all this political pressure was counterproductive.

The city manager scoffed at the suggestion that we relax and so did the newspaper. Milnes believed that the only way we were going to get out of this jam was by applying intense pressure. *The Record* editorialized that Feinstein's support of mandatory insurance was only slightly less devastating than the halt in building that would occur were the maps issued. It noted that thousands would be forced out of the moderate-income housing market with monthly insurance payments of $50 to $100. With respect to the value of political pressure, a columnist wrote, "If Witt and Braddock can't stand the heat, they [should] get out of the kitchen. We also suggest turning up the heat."[4] Word got back to us that Braddock was not pleased.

That was April. By early August the local headlines announced, "Feinstein Supports a Delay in Maps."[5] The significant factor in Dianne's change of heart was not the bad press; it was legislation Milnes had designed, in consultation with an excellent Washington lobbying firm, that gave us the delay we wanted in exchange for our commitment to almost immediate levee construction. What the special legislation did was to put a prohibition in the 1996 federal budget against FEMA's spending any money during the 1996 fiscal year on maps that would designate Stockton a flood zone. Milnes had our congressman introduce the legislation in the House, where it was approved, but it also needed Senate approval.

The Stockton contingent of four returned to Washington. This time Senator Feinstein saw us, and she was ready to support the legislation. She wanted to make sure, however, that we local officials had the political will to assess homeowners $500 to $1,000 to pay for the $70 million bond required for levee improvements. To this end, she required a proviso in the legislation that levee construction begin by July 1, 1996. What she did not want to see happen, she told us, was a possible flood, many left without insurance, and a big bill going to the federal government. She also promised to work with FEMA and the Corps of Engineers to facilitate the permitting process.

As I left her office, I made a point of handing her a copy of her good press in our city, frankly to make up for the bad press for which I had been partially responsible. I wish I had added that she was right: Public safety certainly is something for which elected officials should hold themselves responsible. In our distress over the impact of the FEMA maps on economic development, city staff had underplayed that part of our job. Dianne looked at the whole problem—flood conditions, development, and public safety—before she accepted a solution.

We then went to see Barbara Boxer and as before were met promptly by Rob Alexander. Again he escorted us to the Capitol where he asked us to wait for the senator in a prearranged location, which turned out to be the office of Vice President Al Gore. In a few minutes Senator Boxer arrived. She was exquisitely dressed in a lavender dress of soft, thick fabric complemented by a matching necklace that held a large jade pendant. She was "all over" the reason for our visit. Yes, she knew the problem. We wanted her to send a letter to Senator Kit Bond, the head of the Senate committee on appropriations, asking that the new legislative language delaying the flood maps be inserted. We had sent her a sample letter, but she had rewritten it in a far more concise and compelling form. Yes, she would do all she could to get this budget proposal passed. In past visits Milnes did most of the talking, but this time I presented our case. I knew she would expect and prefer hearing the story from me. I told her that we needed this letter to Senator Bond signed by the two senators from California. She agreed. As she was leaving the office, I complimented her on exposing Oregon's Senator Packwood's sexual harassment. She beamed and turned around and said, "There's a lot more to come; many women are stepping forward."

At just that moment the Senate was adjourning. My favorite memory of Washington is Senator Boxer, short of stature, looking up at Senator Feinstein, tall of stature, and gesticulating energetically, asking her to join in signing the letter to Senator Bond. Feinstein, looking down at Boxer, nods in agreement, and Boxer turns to me and says, "You've got what you want."

Although the appropriations committee was normally loath to make an exception for one city, the legislation passed. Senators did seem to see the rationale for the affected local people's paying for the work themselves, at far less cost and with much greater speed than the federal government could ever do it. They were ready to give us another delay in 1997, so the final maps were never issued. By August 1998, the work was finished. Not only finished, but famous! Even before the levee reconstruction was completed, Stockton received a national award from the American Association for Flood Plain Managers for effectively dealing with this designation. We became FEMA's model city! Last but not least, our local state assemblyman introduced a bill in the state legislature to provide $12 million to partially reimburse the residents of Stockton for their assessment for levee construction. The bill passed. The checks have arrived.

Many people played a part in our success: All those Stocktonians who wrote letters to Washington, *The Record*, which made sure FEMA was harassed daily, a few politically powerful people who contacted the White House and senators they knew, our city council and county board of supervisors who voted consistently and unanimously in favor of every stage of the project, and finally the remarkable city staff, principally our city manager, Dwane Milnes, who was the mastermind of our effort throughout, and his project assistant, Wayne Smith. Milnes worked steadily on the project for more than a year, in addition to fulfilling his regular full-time duties as chief administrative officer of the city. If you ask him who helped us the most, he will squint his eyes and say that there were hundreds, but if you put them all into a vast field, two would stand the tallest, Senator Barbara Boxer and businessman Joe Barkett, the Democrat in our county most connected to the power structure in Washington and my opponent in the casino story. I would add to this list Senator Feinstein. It was Dianne who insisted that we find a way to reconcile the government's—and her own—concern for public safety with our city's need for economic growth.

During my last year in office, wanting very much to retire my $8,000 campaign debt, I invited Senator Boxer to be the keynote speaker at my annual Women Leading luncheon. She was dynamite. Her presence that day before a crowd of three hundred enabled me to leave office debt free. Two years later, in the summer of 1998, when she was up for reelection to the Senate, her campaign manager asked me to put on a fund-raising event for her. The minimum to be raised was $10,000. Our final figures showed a profit of $13,000. Though a small contribution to her $20-million-plus campaign budget, nevertheless it did get her excellent publicity in *The Record*.

In my introduction of her that August night, I touted her efforts on behalf of Stockton with FEMA. I noted that she had also secured $4.3 million for our Downtown Transit Center, budgeted at $8 million. If we wanted the remaining funding, we had all better get out and work for her. Further, she had helped secure for us a $750,000 grant for cleaning up the channel waters, a vital part of the downtown renewal program. At my son-in-law's urging, I submitted my speech as an op-ed piece for *The Record*, which gave it a great headline: "Barbara Boxer a Proven Friend of Stockton."[6] Barbara came back to Stockton once more during the election, to speak of the importance of community-oriented policing and to applaud STAND for its remarkable achievements. Even though I was no longer in office, she insisted that I stand with her while she spoke of the importance of having effective local politicians. She received great press for this visit also. Her opponent received practically none.

Just four days before election day 1998, Boxer invited me and twelve other elected officials to walk with her, Hillary Clinton, and Dianne Feinstein into the main dining room of the Saint Francis Hotel in San Francisco at a huge fund-raising event. When she came up to our group, just before entering the dining room, I could not help myself. "Barbara, you look beautiful," I said. And she sure did. Though Boxer was returned to the Senate by a ten-point margin statewide, she won by only 260 votes in San Joaquin County, actually an excellent showing for an outspoken liberal woman in our very conservative, male-dominated city and county.

Two months before I left office, Assemblyman Mike Machado invited me to host an event at my house where the star attraction was to be Senator Feinstein. The event got so large that it was moved to Dianne's favorite museum, Stockton's Children's Museum. I got sick and could not attend. Dianne had designed and had framed a farewell statement that applauded my work as mayor and stressed how much she valued the contribution of local leaders, having herself been a mayor. She concluded her remarks by saying, "I hope you are called back to duty before too long." What the future holds for me I cannot say, but I can say with all my heart that I am fortunate indeed to have had Barbara Boxer and Dianne Feinstein as role models, colleagues, supporters, and friends.

Redesigning Stockton's Waterfront: The Legacy

In the first week of June 1994, I received a letter from the Institute on City Design that made a surprising proposal: "On behalf of the National Endowment for the Arts, it is my honor to join Mayor Joseph P. Riley in inviting you to attend the Mayors' Institute on City Design in San Antonio, Texas, on October 6–8, 1994." I was one of seven mayors in the United States who were invited to attend a national conference on city design. Each mayor was asked to bring a significant design problem from his or her city to present to urban planners and other experts. Although the conference sounded interesting, no special problem came to my mind. Design problem? Like what? Besides, I had already planned a trip in October, at the same time as the conference, to China, Japan, and the Philippines, where Stockton had three "sister cities." Everyone in our sister cities was expecting the mayor of Stockton; the arrangements were in order; it sounded like a lot of fun. I was vacillating over this change of plans when a friend said bluntly, "Skip the fishing village of Shimizu. Go to San Antonio." I sent a copy of my letter from the Institute for City Design to Dwane Milnes, the city manager, and asked him to develop a design problem. What the staff prepared for me was a magnificent document, which they entitled "The Channel Study."

"The Channel" is a deepwater channel that flows from Stockton eighty miles west across the Central Valley into San Francisco Bay. Its inland end is a deepwater port, Stockton, in the heart of the Central Valley. Looking at the Port of Stockton from the air, the channel head forms a Y-shape. Weber Point, named for Stockton's founder, Charles M. Weber, is the ten-acre peninsula that protrudes into the water to make the fork of the Y at the head of the channel. The land outside of the prongs of the Y is known as the north and south shores. "The Channel Study" presented for the experts at the San Antonio conference the question that had defeated city governments and public leaders in Stockton for decades: what to do with Weber Point and the adjacent areas? In order to explain why this was such a crucial question, in fact *the* question for Stockton, I will need to sketch in a little history.[1]

Like many cities the world over, Stockton was built on water; it owes its existence to a river channel to the sea. The city was put on the map by the arrival of the Gold Rush immigrants in 1849, many of whom came to California by sea via the channel—from China, from other parts of the U.S., from everywhere. Stockton was the place near the foothills of the Sierra where they landed to begin their search for gold. The businesses that supplied and supported the miners—teams of twenty-four horses at a time hauled their equipment up into the hills—sprang up and flourished here.

At almost the same time, agricultural production began in the immensely fertile lands of the Central Valley, lands which extended to the horizon on every side, and for this agricultural economy, too, Stockton became the commercial hub. Farm machinery was manufactured, canneries and a flour mill were built, as well as boarding houses and saloons for the workers. The key to it all was the deepwater channel—its port, its warehouses, its access to national and overseas markets. Railroads linked Stockton to Sacramento in 1869 and then to the East Coast via the Central Pacific by 1870. Not one but three transcontinental railroad systems ran through Stockton by 1910.

For a hundred years, from the Gold Rush to the end of World War II, Stockton's rapid expansion and economic prosperity steadily increased. In the year 1893, for example, five manufacturers in Stockton produced 450 different kinds of combined harvesters. Fortunes were made, and the look of the city began to reflect this affluence in a number of impressive private houses as well as handsome public buildings and grounds—the county courthouse, an agricultural pavilion, schools, the county jail, hospitals, warehouses, parks, and imposing office buildings. By the early twentieth century the city's sense of itself was embodied in even grander structures: the municipal baths, the ornate Fox Theater, the second county courthouse, and, most splendid of all, the "Spanish Renaissance" style Hotel Stockton, located at the water's edge at the head of the channel. Looking out from its roof garden, one could see large stern-wheelers, two to four abreast, lying gracefully at anchor at the channel terminus.

During both world wars, especially the second, Stockton had a boom economy based on war production. Its most famous contribution to the First World War was a modification of the caterpillar tractor, developed by Benjamin Holt of Stockton for use in the friable soils of the Delta farmlands. His use of caterpillar tracks to replace wheels later influenced the design of the armored tanks that were used during the First World War.[2] During World War II, Stockton became a huge supply base for the whole Pacific theater. Its main activity from 1941 to 1945 was shipbuilding, with no fewer than ten shipyards, employing ten thousand workers. The expanded port facilities included a cement dock long enough for thirteen war ships to tie up in single file. Even after the war, several of the military depots remained, though operation of the port passed back from the Army to civilian control.

With the end of large-scale wartime activity in 1945, the area's decline began. Shipyards lay empty in the port area, and not many boats were moored at the channel head. In Stockton, as in many cities across the country, intensive residential and commercial development in the suburbs led to the whole downtown area's being increasingly abandoned and neglected. Beginning as early as the late 1940s, businesses and residences moved out of the downtown area in droves. Some downtown buildings were boarded up; others were torn down to make way for parking lots that were in turn abandoned; still others were left vacant and became sanctuaries for vagrants and criminals. Like much of downtown, Weber Point and the area around the channel head became a scene of desolation.

Successive city governments were concerned about what was happening. No fewer than five major studies of the Weber Point waterfront area were undertaken in search of remedies. The first, in 1954, was appropriately called "A City of Blight." The next four, in 1974, 1981, 1983, and 1989, urged major building projects on Weber Point. R/UDAT (Regional/Urban Design Assistant Team) recommended the construction of high-rises. The $250,000 Central Stockton Plan of 1989 imagined a convention center and hotel, the expansion of the redevelopment area downtown, and the hiring of staff to supervise the implementation of its plans. Even this study produced no perceptible changes for the waterfront; consequently, like the others, it only increased popular mistrust.

By 1994, because nothing existed on Weber Point except weeds and overgrown trees and cracking asphalt and heroin syringes and prophylactics, because nobody but transients and bums and an occasional fisherman was to be seen there, public confidence in the possible transformation of Weber Point became virtually nonexistent. The perception and, in fact, the reality was that nothing had happened on Weber Point in decades. Sure, people remembered the broken-down Holiday Inn and the Chili Pepper restaurant, but even they were long gone. Visible inaction in the past led people to believe that nothing could ever happen, a self-verifying prophecy if ever there was one, because without intense and sustained public support nothing would happen this time either. If the city government—if my administration—could do something about that area, we might begin to reverse almost fifty years of decline. We might even be looking at the possibility of bringing the whole central city back to life.

What I took to San Antonio, "The Channel Study," was a marvelous slide show and pictorial boards that depicted the importance and challenge of the waterfront. There were nineteen experts at the conference—urban planners, a transportation expert, a developer, a landscape architect, an expert in leadership for public involvement—who discussed each of the design problems brought by the seven mayors. It is not a boast but a simple fact to say that these experts were far more excited about Stockton's waterfront than about any of the other design problems. They were amazed that there was a piece of land in the center of the city that was unencumbered and available for development. They saw it as a fabulous resource. They stressed the importance of planning—our decisions should be made for a year from now and fifty years from now—and of a sense of place, too. This location should be owned by the whole community. It should be the heart of the city, the place where the city came together.

There were some people at the institute who especially impressed me. One was Samina Quraeshi, the director of the Design Program for the National Endowment for the Arts, an author and an artist. She had taught at Harvard and Yale and had been involved in revitalizing the waterfronts of both Boston and Miami. There was also Sharon Kafka, who was extremely knowledgeable about the River Walk in San Antonio. She took us on a boat tour and explained how the River Walk, much of which was built by WPA workers in the early 1930s, had developed. I was especially interested because several Stocktonians had told me that San Antonio provided a model for Stockton's waterfront.

One must begin with a design and a dream, explained Kafka, which everyone in the community needed to understand and embrace. It should not been seen as the pet project of one or more small groups—urban planners, politicians, developers. Once it was understood and supported by the public at large, competing projects, which are often proposed in the course of large-scale redevelopment, could be measured by their fidelity to the plan the community supported. Intrinsic to the River Walk's plan, for example, was river access from the River Walk to the Alamo. When the first big hotel came along, the residents of San Antonio required Hilton to construct a tunnel through its first floor to allow the river to flow through to the Alamo.

Another key element of any plan for long-term city renewal, as I learned at the conference, is a continuing committee structure that will carry forward the goals and the policies of the plan into succeeding municipal administrations. Like the factor of community involvement, this political longevity is essential to putting a large design plan into practice, moving it from the drawing boards to the streets. Listening to Sharon's remarks also gave me a lot of respect for how long it takes to develop an area. The River Walk had been in process for six decades! Our project could take several years, too, and Stockton could do it, but only if we could move beyond four decades of studies that had led to nothing except a pervasive popular mistrust of people with plans in their pockets.

I came back to Stockton all fired up about a large-scale renovation for Weber Point. "Community involvement is the key," I told my staff, "and planning and expertise." We decided to begin with a large committee or "task force," and the deputy city manager came up with a list of people who might serve. Although Samina Quraeshi advocated an all-inclusive community meeting, followed by subcommittees that would continue public participation, we did not start that way. Instead, we handpicked a group of twenty-eight people who seemed to us to represent a cross section of the city. Above all, they were widely known, trusted and admired, people who could lead a skeptical public to say, if this or that person is a member of the task force, it may just work. We avoided people with special agendas.

At first, I made the mistake of thinking that one of the major developers should serve, but one of the new council members cautioned against it. "Alas, same old thing, big shots are going to run this effort," he objected. We dropped both that developer and another one who had been active downtown and who wanted to see a ball park on Weber Point. Had such people been included, the committee would have been perceived as their pawn and as incapable of expressing the collective will of Stockton.

Fortunately, we had very sensible people in key positions at the time: Victor Wykoff, the chairman of the city planning commission; Carl Brooking chairman of the redevelopment commission; Leslie Crow, the chairwoman of the Cultural Heritage Board; and Tom Shephard, the managing partner of a law firm whose property was on the waterfront. Because we needed the downtown business and developer interests represented, we selected an accountant, Rudy Croce, who was treasurer of the Business Council, and Don Geiger, chairman of the downtown improvement district.

We signed up a land developer, Mike Atherton, who represented the Building Industry Association, and Nel Tarwater, president of the Stockton Board of Realtors. The owner of a highly successful Latino enterprise, Humberto Sanchez, agreed to serve. We also asked the members of the city council to select committee members, a process that brought in an African-American business leader, Ernie Boutte, and a restaurant owner of Chinese descent, Sam Louie, and, in response to the demand of one council member for greater community participation, a student from Delta Community College, Jeanne Sibert, and a senior citizen, Robert Rimington.

We had two representatives from small business, Norena Badway and Ken Davis, and two from business organizations, Steve Anthony and Jeanne Zolezzi. Big business had its representation in the figures of three bankers, Ray Graetz, Robert Kavanaugh, and Luis Sanchez.

Giving balance to the group, we appointed Robin Kirk from the Sierra Club, Joe Winstead from the Building Trades Council, Beth Horton, chair of the Stockton Arts Commission, and Diane Trainor, principal of the Woodruff Regional Occupational Center, which had its facilities adjacent to the waterfront.

An outspoken critic of the general design of downtown was an organization called Stockton Beautiful. We asked its president, Gerry Dunlap, to serve. Two council members, Mel Panizza and Duane Isetti, were also on the task force. Mel served as its vice chairman and I as the chairwoman.

In all, the group of twenty-six was representative of the major components of Stockton, particularly its business leadership, its downtown interests and its ethnicity. No one had an axe to grind. I had worked with most of the members prior to becoming mayor, particularly Victor Wykoff, who had been a key player in United Way when I was president and who had been my appointee to the Stockton Planning Commission.

As this task force was being formed, I had my annual Women Leading Luncheon, a campaign fund-raiser. What better speaker could I possibly invite than Samina Quraeshi! After an inspiring speech at the luncheon, she was interviewed standing at the tip of Weber Point. She had visited urban waterfront renovation projects throughout the United States, she told the reporter, and she thought that Stockton had the greatest potential of any she had seen: "You have to give people a place to nurture their spirit." Weber Point could be that place, the heart of the city. Stockton could recapture a sense of itself by recapturing its history. Noting that Stockton's founder built his house on Weber Point 144 years ago, she said, "His house and his vision should be put back."[3] And quoting Wallace Stegner, "No place is a place until the things that happened in it are remembered."

At the first meeting of the task force, I sought to reinforce the sense of urgency. I talked about an "action plan." The object of this committee was *not* to produce yet another study. This time the community needed to come together, and things would happen. We talked about what we could accomplish by the summer, about short-range goals in addition to a realistic long-term vision. The sense of the group favored both open space, a parklike environment, and commercial development that would make the project self-supporting in the long run. As for the early concerns of the task force members, some questioned whether our city would have the will to make waterfront development a reality. "In some quarters in Stockton," the task force was told by one of its own members, "the committee here has been referred to as Mission Impossible."

Basic to this skepticism was the pervasive belief that nothing would happen. There was also an all-consuming preoccupation with crime in the area. The committee closed its first meeting with the decision to contract for expert advice and look for ways to involve the community in the waterfront's revival. The city had set aside $100,000 for a design consultant. From the nine applicants, we selected Lyndon Buchanan Associates. Bay Area Economics, an organization that also impressed us greatly, became associates on the project.

Even though *The Record* criticized the committee appointments, insofar as certain friends of the publisher were not included, the paper applauded the city council's initiative. "What we have not had until now is a high priority, high-profile government commitment," it said.[4] In his column of January 27, 1995, Michael Fitzgerald wrote these memorable words: "First allow me to congratulate Darrah and all who support her desire to rebuild the waterfront. The waterfront is a key to fixing Stockton's tenacious crumminess; perhaps also the prescription for alleviating Stockton's spiritual malaise, the shame we feel about our decayed downtown."[5] That said it all. However many experts we had, there was a profound disenchantment among people in the city about the city. But how, exactly, does one go about "fixing...tenacious crumminess"? What heals "spiritual malaise" or civic "shame"? Can a mayor or a committee accomplish those things?

As long as I had lived in Stockton, which by then was thirty-four years, I had never thought in a specific way about downtown. One of the first things the consultants did for the task force was to take us on walking tours that taught us to see our own city from the perspective of city design. We started out at the heart of downtown, at Main and San Joaquin streets. What businesses were generating traffic along Main Street? we asked. What places, what doorways were people going in and out of? Where were people buying bagels or flowers, getting a cup of coffee, picking up the newspaper or a gift? The shops on Main Street were closed and out of business. The Canliss building was a government building with no retail dimension. We walked west by the Hunter Square Fountain and the mall towards El Dorado Street, a part of town that was very attractive to look at but practically deserted because there was nothing for people to do, nowhere to eat, and nothing to buy there.

Also there were arterial barriers, El Dorado and Commerce streets, where heavy, fast traffic threatened pedestrians. Very little was happening in the downtown area that made one want to go there. Remarkably, there was no access to the waterfront. The dominant feature of this part of the city was the historic Hotel Stockton, once a magnificent structure at the head of the channel, the focal point of the city from all directions. It had been boarded up for years.

Many other walks followed. On one walk through the northern part of the waterfront area, coming from Fremont down to the waterfront, we examined barriers to water access, and another walk took us along the south shore. On a boat trip later we were appalled, when we came to a crucial location at the channel head, to see a four-story office building rotting. Windows were broken out, a curtain flapped in the wind, graffiti covered the walls, and weeds and debris lay on the ground. At the same time, our walking groups saw some beautiful features of downtown, such as the all-marble lobby of the historic Bank of Stockton, and the formerly magnificent Fox Theater, completed in 1930, recently renovated and reopened amidst much ceremony.

After this particular walk, I wanted to share my new-found understanding of downtown with everyone. At a Youth-in-Government Day session, I proudly took a group of Stockton High School seniors on that same walk, from the Court House to Weber Point. I held forth enthusiastically about the importance of this historic ten-acre peninsula. I asked for their comments and responses. One girl scrunched up her face and said, "It's disgusting. Obviously druggers and prostitutes hang out here."

On another occasion, one of the principal people for Bay Area Economics, Terezia Nemeth, was sitting by herself on a bench near Weber Point when a security officer came by. "Hey lady, you better not sit here. You could get in real trouble in this part of town," he warned. Terezia got the message: Public perception had to change. She promptly advised us to institute a series of quick actions to publicize every success, no matter how small. We took down the chain-link fence that blocked access from the north shore to the street. We repaired the clogged waterspout on a fountain in McLeod Lake, just north of Weber Point, and a beautiful spray of water shot up into the air. Both actions were cheap and visible.

One Saturday, two committee members and I, with help from city staff, mounted a huge cleanup of Weber Point by community volunteers. The city was so uptight about the dangers of the area and the possibility of a lawsuit that all the participants were required to wear rubber gloves and to use a special device to pick up the debris. Some sixty of us collected nearly five thousand pounds of garbage, had a lunch afterwards, and received good press in *The Record*. In a small way, something was happening on Weber Point.

Large-scale community involvement was the next priority. I knew that a questionnaire would be sent out, but I thought the experts would write it. Not so. With the help of the consultant, we had to devise our own, and as a result we really "owned" that document and became committed to having it filled out by as many people as possible. The twenty-five members of the task force took questionnaires to their personal constituencies—the Rotary Club, the Sierra Club, Latino groups, the Building Trades Council, Junior Aid, and several Southeast Asian groups. We contacted eighty-two groups and had eighteen hundred questionnaires completed. The strength of that result was undeniable. Subsequently, whenever a question arose about any aspect of the final waterfront plan, one simply said, perhaps a little self-righteously, "Look, we got input from eighteen hundred residents, and this is what they want."

Another effective method for community inclusion was a series of three public meetings, each attended by some fifty to one hundred people. Participants were divided into groups of eight, and each group was given a blank map of the waterfront. We asked them to discuss among themselves what they wanted to see in the several locations and to fill in the map accordingly. At these meetings a major point of consensus emerged: Weber Point was to be an important outdoor space, not a place for dense development. People wanted to see an open, parklike area that could feature an amphitheater, a band shell, or an international marketplace that promoted cultural activities. They wanted to see a lot of green park area and recreation space and have clear views of the water from all vantage points. They wanted improved linkages, such as promenades and bridges across the channel, to enhance everyone's enjoyment of the entire site.

For me, perhaps the most brilliant aspect of the consultants' work was the way they shaped our thinking. Most people on the committee, though prominent in various ways in public life, had no preparation for making decisions in the area of city design. We knew next to nothing about the layout or landscaping of city streets or about the architectural merits of historic preservation as compared to income-producing structures. The walks taught us to see familiar sights in our city with new eyes. With the help of the consultants, we established six guiding principles for the ultimate plan: 1) Gathering, making the waterfront a place where people from all parts of Stockton came together; 2) Vitality, enhanced economic vitality; 3) Connection, between the waterfront and downtown; 4) Identity, the waterfront as a place that consolidates the specific identity and special history of Stockton; 5) Environmental Quality, enhancing natural conditions; and 6) Economic Consequence, the immediate financing needs.

Ours was not the only game in town. Once the council began discussing Weber Point as a focus for city planning, a number of private developers came forward with competing proposals. One person wanted to build a baseball stadium, a waterfront sports and events center. A ball park, we were told, could be designed to resemble the urban-style, ivy-covered stadiums, such as Wrigley Field. It could be a multi-use center, with approximately six thousand seats, but at $9 million the estimated cost for this proposal was out of sight. I certainly was not ready to put it on the ballot as a bond issue, yet I liked the idea of using Weber Point for large events. I think they are fun, they build community and promote public spirit, and they are a way that nonprofit organizations can fund their operations. So, I began to listen carefully to any talk of festivals or concerts or corporate picnics, but only baseball—no. It would not pay off, and the public did not want it.

A second proposal was a nine-hole executive golf course on the north shore. Although a golf course would have been pretty to look at, it would have required the city to purchase several additional acres of property along the north shore, acres that were already home to small businesses. Such an acquisition would have been impossibly expensive for the city. That idea did not go anywhere.

Then a major local developer came up with the "Stockton Foundation." This plan also called for a ball park, and it called for a $50,000,000 commitment by the residents of our city to a nonprofit corporation, a proposition that would have to come to the city for a vote. Knowing that the vote would fail, this particular developer could then say, "The community does not want to invest in a downtown, so surely the city should support investment out at the airport," where this developer had major property interests.

Another resident suggested an amusement park on Weber Point, with a carousel. And finally, there was a proposal for an educational institution. While all of these large projects were being discussed, there were also a couple of smaller ones. One man wanted to start a paddle boat business on the south shore. Another dreamed of a sailboat business. Subsequently, through some help from the city, both got started; both failed. As the committee listened to all of these proposals, we came to an understanding: Any proposal would have to pay for itself. It could not require large public subsidies. At the same time, it became apparent that private money was not waiting in the wings to take control of the future of Stockton's waterfront. The task force turned its attention back to the challenge of public design. We still had a long way to go to convince the residents of the city that major change was possible.

Bay Area Economics subtly kept us moving forward when the going got tough. At just this point, when we were quite discouraged, it came up with a land-use map that helped return our focus to practical matters. Weber Point and Banner Island would be open recreation areas; the north shore would be designated for mixed use, the south shore would have education and entertainment facilities, and the parking lot on Weber Block would be removed and the block redesigned with fountains, pools, and greenery. The civic center area (city hall, the public library, and the civic auditorium) would remain as it was. These recommendations seemed consistent with what was already in place and with what was needed in the area. The Children's Museum had located on the south shore and was doing quite well; Griffin Associates had signed a contract for land at the end of the south shore for a giant volley ball and sports complex; and the waterfront warehouse was, we believed, on the way to becoming a successful retail outlet. What happened next, however, did not go according to our expectations. Griffin Associates gave up on the idea of coming to Stockton, the Children's Museum developed serious financial problems, and the warehouse was sold to a businessman who turned it into office space.

Despite controversy and disappointment, the waterfront task force put the "Vision and Action Plan for Weber Point" on the council agenda for a meeting in January 1996. Several members of the task force gave brilliant presentations. No one raised an objection. The experts who had gathered in the council chamber were quiet. The plan passed unanimously. There was a lot of joy and hugging and backslapping that night after the council meeting.

As I evaluate the several factors that made for success in getting the plan accepted, I think first of the task force members' regular attendance before the council to discuss the progress of the committee. Second was the positive influence of constant public input. This is what the community wants, the report maintained. Further, the members of the task force were individuals who commanded public respect. Fourth, the city staff was united and fully in accord. Lastly, the money was there—funding, at least for the phased development of Weber Point, appeared to be in the budget.

The whole project, including Water Square, was estimated at $17,000,000, with some $6,000,000 coming from donations. There was sufficient funding, $3.6 million, to get started on Weber Point. Only one year later, Bay Area Economics received a prestigious statewide award from the California Chapter of the American Planning Association for its "Stockton Waterfront Revival Vision and Action Plan."

We had to move quickly. A new council would be taking over in January of 1997. We set the deadline for a completed design for March 1996, only two months after the first council vote. The next step was to hire the design consultants. After looking at proposals from nine outstanding design firms, we chose RHAA, Royston, Hanamodo, Alley and Abby. Although the estimate for their services turned out to be $130,000, the highest of the nine, we never regretted our choice, though the newspaper grumbled about it for quite a while afterwards.

At every point we needed to sustain citizen involvement and have our residents embrace the design. We put together a slide presentation to take throughout the community. Fifty groups and a thousand persons were contacted. Also, a number of public workshops were presented where people could tell us what they wanted were. Yes, they did want the fountain for children and the entry way to Weber Point. They did want a big space in the middle for events and a stage for concerts. They did want a twenty-foot promenade around Weber Point, where people could walk and roller blade and bicycle. They did want a children's play area. In one of its slide presentations, RHAA showed a sail-like structure over a central events area of Weber Point that would be supported by columns that the designers called masts. Knowing how hot it can get in the summer in Stockton and how windy it can get on the point, and how it even sometimes rains in April, the idea of a cover to protect visitors from the elements, coupled with a lookout to the water and to Mount Diablo, was very appealing.

We set up an events committee, and it got very energetic. In the beginning, Weber Point was going to be mainly an open space with only an occasional concert. Little by little, however, the idea of sponsoring community events took over. We were afraid that if the area featured only a park, no one would come to it. The plan might be approved, but residents still needed a reason to come downtown. Major events would attract people, and the sight of a big crowd would, in turn, ensure safety; that combination—the crowd and safety—was necessary for the economic viability of the project.

At one point, although there were already others in the city, we organized a farmer's market on Weber Point. It failed after three sessions because nobody would come down there. In other words, after all of the public meetings, the questionnaires, the slide shows, the discussions, that old despairing feeling among Stockton residents that "nothing would happen" on that large blighted piece of land was alive and well. Organized events became more and more the committee's answer to this public skepticism. We had a business plan drawn up for Weber Point, which was approved in June 1997. It called for theatrical productions and concerts and corporate picnics. It also required that a gate for evening safety be added to the design, a compromise with the popular ideal of openness.

On September 7, 1996, three months before I left office, the council approved a $4.1 million expanded project and established a continuing waterfront committee with the new mayor, Gary Podesto, as chairperson. We paid RHAA $133,000 and contracted for the company to proceed with the engineering plans for Weber Point. The Bank of Canton gave up its 40 percent holding on Weber Point in exchange for land in Stockton to be donated by the city to the Mercy Charities to use for the construction of low-income housing.

On a lovely day in San Francisco, almost at the end of my term, I met with the leadership of the Bank of Canton and accepted the land of Weber Point for the city of Stockton. On October 28, 1996, we broke ground at Weber Point and put up the sign reading, "Weber Point Events Center." I worried that we had moved too far away from the original concept of a community park, but Terezia Nemeth of Bay Area Economics reassured me: "So long as they are not putting up a building, the space can have changing uses."

No one could have predicted that 1997 would be the second wettest year in Stockton's history. Construction delays slowed the anticipated completion date by several months, well into 1999. The price tag climbed to $5.3 million, mainly because of the additional design requirements for large-scale events. The plan for an interactive fountain was taken out of the budget and then restored at a cost of $1 million, and the shade structure was scaled back. Some people continued to complain about not having a ball park. *The Record* carried on about the high cost of consultants. Nevertheless, the council held to the original plan for Weber Point and allocated the funding necessary to complete the job.

Amidst great fanfare, Weber Point Events Center was formally opened and dedicated on July 3, 1999 (by then the price was $6.5 million), five years after "The Channel Study" had been written. Thousands of people gathered that night for fireworks and a concert by the Stockton Symphony. As I walked through the big, joyful, relaxed and very diverse crowd, I felt the goals of all of our planning were taking physical shape. It was one of the thrilling moments of my life. The city's most long-term editorial writer, Richard Marsh, called the new reality "astonishing." Referring to the commitment by Civic Partners of Costa Mesa of $38 million for the renovation of the Hotel Stockton and an adjacent twenty-screen Cineplex, he said "It's just one of the multimillion dollar projects transforming Stockton."[6]

An office complex and parking facility, the Stewart Eberhardt Building, opened in 2001. The city received $3.5 million in federal grants and loans to transform Weber Block from a sinking parking lot to a plaza, the Dean DeCarli Waterfront Square, which will eventually connect Weber Point to the Hotel Stockton and the downtown. The guiding principles of the Vision and Action Plan were being realized: The downtown area around the channel head was coming back to life. People and money seemed to be flowing in.

It sounded too good to be true, and to a degree, it certainly was. The situation became more complex. In June 2002, the city council, citing nonperformance, canceled its contract with Civic Partners. Three years after the opening of the Weber Point Events Center on that heady July evening, both the United States and the California economies found themselves in troubled waters. Finding financial backers for large public projects became more difficult. Yet, even in the uncertain environment of 2002, the Stockton City Council made a commitment to renovate the Hotel Stockton and to build a state-of-the-art movie theater next to it. Under the earlier contract with Civic Partners, ground was to be broken for the Cineplex in November of 2002. As of this writing, the council is determined that this will happen and that the hotel renovation will go ahead as well. The council is seeking private developers for both projects and is reapplying for state tax credits to help finance the renovation of the historic hotel. Unwilling to accept defeat, the council is exploring public/private partnership arrangements with potential investors. They are prepared to sell bonds backed by funds from the city treasury. When I think of the cynicism and hard core disbelief that existed when we first began talking about the waterfront redesign, this uncompromising stance by the council is very gratifying.

Because Weber Point had become the essence and symbol of our blighted downtown, once it changed, once the physical site was transformed and reshaped, people's perceptions changed dramatically. By the summer of 1999, articles and editorials singing the praises of the glorious renewal of Stockton's downtown had become almost commonplace. This new perception is both the cause and effect of new investment. A momentum seems finally to have built. That is ultimately what is behind the city council's commitment to see to it that the Hotel Stockton renovation and the high-tech film theater become realities. The residents of Stockton now want and expect those projects to be completed and they will be, in spite of more difficult economic times.

When people return to the old parts of a city and see renovated structures, they re-imagine the city's past. This historical understanding of a common past, in addition to the personal histories that people from different parts of the world bring with them when they move to Stockton, can underpin a new sense of community. People have fun in a city's historic places. If the waterfront plan at Weber Point does its job well, it will lead to recovered awareness of a dramatic past when Stockton's unique position at the head of the deepwater channel brought the world to its door. Soon we will once again be able to look westward from the verandas of the restored Hotel Stockton, across the fertile plains, to the outline of Mount Diablo in the distance. As people before us have done, we will see new possibilities and dream new dreams.

Getting Out of Politics

Running For Congress:
What the Party Recruiters Don't Tell You

*W*hat you do not know when you get elected is that other people (and you yourself) immediately begin to think of you as a candidate for higher office. Your brother says, "You're going on to be governor?" or a seat opens up and you ask yourself the crucial question: Is it a job I could get, a position I could win? As you work at your current job, you begin to consider what your next step will be. I could not consider a state legislative office as a next step because the two representatives from my district were two popular Democrats whom I liked a lot, Mike Machado in the assembly and Pat Johnston in the senate. But what about the U.S. Congress?

Richard Pombo, a conservative Republican, was thirty-one years old and had been on the Tracy City Council for two years when he successfully ran for Congress in 1992 from the eleventh congressional district in California, where I live. I was disappointed when Patti Garamendi lost to Pombo in 1992, and I supported Pombo's opponent, Randy Perry, in 1994. Watching the final returns on election night 1994 was a lesson in how a campaign can end in disaster—Perry got only 39 percent of the vote. Despite this precedent I saved articles about Pombo, thinking of the possibility of running against him when term limits forced me to leave the mayor's office.

As I was considering this question, I heard a talk by Ellen R. Malcolm, president of EMILY's List, who spoke on July 10, 1993, at the University of California Davis.[1] Despite her interest in women candidates, Malcolm's talk contained one of the most discouraging political ideas I had ever heard. EMILY's List (Early Money Is Like Yeast), a national feminist lobby, is said to be one of the most successful fund-raising PACs (political action committees) in the country. Malcolm's message that day was that it is almost impossible to beat an incumbent. In 1988, 401 out of 408 incumbents won reelection. Among non-incumbents, however, 81 percent had won in races for open seats. Since Pombo was already a member of Congress, I would be in the position of running against an incumbent.

Malcolm also presented an interesting analysis of the qualities of women who did win. First, they had both a local consultant and one with national expertise—one person if possible, two if necessary. Second, they had a fund-raiser on the campaign staff who would eat and sleep fund-raising. The quality of the woman candidate was important, too. Winners had a clear sense of themselves—they had high energy and were warm and decisive. They had helped others win, worked on their campaigns, and could tap into existing networks. They had a clear sense of what was going on in the district, and they had many local ties in the community. Furthermore, they were people who were willing to fight back. Women who won their races were willing to go negative against their opponents. If they held back, they lost. What voters really cared about, said Malcolm, was the candidate's value system. Voters believed that women understand domestic issues, such as health care, and will fight for them in Washington. Measured by this checklist of traits of winning women, I thought I looked pretty good, but Malcolm's main point about the advantage of incumbency argued against my aspiring to the U.S. House of Representatives.

Nevertheless, I kept track of the press, and I soon found that Pombo had a remarkable ability to get good publicity. One major reason for this was that his very conservative philosophy was consistent with that of *The Record*, then owned by the very conservative *Omaha World Herald*. Beyond that, his press officer must have been a genius. The first piece about him to appear after his election announced, "Pombo makes right office move, spares taxpayers." Pombo had passed up an office in the downtown State Office Building for an office in North Stockton and saved $600 a month, and he had furnished his Stockton office with tables and chairs from his home and government surplus. The article ended with a flourish about the responsibility of elected officials to save taxpayers money.[2]

Cost-cutting efforts by Pombo were again featured on March 19 in an article lambasting the president's budget because it "raises taxes and fails to significantly cut federal spending." At a time when presidential appointees were being rejected for their failure to pay social security taxes on domestic employees, an article in *The Record* reported that Pombo's family had hired undocumented workers for their farm and ranch near Tracy. Yet even this episode was presented by the paper in a way to flatter him; the article noted that his family had not hired such workers since 1986, when a federal law made it a crime. The article did *not* say that this practice had actually always been illegal. Indeed, the focus of the whole story turned out to be that Pombo had been put on the spot by the daughter of Patti Garamendi, his opponent for a congressional seat in 1992, who had phoned in the question on a talk show.[3]

Another example of *The Record*'s special treatment of Pombo occurred in connection with the Fourth of July 1993 Waterfest celebration in downtown Stockton, where there was to be an awards ceremony that I had initiated and for which my office had done all the work. Accompanying a pre-Waterfest article on these awards and the lists of students who would receive them, whose picture appeared in the paper? None other than Representative Richard Pombo, bringing holiday greetings to the residents of Stockton.[4] He was the only politician who had his face in that issue of the paper. Most incredibly, when Pombo voted for a pork barrel project called Steam Town, a railroad park in the Pennsylvania district of Representative Joseph McDave, the headline read, "Pombo Proving He's His Own Man."[5] The article explained that he had originally planned to vote against the project, but when he saw Republicans and Democrats alike lining up to vote against it, he got so mad that he voted for it.

Richard Pombo's special relationship with the press was also evident in the area of environmental issues. When he tried to destroy the Endangered Species Act, the fact that his opposition to it was utterly self-serving was never pointed out. Pombo's family business, a big real estate company, has benefitted enormously from massive building and development in Tracy, which is one of the fastest growing cities in California. The first thing one sees upon entering San Joaquin County is a Pombo real estate sign. The Endangered Species Act had resulted in some residential developments being halted or delayed, and for a time, a major developer could not go ahead with his Tracy Hills project because it provided a habitat for the kit fox, an endangered species. While conservationists claimed that the act had succeeded in saving such species as the

California gray whale and the bald eagle, Pombo claimed that the act was no more than a measure to prevent growth.

What Pombo proposed was a radical initiative which environmentalists said would weaken efforts to save wildlife, set up an expensive new entitlement program for landowners, and bog down new listings of endangered species in red tape and litigation. The bill passed in committee but was stalled in Congress when polls showed strong public support for laws preserving wildlife, clean air, and clean water. The Sierra Club labeled Pombo an "eco-thug," but once again, faithful to Pombo, an editorial headline in *The Record* called the Sierra Club "a narrowly focused special interest group." "Representative Richard Pombo needs to hang in there" said the editorial, which not only endorsed Pombo's position but also demanded that the Sierra Club give him a public apology.[6]

The conservation chair of the Sierra Club did apologize, but not without criticizing *The Record* for its derogatory language and biased, uninformed reporting. One final item: One marvels at Pombo's gall when he came out with a book called *This Land Is Our Land,* described by its publisher as a manifesto for property rights.[7] Environmentalists gave blistering reviews and characterized the work as "ludicrous," "inaccurate," and "funnier than vintage Saturday Night Live." Nonetheless its coauthor, Joseph Farah, a conservative writer and a former editor of the now-defunct *Sacramento Union*, defended it as an alarming revelation of the threat to private property rights.[8]

During the time when the battle was being waged between Pombo and the environmentalists, the city of Stockton had been included on the 100-year flood plain map drawn up by FEMA (Federal Emergency Management Agency). As explained earlier, this designation would have been economically very damaging to Stockton residents as well as to builders and potential investors and new businesses, which in turn would have had a ripple effect on labor, tax revenues, and other matters.

The sustained and finally successful effort to avoid these consequences was directed by City Manager Dwane Milnes and involved a delegation from Stockton to Washington and several key players there, including Senators Dianne Feinstein and Barbara Boxer. We also worked with Stockton's business leaders to solicit the support of national politicians. Characteristically, Pombo grabbed the press on this effort and the headline read: "Stockton Flood-Map Delay Dies in Congress" with the subtitle "Pombo cooking up new plan to halt designation." Under his photo is the caption, "At this point, I think we will get what we want."[9] Pombo, a minor player in the whole affair, was presented by *The Record* as the fighter and savior of Stockton from the dragon of flood plain designation. The prospect of running for Congress against someone who was both an incumbent and the beneficiary of such consistent flattery from the only newspaper in Stockton was not reassuring.

In November 1995, a year before I would be out of office because of term limits, I received a call from Jennifer Burton, a representative of the Democratic Congressional Campaign Committee (DCCC), Congressman Richard Gephardt's operation in Washington. Ms. Burton asked if I would be interested in running for Congress. Yes, I said, I would think about it. She said I would receive a call from Gephardt and I did, on November 27. The reason Burton called was that our state senator, Patrick Johnston, had been contacted by Richard Lehman, a former Congressman and now an employee of the DCCC, to ask who Pat thought would be a strong candidate. Pat himself had no interest in running for the seat. Instead, he recommended John Garamendi and me. John, who had recently been appointed undersecretary at the U. S. Department of the Interior, had declined.

Recruiting was occurring on more fronts than just the DCCC. EMILY's List was also sending recruiters to visit potential candidates. On November 21, I received a phone call from Karin Johanson, the West Coast representative of EMILY's List. "If anyone could give Pombo a scare, it would be you," she said. She had worked for Randy Perry's campaign in 1994, and she believed he had lost because he simply could not get it together financially. She did not want to see the entire Central Valley go to the Republicans. December 29 was the filing date—I would need $1,300 and fifty signatures. Karin felt that Newt Gingrich was so unpopular that the Congressional elections of 1996 would become a national referendum on him, and because Pombo was so closely aligned with Gingrich, Gingrich's unpopularity would work to my benefit. Further, my district, the eleventh, was 51 percent Democratic. In San Joaquin County there were 204,000 registered voters—115, 000 Democrats and 89,000 Republicans. There were also 61,000 voters in Sacramento, with the majority being Republican.

To me, the overriding challenge of a possible candidacy was raising money. Although I could and had raised significant funds in San Joaquin County not only for my own elections but also for nonprofit corporations, I had no idea how fund-raising worked nationally. Karin Johanson explained the basic picture: the Democratic Party could give up to $60,000; other sources were individuals, PACs (primarily organized labor PACs), organizations like EMILY's List, and other progressive groups. She anticipated that I could receive from $20,000 to $100,000 from EMILY's List. My biggest expense would be TV in Sacramento. She thought my campaign would cost about $600,000.

Frankly, I could see raising $250,000 to $300,000, but I did not know where the remainder would come from. She mentioned mail solicitations, fund-raisers, etc. She said the Democratic Party would go for broke in the 1996 campaign. It wanted to regain the majority in the House. Districts that slated strong candidates would be favored with dollars. To get started, I would need to conduct a poll in order to assure me that there was interest in my candidacy, to assess the voters' concerns and identify issues, to evaluate Pombo's popularity, and to determine how well known I was throughout the district. She thought the poll would cost about $10,000, and she was optimistic that the party would pay for it. She said I should expect calls from members of Congress, and she mentioned Anna Eshoo, who was recruiting in California.

Karin made a personal visit to my house and stayed for about three hours. We really hit it off; later she said that if she could have stayed with me during the entire decision-making period I probably would have chosen to run, and I think she is right. She noted that Pombo was extremist on the issue of endangered species. I was known and local. I raised my own concerns: What about my age, then sixty-one? What about fund-raising within the business sector? Gingrich had discouraged people from giving to both parties, and although in the 1980s, Tony Coehlo had got business PACs to give to Democrats, it was now very tough to get dollars from corporate PACs for Democrats. Corporate trade was beholden to Republicans.

On the other hand, organized labor, which supported Democrats, saw this election as critical. Karin felt that in my fund-raising, I could sell myself as a popular politician and a good risk. I had first to raise dollars in the district. At the end of December, there would be a reporting period, followed from then on by quarterly reports. People would look at how many dollars I had raised and how many donors I had. EMILY's List would provide me with a person to help with phoning and doing follow-up.

Karin also made an appealing point about how much candidates grow in the campaign process. She gave me names of persons who would be helpful to a campaign, people like Richard Lehman and Assemblywoman Jackie Speier. By the time she left, I felt excited about the possibility of running. On November 29, I received a very nice letter from her stating that "the Democratic Party would be very fortunate to have you as a candidate next year, not to mention the people of your district."[10] She had talked to Gephardt's office and the DCCC and felt that everyone was "in sync" on getting a poll conducted on my behalf. She was also hopeful that EMILY's List could contribute to that effort.

Because Senator Pat Johnston is a good friend of mine and a politically astute state senator, I called and asked his opinion about my running. He said it would be terrific from his perspective, if I had an interest. He certainly would support me with photos and any way I wanted him to. He thought it was a good idea to get a poll. He felt that Pombo was not settled in the district; he was not unbeatable.

Of course, I told my family that I was considering running for Congress. My husband, as always, was extremely supportive. My son-in-law was the biggest help of all, principally because a close friend of his from high school was at that time a knowledgeable insider in California politics. He put me in touch with her. Our conversation was quite different from those I had had with the recruiters. She began by saying that the campaign, in order to be successful, would require a fantastic amount of money—Pombo could be expected to spend at least $750,000. The poll to assess the feasibility of my candidacy would need to show that I had a chance of winning. If I had no chance, I would get no money.

Regarding EMILY's List, she understood that they were not supporting many individuals this time around; they were focusing more on voter registration. She advised me to be very cautious. In fact, she did not want to be encouraging at all. She felt that Pombo, as one of the Gingrich group, could raise a lot of money and would give a lot away to other candidates as well. If Clinton turned out to be extremely popular, that would help. But, she said, the campaign would be really dirty. Pombo is an extreme right-winger and that kind gets personally nasty. Recalling his vicious campaign against Patti Garamendi, I had to agree. "There's nothing that they wouldn't stoop to," she warned. The campaign would be vicious, grueling and ugly. She advised me not to run unless I really thought I could win. She also commented, correctly I believe, that I would never hear from the party recruiters the kind of points she was raising.

Lastly, she warned that I should never underestimate the demands of the job itself; it would be a round-the-clock job. She related that Barbara Boxer seldom had the time to see her granddaughter and that Barbara had complained about that fact. At that point, being a member of Congress did not seem like much fun to me. And Karin reminded me, traveling is the worst—there's a lot of flying. She concluded by saying that she would be surprised if the DNC would pay to conduct my poll. She also recommended other people for me to call to continue to assess my viability as a candidate. Needless to say, this conversation was very sobering.

On November 27, Richard Gephardt himself called, indicating that he was very excited about the possibility of my entering the race. He reported with enthusiasm that Clinton was nine points up in his popularity rating. He said that much of my money would need to be raised at home, and he referred me to Vic Fazio and Nancy Pelosi (both Democratic members of Congress from Northern California at the time) for fund-raising advice. He felt that my opponent was vulnerable on issues. "I hope you decide to run," he said. "Everyone here thinks you would be a terrific candidate and a winning candidate."

The next call I got was from Congresswoman Rosa D. Lauro from Connecticut. She was serving her fifth year (during her third term) in the Congress. She had managed Senator Dodd's campaign, had worked for EMILY's List, and had run for governor. She said that serving in the House had exceeded all her expectations. It was an unbelievable job. She participated in debate on critical issues—sometimes winning, sometimes losing. "I love it," she said. She stressed the importance of the Democratic Party winning back the House, especially at this time when there were so many issues at stake, such as education and health care. She thought I had gained ideal training in my job as mayor since I had dealt with many of the same issues every day that came before the national legislature.

Barbara Boxer's chief of staff in the Valley, Tom Bohigian, was also very encouraging. He felt that 1996 would be a good year for Democrats. He thought I had a good base of support, a reputation as a moderate in the community, great name identification, and I had been able to win reelection. "I will walk precincts for you," he said.

Soon after, I received a call from California Congresswoman Anna Eshoo, who came on very persuasively. Serving in Congress was an extraordinary opportunity. There would be many resources at my disposal, including good advice on campaign building. She decried what was happening in the House, where the Republican majority was voting against education bills and at the same time throwing money—seven billion dollars—at the U.S. defense budget. Like Karin Johanson from EMILY's List, she felt that my major support would come from women's groups, progressive groups, and organized labor. Women—including women candidates like me—forge consensus. I would be able to speak out, to have an impact on important issues, such as the ban on assault weapons, the regulation of the placement of nuclear power plants, and education. She argued that there was not an issue that I had not dealt with already and that local elected leadership was the best experience base one could have. She herself had served on the board of supervisors of San Mateo County. She felt that EMILY's List was great and that its members had killed themselves for her in 1988. She felt that Pombo's voting record was the most obnoxious possible, especially when it came to environmental laws. She thought that I would have instant credibility and that I would be knowledgeable on issues. She closed by saying that I needed to look at what had motivated me to get into politics to begin with and to consider the political results that could come from my being in Congress.

The Record got wind of these phone calls and ran a front-page article on December 10, 1995, entitled "Democrats Luring Darrah to Challenge Pombo."[11] I responded by saying that the attention was very flattering but that I had not decided whether to run. One thing I noted at this time was that I received no phones calls from local people urging me to run. I got maybe two letters, but there was certainly no spontaneous expression of support following the story in the paper, and that impressed me. Looking back, I continue to find this silence distressing, and it certainly increased my reluctance to run for Congress. It is one thing to undertake a "grueling" campaign when you have a big cheering section behind you and quite another to go it alone.

The poll was conducted by the Democratic Congressional Campaign Committee December 1-13, 1995, and initially I thought the results sounded promising. Answers to general questions—"Is the country going in the right direction?" and "Are things severely off on the wrong track?"—indicated a fairly high level of discontent with the status quo.

Almost two to one, people felt "the country was not going in the right direction." Yet this same dissatisfaction did not seem to hurt Pombo, to whom 43 percent of respondents were favorable, compared to 28 percent who were favorable to me. However, only 39 percent felt Pombo should be re-elected; 24 percent thought someone else should be elected. Asked whether they and their families were better off with Democrats in charge, 27 percent preferred Democrats and 26 percent Republicans; 44 percent felt it made no difference. As for the cruncher, "Who would you elect for Congress, Pombo or Darrah?" 47 percent were for Pombo and 29 percent were for Darrah.

The poll also probed the potential for negative campaigning, listing a series of possible reasons to vote against Pombo, framed as questions that identified some of the most conservative elements in his congressional voting record. These questions pointed out that Pombo had voted against cutting defense spending and for cutting school lunch funds; he had voted to make it easier for polluters to release waste into waterways; he had voted to cut Medicare and he had opposed the ban on assault weapons and the mandatory waiting period for purchasing handguns. He had also opposed Clinton's proposal to put 100,00 new cops on American streets. The results of these "questions" about his voting record showed that 57 percent of the respondents saw a reason to vote against him on the basis of some portion of this record.

Next, the poll made a series of statements about me—being mayor, my age, my past work experience, my focus on fighting crime, my leadership in the revitalization of Stockton's downtown and in creating jobs—and asked: "Knowing what you now know, for whom would you vote for Congress in November?" Given this negative information about Pombo, 39 percent would vote for Darrah and 34 percent for Pombo. Of course, there were no comparable negative "questions" about me that referred to my voting for tax increases for water and sewer rates or the expenditures on remodeling my office or the "lavish" gala I had thrown for my inauguration, items that would surely become sources of Pombo's negative television ads during a campaign. The negatives about Pombo, to be useful to me, would require sufficient funding for a convincing television attack. Finally, asked about party affiliation, 40 percent identified themselves as Republican, 41 percent Democrat, 16 percent Independent. Yet in the 1988 and 1994 elections, 48.5 percent had voted Democratic and 51.5 percent Republican.

I talked to Pat Johnston about the results of this poll. He noted that Pombo did not command a decisive majority of the voters. That was clear. Also, his position on several issues certainly left room for attack. On the other hand, Pombo would have an overwhelming advantage in a traditionally very conservative portion of Sacramento that lay in the eleventh congressional district. And Pombo's ability to get credit in the newspaper for achievements in our district was troublesome.

Next, I returned to the political expert who went to school with my son-in-law. She thought that on the question of who would you elect for Congress, Pombo or Darrah, the figure of 19 percent "strongly" for me, together with the total of 29 percent support, was really good. She thought, too, that Pombo's approval rating in the high 40s showed some vulnerability. On the down side, she pointed out that being a challenge candidate always made for an uphill battle. On the basis of the poll data, she concluded that I would enter the race fifteen points behind Pombo. Many challengers start from an even less favorable position, she said. A poll like this would not eliminate potential donors to my campaign. I was certainly a candidate they would consider supporting. She thought the size of the poll, just 400 respondents, was small and lessened its usefulness. It was good, she said, that there were so many negative responses about Pombo's position on issues, but there were no biggest issues, nor any single "hot button" issue.

In terms of raising money, she thought that I would get serious organized labor support and support from EMILY's List. I could go to Washington to meet with PACs and enlist financial support. My first target would be the Democratic Party's list of the twenty most favorable districts for Democratic success. There would be a second list of thirty targeted districts. The maximum that a PAC could give was $5,000, and the top twenty races would get a lot of this PAC money. If I were not on the list of the top thirty, my chances would be weak. She was concerned that there had not been a commitment to put me on a list in advance. There were a lot of open seats in 1996, and they were the ones on the targeted lists.

On December 22, *The Record* reporter Diane Barth called and asked me if I were going to run for Congress. My response was that I would not. The reason I gave her was that the campaign would take me away from my job as mayor and from several major city projects. I cited the revival of Stockton's waterfront, my fight against large-scale card rooms within the city limits, and the library campaign. The truth of the matter was that the first two of these projects were well in hand at that time. However, my involvement in the library campaign, a factor that was crucial to that campaign doing as well as it did, would indeed have been impossible had I decided to run for Congress.

The real reason I said "No" was that I had become convinced that Pombo could raise far more money than I could. I thought he would spend $1.2 to $1.5 million on his campaign, and that I would be lucky to raise $600,000. Moreover, I would be portrayed very negatively. Pombo, if he felt challenged, would become ruthless. I also thought that in my desperation to win I could go seriously in debt, and I did not want to risk that. Speaking bluntly, I felt that my chances of winning were not strong enough.

It was therefore with a mixture of outrage and relief that I read *The Record* editorial of the September 30, 1996, only five weeks before the November election: "45 million thank yous are due to Representative Pombo."[12] Once again, he had claimed all the credit for something he had had very little to do with, in this case reimbursing area residents for their outlays for flood control. All Pombo actually did was to introduce the bill in the House and to ruffle some feathers in the process. It was once again Dwane Milnes and a consultant from the flood agency's Washington lobbying firm who prepared the legislation, educated the staffs of the appropriate Congressional committees, and secured the support of Senators Boxer and Feinstein. At most, Pombo's contribution was the bare minimum. An opponent who could lead the press into this kind of misrepresentation just before election day was not one I was eager to run against.

An important asset for my campaign for Congress, and one that I did not properly evaluate at the time, was my leadership in the defeat of the casino proposal. Stocktonians had voted that down two to one. A gambling casino would have been equally unpopular if not more so in the other six cities of the county. The idea of Darrah as a fighter against corruption would have been a vote getter too. The only trouble was that Pombo had thus far not been involved in corruption.

There were still further considerations. So far, I was not on the Democrats' targeted list, presumably because the eleventh California district was not an open seat. I knew that Pombo had been a Gingrich boy and that Gingrich's supporters would donate whatever was necessary to keep him in office. Pombo voted the straight conservative line. As for my funding, where would it come from? Whereas the mayor is a nonpartisan office in Stockton, a congressional candidacy would certainly be partisan, and all my business friends, who supported me for mayor, would return to their Republican loyalties and support Pombo. In fact, I even asked one of them, a developer, and he said he liked Richard Pombo, that he was one congressman who seemed to be getting results for business interests.

So where would the initial, locally raised $300,000 that would make me look like a reasonable candidate come from? I thought that most of it would come from my own pocket. Granted, organized labor was supposed to be supportive, but Richard Pombo had voted against NAFTA early on, and I well remembered labor's luncheon in December of 1994, where Pombo was greeted enthusiastically. At the 1995 December luncheon nobody from labor came up to me and encouraged me to run against Pombo. With weak labor support, and no organization other than EMILY's List promising significant help, it would all be up to me.

As things turned out, Richard Pombo ran in 1996 against Jason Silva, an unknown who raised very little money. Even against Silva, Pombo spent $323,000 on the campaign. As in 1994 against another relative unknown, Pombo won by 61 percent. I will keep my eye open for a promising candidate for the Eleventh Congressional District, but I now know that she will not be me.

In Retrospect

The main lesson that I take away from my seven years as mayor of Stockton is that many women in many cities, large and small, can do what I did. There must be a lot of women out there with backgrounds like mine in business and nonprofit organizations who have the skills and experience to step into the fray and assume the responsibilities of public office.

American politics, in other words, still has room for the amateur. You will have to work your tail off and you will get a lot of resistance from the old boys in both politics and business but you can survive and you can prevail. Indeed, American politics always needs new amateurs, especially women.

A couple of years ago, at a conference sponsored by the Junior League of Oakland-East Bay entitled "Women in Business," which six hundred women attended, I offered a workshop on my experience in moving from work with nonprofit organizations to the mayor's office. Only four women attended! I agree with what Senator Feinstein says in her foreword to this book: Although women have "chipped away at the glass ceiling...we have a long road to travel before [we] are accepted in every office as equals to our males counterparts." And I agree with her that women are not going to move down that road unless they, we, get involved in electoral politics. I want to close, therefore, with a call to women like me, those with some experience in business and/or in organizations who are concerned with public issues, to make the move and run for office. I hope my story makes this idea look not only possible, but exciting. Run for school board, perhaps, or work on the campaign of a friend who is running for city council. It feels good to get involved. Give yourself one of those terrifying, white-knuckle election nights that turns out right after all. I know your kids will want to help!

As for my legacy, I have a lot to brag about. The changes that are occurring in downtown Stockton in the waterfront area and around Weber Point are wonderful to behold. At no point in the long and demanding effort to launch this massive project did I fully imagine what it would be like to see it actually happening as it is today. The park and events center are built, and people use and enjoy them. The renovation of the Hotel Stockton—be it retail, office, or residential—will be fabulous someday. The big cineplex will come too, eventually; meanwhile, other buildings are getting a face-lift. The lunch crowds on sunny days move easily, and children run around the new fountain on Weber Point. What a difference from how it was a mere ten years ago!

Although I would never claim personal credit for all of this, because hundreds of people have contributed to it in many ways, I was a key player, and I feel tremendous pride in it. Had it not been for my going to San Antonio and then working long and hard on the project for the rest of my time in office, it is unlikely that the rebirth of downtown Stockton would be happening the way it is today. This culminating project of my mayoral career required all of my political education to accomplish: how to initiate a big project and get key staff on board; how to involve many and diverse elements of the city population in accepting a successful design and in winning reliable, sustained public support; how to fend off the opposition; how to build it into the committee structure of city government so that it would continue after my term ended.

The changes to the waterfront area cover many city blocks in the heart of downtown. Stockton is safer than it was ten years ago. Crime is down throughout the city, and whereas crime, drugs, and violence of all kinds are an ongoing problem in Stockton as elsewhere, they are—and are seen to be—much more under control here than they were when I took office.

The city council now attracts candidates with a sense of citywide responsibility, people who are respected in the community and who work for the public good. That's a big difference, too, from how things had been before the passage of Measure C and also since the days of my first city council.

And let us not forget that what you *don't have* in a city can be just as important as what you do have. Stockton does not have the biggest casino in Northern California! For all of these things, I have a sense of accomplishment, a sense that I did make a difference in the city.

Turning to the personal, I was fifty-four when I became mayor.

Because I started late, politics was never a career for me in the sense that a career gives shape and definition to a person's life. I see my political activities as a culmination of my earlier public service work and compatible with my role in a traditional family life, which now includes five grandchildren. These days I serve on two boards: Planned Parenthood Mar Monte and the Jacoby Center for Community and Regional Studies at the University of the Pacific. Both organizations allow me to continue to work for causes to which I have always been committed, such as women's choice and the needs of the Stockton community.

Once you have been a mayor, you are invited to do other things. And you can take action on local issues in an effective way, as I did in March 2000, working against a change in the city charter sponsored by my successor that would increase the powers of the mayor and raise the salaries of the mayor and council. My side lost, but I had the opportunity to weigh in. I get calls asking me to sit on boards of various sorts and, of course, requests that I do fund-raising for worthy causes, most of which I have so far declined in order to have time to work on this book.

My daughter is involved with public issues in her community. Jeanne has fund-raising events at her house for candidates for the San Francisco School Board. That's a good place to start. I like to think that she does this partly because of my example, as well as because of her own experiences in my campaigns and during my time in office.

I was fortunate to have a dad who pushed me to get a fine education and who seemed to endorse the more aggressive side of my nature. Once I decided to get political, my mother gave me love and support, as she always had, and became my chief financial benefactor as well. I am lucky to be married to a man who is extremely supportive and open, and to have wonderfully supportive friends. My children were gung-ho too. They participated in all sorts of ways in my political activities.

If you go into politics, it is good to have a certain sort of temperament. I always liked to be a star. When I was in high school in Los Angeles, doing the dishes at home after dinner, I would imagine myself a star in the movies. When the time came for me to step up onto a real stage, I just loved it.

Notes

I Setting the Stage

1. Candidates are not party nominees. Anyone can run in the primary and the two who receive the highest number of votes compete in a runoff.

II Meet the Candidate

1. Mary Baker Eddy. *Science and Health with Key to the Scriptures* (Boston: Published by the trustees under the will of Mary Baker G. Eddy, 1934), 475.

2. At this time, *The Record* was called *The Stockton Record*. In March 1994, in support of a marketing effort called "regionalization," its name was changed to *The Record*. In this book, I have referred to the Stockton paper as *The Record*.

3. Helen Flynn, "Learning Where Income Goes Fringe Benefit at Darrah Home," *Stockton Record*, 8 October 1978, p. 27, col. 4.

III Getting Elected

Ralph White and Measure C: Closing Down the "Monday Night Circus"

1. Detailed information about the structure and provisions of Measure C was provided by Dean Andal, its chief architect. Personal interview with Alice Crozier, July 6, 1998.

2. Christopher Woodard, "White-Profile of an Enigma," *Stockton Record*, 21 June 1987, p. A-1, col. 5.

3. "Easing Racial Tension," *Stockton Record*, 9 August 1967, p. 25, col. 3.

4. "General Mills Bias Probe 'Top Priority,'" *Stockton Record*, 16 January 1971, p. 10, col. 2.

5. "Jesse Jackson in Stockton, Urges New Political Tack," *Stockton Record*, 12 May 1983, p. 1, col. 3.

6. Bill Cook, "3 on Council Sold Out, Sousa Claims," *Stockton Record*, 21 September 1979, p. 1, col. 2.

7. Judy Keen, "A Renegade on the Loose," *Stockton Record*, 12 August 1986, p. A-1, col. 2.

8. "Monday Night Circus" was a popular name during the 1980s for Stockton City Council meetings, which were held on Monday nights.

9. David Judson, "White Leaves Message in a Bottle," *Stockton Record*, 12 August 1986, p. A-1, col. 2.

10. Ken Mimms, "Council Dialogue Turns X-rated," *Stockton Record*, 13 September 1983, p. 13, col. 3.

11. See note 5 above.

12. Ken Mimms, "City Council Candidate Assails Racial Questions, *Stockton Record,* 26 August 1983, p.1, col.. 1.

13. Richard Hammer, "White Ordered Off Council, *Stockton Record,* 10 October 1985, pp. A-1, col. 2.

14. Editorial, *Stockton Record*, 18 June 1987, p. A-12, col. 1.

15. B. Riplese, "White: Run Him Out of Town on a Rail?" *Stockton Record*, 6 April 1988, p. A-17, col. 2.

16. Christopher Woodard, "'Fire Petition' Said to Target Nisby for Recall," *Stockton Record*, 23 January 1988, p. A-1, col. 5.

17. "White's Recall Plans Challenged by Darrah," *Stockton Record*, 1 September 1987, p. B-6, col. 1.

18. Hugh Wright, "Ruling Hurts Election Hopes of White," *Stockton Record*, 10 October 1987, p. A-1, col. 2.

19. Christopher Woodard, "White May File Federal Rights Suit," *Stockton Record*, 10 November 1987, p. B-1, col. 5.

First Mayoral Campaign

1. Editorial, *Stockton Record*, 4 February 1990, p. A-12, col. 1.

2. Andrew Pollack, "Mayoral Candidate Sets Record for Fund-Raising in Stockton," *Stockton Record*, 27 January 1990, p. A-1, col. 5.

Inauguration and Settling In

1. Paul Feist, "Lavish Open House to Usher in New Council," *Stockton Record*, 22 February 1990, p. A-1, col. 2.

2. Victoria Colliver, "City Called on Carpet Over Office Remodeling," *Stockton Record*, 23 May 1990, p. A-1, col. 1.

3. Ibid.

IV First Term

Relations With Council and Staff
The Departure of Alan Harvey: Politics is Not Junior Aid.

1. In March 2000, Stockton voters approved a charter change that increased council salaries and provided additional mayoral power in the selection of the city manager, the council committee appointments, and the budget process.

2. Christopher Woodard, "Bitter Harvey Rips Panizza's 'Gang of 3,'" *Stockton Record*, 30 January 1991, p. A-1, col. 2.

3. Ibid.

Mrs. Nguyen, the City Attorney, and Gracious Me

1. *Stockton City Council Meeting*, prod. and dir. Continental Cablevision, 8 April 1991, videocassette from the Melvin J. Panizza Collection, Stockton, CA.

2. Nguyen, pronounced "Wen" in Vietnamese, is a far more common sur-

name in Vietnam than ever Smith is in the United States. A married woman would continue to use her birth surname as her legal last name, but in verbal address would be called by the first name of her husband.

3. *Stockton City Council Meeting*, prod. and dir. Continental Cablevision, 11 March 1991, videocassette from the Melvin J. Panizza Collection, Stockton, CA.

4. *Stockton City Council Meeting*, prod. and dir. Continental Cablevision, 1 April 1991, videocassette from the Melvin J. Panizza Collection, Stockton, CA.

5. *Stockton City Council Meeting*, prod. and dir. Continental Cablevision, 8 April 1991, videocassette from the Melvin J. Panizza Collection, Stockton, CA.

6. *Stockton City Council Meeting*, prod. and dir. Continental Cablevision, 1 April 1991, videocassette from the Melvin J. Panizza Collection, Stockton, CA.

7. *Stockton City Council Meeting*, prod. and dir. Continental Cablevision, 28 March 1994 videocassette from the Melvin J. Panizza Collection, Stockton, CA.

8. Michael Fitzgerald, "Brother Finds Homeless Sister in Stockton," *The Record*, 26 February 1999, p. A-1, col. 2.

The Agenda: Crime and Drugs
Cleveland School: A Defining Moment

1. Tony Sauro, "5 Children Die, 30 Hurt During School Rampage," *Stockton Record*, 18 January 1989, p. A-1, col. 5.

2. Michael Fitzgerald, "Tranquil Playground Turned into War Zone," *Stockton Record*, 18 January 1989, p. A-1, col. 3.

3. Tony Sauro, "Purdy Led Violent Existence," *Stockton Record*, 20 January 1989, p. A-1, col 5.

4. Ibid.

5. John Hurst, "Stockton: An Inferiority Complex on a Rampage," *Los Angeles Times*, 26 September 1986, home edition.

6. Gary Swan, "Merchants, Residents Delighted to Host 49ers," *San Francisco Chronicle*, 18 July 1998, final edition.

7. Amy Starnes, "Stockton Cineplex Becoming Reality," *The Record*, 27 July 1998, p. A-1, col. 3.

Police Funding Committee: A Popular Tax Increase

1. Paul Feist, "Council Makes More Police Top Priority," *Stockton Record*, 6 March 1990, p. A-1, col. 5.

2. Victoria Colliver, "Stockton Plans Tax Increase for Additional Police Officers," *Stockton Record*, 5 June 1990, p. A-1, col. 4.

3. Editorial, *Stockton Record*, 10 June 1990, p. A-10, col. 1.

4. P.F. "Jack" Calkins, letter to author, 29 October 1990.

STAND and "A Mayor Who Is Not Afraid To Make House Calls"

1. This section benefits from Mary Delgado's detailed account of many of STAND's activities, especially their encounters with the school board and their later legal undertakings. Interview with Alice Crozier, July 20, 1998.

2. L. Michelle Henagan, "Residents Demand Protection," *Stockton Record*, 21 May 1992, p. A-1, col. 2.

3. Dana Nichols, "You Can Fight to Regain Control," *The Record*, 27 August 1994, p. A-1, col. 2.

4. Editorial, *The Record*, 18 February 1998, p. B-4, col. 1.

5. Thomas J. Owens, letter to author, 24 May 1991.

A Visit to Taylor School: Follow-up to a Drive-by Shooting

1. Cindy Sui, "Car Gunman Hits Girl, 13," *The Record*, 31 August 1994, p. A-1, col. 1.

2. Michael Fitzgerald, "Fear a Part of Childhood in Stockton," *The Record*, 1 September 1994, p. A-1, col. 2.

3. Christopher Lewis, "'Was Blind, But Now I See,'" *The Record*, 19 September 1999, p. A-1, col. 2.

Downtown Cleanup: Early Days

1. Jim Nickles, "Downtown Task Force Proposed," *Stockton Record*, 6 April 1991, p. C-1, col. 2.

2. *Stockton City Council Meeting*, prod. and dir. Continental Cablevision, 8 April 1991, videocassette from the Melvin J. Panizza Collection, Stockton, CA.

3. Editorial, *Stockton Record*, 18 July 1991, p. A-12, col. 1.

4. Jim Nickles, "Bronx Hotel SMAC'd with $115,800 Penalty," *Stockton Record*, 31 January 1992, p. B-1, col. 2.

5. Andrew Pollack, "Downtown Hotel Owners Must Pay Up," *Stockton Record*, 14 July 1993, p. A-1, col. 3.

6. Bill Cook, "Increasing Police Patrolling Is Decreasing Crime," *The Record*, 17 April 1994, p. E-1, col. 2.

7. The term refers to a blighted area where the city has the power of condemnation and where property taxes generated by an increase in property values are returned to the redevelopment agency to finance further projects.

8. Editorial, *The Record*, 3 August 1998, p. B-4, col. 1.

9. Don Geiger, speech presented in acceptance of Stocktonian of the Year 1995 Award, 31 January 1996.

Statistics: Seeing Results

1. Howard Lachtman, "ABC Special Turns Stockton into Dodge City," *Stockton Record*, 24 January 1990, p. D-1, col. 2.

2. Editorial, *Stockton Record*, 12 July 1993, p. A-4, col. 1.

3. Editorial, *Stockton Record*, 5 January 1994, p. A-10, col. 1.

4. Editorial, *The Record*, 2 January 1995, p. A-4, col. 1.

5. Editorial, *The Record*, 22 February 1996, p. A-6, col. 1.

6. "California Crime Rate Way Down, S.J. County, Stockton Join Trend," *The Record*, 3 October 1997, p. A-1, col. 4.

7. Editorial, *The Record*, 6 October 1997, p. B-4, col. 1-2.

8. Christopher Lewis and Amy Starnes, "Stockton Crime Down 5 percent," *The Record*, 18 May 1998, p. A-1, col. 2.

9. Editorial, *The Record*, 19 May 1998, p. B-4, col. 1.

V Getting Re-elected

Gay Issue: Stockton Is Not San Francisco

1. *Stockton City Council* Meeting, prod. and dir. Continental Cablevision, 8 June 1992, videocassette from the Melvin J. Panizza Collection, Stockton, CA.

2. Ibid.

3. Michael Fitzgerald, "Gay Parade is a Milestone for Stockton," *Stockton Record*, 10 July 1992, p. B-1, col. 1.

4. Michael Fitzgerald, "Stockton Speaks Out About Gay, Lesbian Parade," *Stockton Record*, 14 June 1992, p. B-1, col. 1.

5. Jim Nickles, "Gays Parade on Streets of Stockton," *Stockton Record*, 15 June 1992, p. A-1, col. 1.

Learning to Speak: Getting Tough, Staying Sweet

1. Toastmasters is an international organization that gives instruction in public speaking. There are seven Toastmaster clubs in Stockton.

2. Dawne Bernhardt, Executive Communications, San Francisco, CA.

3. All quoted material from my meetings with Dawne Bernhardt is taken from my videotapes and audio tapes of our sessions, July 23, 1992, August 17, 1992, August 21, 1992.

4. *League of Women Voters, San Joaquin County, Candidates Night*, prod. and dir. Continental Cablevision, 30 September 1992, videocassette from the Joan Darrah Collection, Stockton, CA.

The Campaign for Re-election

1. Jim Nickles, "Political Veterans Take Aim at Darrah," *Stockton Record*, 25 May 1992, p. B-1, col. 5.

2. Jim Nickles, "Fargo Runs for Cover at Debate, Mayor Pulls Record on Ex-City Manager," *Stockton Record*, 1 October 1992, p. B-1, col. 5.

3. Jim Nickles, "Fargo Aims to Dispel Reports of Shaky Past," *Stockton Record*, 26 October 1992, p. A-1, col. 5.

4. Hildegarde Poehner, "Widow: Fargo Unfair to Blame Finance Director," *Stockton Record*, 4 November 1992, p. A-14, col.

5. Eunice Trotter, "Mayor Darrah Hangs On, Defeats Fargo in Squeaker," *Stockton Record*, 10 November 1992, p. B-1, col. 1.

Women Leading Luncheons: Redefining Power

1. Pat Meredith, speech presented at the Women Leading luncheon, Stockton, CA, 14 October 1995.

VI Second Term

Ethnic Politics
Sylvia Sun Minnick: The Race Card

1. Eunice Trotter, "Stockton Councilwoman Accuses Darrah of Racism," *Stockton Record*, 23 December 1992, p. A-1, col. 1.

2. Ibid.

3. Editorial, *Stockton Record*, 1 July 1990, p. A-12, col. 1.

4. Ibid.

5. Renee Sanchez, "Stockton Rejuvenates Downtown with Vigorous Cleanup Campaign," *Stockton Record*, 3 July 1990, p. A-12, col. 2.

6. Jim Nickles, "Proposed $1 Billion Theme Park Would Bring Gold Rush Downtown," *Stockton Record*, 24 October 1990, p. A-1, col. 1.

7. Jim Nickles, "Gold Rush Theme Park May Not Pan Out," *Stockton Record*, 30 October 1990, p. A-1, col. 2.

8. Paul Feist, "Council Willing to Talk About Gold Rush City," *Stockton Record*, 14 November, 1990, p. B-4, col. 6.

9. Ibid.

10. Jim Nickles, "Harvey Felt Like a Victim," *Stockton Record*, 24 January 1991, p. B-1, col. 5.

11. *Stockton City Council Meeting*, prod. and dir. Continental Cablevision, 28 January 1991, videocassette from the Melvin J. Panizza Collection, Stockton, CA.

12. Jim Nickles, "Darrah Will Spend Over $100,000 to Be Elected," *Stockton Record*, 26 October 1992, p. A-1, col. 1.

13. Editorial, *Stockton Record*, 24 December 1992, p. A-6, col. 1.

14. Ibid.

15. Eunice Trotter, "Most on Stockton Council Back Mayor in Racial Dispute," *Stockton Record*, 6 January 1993, p. A-1, col. 1.

16. Ibid.

17. *Stockton City Council Meeting*, prod. and dir. Continental Cablevision, 11 January 1993, videocassette from the Melvin J. Panizza Collection, Stockton, CA.

18. Ibid.

19. *Stockton City Council Meeting*, prod. and dir. Continental Cablevision, 19 January 1993, videocassette from the Melvin J. Panizza Collection, Stockton, CA.

20. Ibid.

21. *Stockton City Council Meeting*, prod. and dir. Continental Cablevision, 25 January 1993, videocassette from the Melvin J. Panizza Collection, Stockton, CA.

22. *Ibid.*

23. *Stockton City Council Meeting*, prod. and dir. Continental Cablevision, 9 February 1995, videocassette from the Melvin J. Panizza Collection, Stockton, CA.

24. Dianne Barth, "Stockton Educator, Historian Inducted into Hall of Fame," *The Record*, 14 June 1998, p. B-1, col. 2.

Parga-Ramirez: Consequences of a Drug Raid

1. Eunice Trotter, "Stockton Officer Killed," *Stockton Record*, 23 January 1993, p. A-1, col. 2.

2. *Stockton City Council Meeting*, prod. and dir. Continental Cablevision, 25 January 1993, videocassette available from the Melvin J. Panizza Collection, Stockton, CA.

3. Ibid.

4. Editorial, *Stockton Record*, 14 March 1993, p. A-12, col. 1.

5. *Stockton City Council Meeting*, prod. and dir. Continental Cablevision, 15 March 1993, videocassette available from the Melvin J. Panizza Collection, Stockton, CA.

6. Ibid.

7. Ibid.

8. Michael Fitzgerald, "Council Shows Good Measure of Maturity," *Stockton Record*, 17 March 1993, p. B-1, col. 1.

Consensus for Change Luncheons: Reaching Out

1. The 2000 census showed 32 percent white, 33 percent Hispanic, 19 percent Asian, 11 percent African American, and 5 percent Other. Statistics obtained from the Council of Governments of San Joaquin County, 31 August 2001.

The Drowning of the Cambodian Children: An Immigrant's Story

1. "1 Boy Drowns, 3 Missing," *Stockton Record*, 28 March, 1991, p. A-1, col. 1.

2. In Cambodian culture, married women are called "Mrs." but use their own family name rather than their husband's last name. In oral address, the "Mrs." is used with the husband's first name. This is also the practice in Vietnam.

3. Jim Nickles, "4th Body Found as Mother Calls on River Gods," *Stockton Record*, 30 March 1991, p. A-1, col. 1.

The Power Game
The General Plan of 1990 and the Loophole of 1993

1. The following discussion benefits from conversations with John Carlson, the director of the Community Planning and Development Department for the City of Stockton, 1981-2001, and Sam Mah, deputy director for the Planning Division, and from "City of Stockton General Plan Background Report," prepared by the City of Stockton Development staff, 22 January 1990, pp. 11-3 to 11-10.

2. *General Plan, City of Stockton*, "Housing Element, Policy 2," 22 January 1990.

3. *Stockton City Council Meeting*, prod. and dir. Continental Cablevision, 22 January 1990, videocassette from the Melvin J. Panizza Collection, Stockton, CA.

4. Interview with Councilmember Richard Nickerson by Joan Darrah, July 26, 1999.

5. *Stockton City Council Meeting*, prod. and dir. Continental Cablevision,

5 December 1993, videocassette from the Melvin J. Panizza Collection, Stockton, CA

6. Ibid.

7. Eunice Trotter, "Developers Fund Council Races," *Stockton Record*, 6 June 1993, p. A-1, col. 1.

8. Editorial, *Stockton Record*, 19 December 1993, p. A-12, col. 1.

9. Michael Fitzgerald, "New Insights May Change City's Politics," *Stockton Record*, 5 January 1994, p. B-1, col. 1.

The Debate Over a Stockton Casino: Cash Cow or Skid Row

1. Michael D. Hakeem, letter to Mayor Joan Darrah and Stockton City Council, 3 May 1995.

2. Dana Nichols, "Making Room for Cards," *The Record*, 5 May 1995, p. A-1, col. 2.

3. Maria Alicia Gaura, "Card Club Boom Puts Asians at Loss," *San Francisco Chronicle*, 3 March 1995, final edition.

4. See note 2 above.

5. Editorial, *The Record*, 11 May 1995, p. A-12, col. 1.

6. National Multi-Housing Council, "Top Multifamily Builders," *Washington Update*, 5 June 1998.

7. Gerald A. Sperry, letter to the editor, *The Record*, 1 June 1995, p. A-8, col. 4.

8. Max Vanzi, "Backers of State Gambling Controls Hope 3rd Try is the Charm," *Los Angeles Times*, 22 February 1995, final edition.

10. Greater Stockton Chamber of Commerce, letter to author, 20 September 1995.

11. Max Vanzi, "Card Club Bill Would Suit Some in Industry," *The Los Angeles Times*, 27 March 1995, final edition.

12. Knight Kiplinger, *The Kiplinger Washington Letter* 72, no. 18, 5 May 1995.

13. H. J. Shaffer, et al., "The Psychological Consequences of Gambling," in *Casino Development: How Would Casinos Affect New England's Economy?* ed. R. Tannenwald (Boston: Federal Reserve Bank of Boston, 1995), 130-141.

14. Olive Davis, "Cardrooms Would Perpetuate Stockton's Bad Outside Image," *The Record*, 18 February 1996, p. A-12, col. 4.

15. Maxine Hong Kingston, *China Men* (New York: Knopf, 1980), 241-242.

16. Larry Barrett, "Stockton Council Delays Playing Hand on Cardroom," *The Record*, 14 June 1995, p. B-1, col. 1.

17. Dana Nichols, "Stockton Residents Back 24-Hour Gambling Proposal, Poll Shows," *The Record*, 20 July 1995, p. A-1, col. 2.

18. De Tran, "Gambling Takes Toll on Viet Emigres," *San Jose Mercury News*, 30 May 1994, final edition.

19. Tamma Adamek, "Pastors Take Stand Against Ordinance," *The Record*, 30 September 1995, p. A-1, col. 2.

20. Bert Eljera, "Cardroom Could Go to Voters," the Record, 29 Septem-

ber 1995, p. A-1, col. 4, and Nancy Price, "Groups Weigh in on Gaming Issue," The Record, 29 September 1995, p. A-1, col. 2.

21. Bert Eljera, "Joseph Barkett: The Quiet Man Behind Cardroom Proposal," *The Record*, 30 September 1995, p. A-1, col. 2.

22. Editorial, *San Jose Mercury News*, 28 September 1995, final edition.

23. Martin Edwards, "Position Paper Against the Delta Park Casino Proposal," paper presented at Stockton City Council Meeting, Stockton, CA, 2 October 1995.

24. *Stockton City Council Meeting*, prod. and dir. Continental Cablevision, 2 October 1995, videocassette from the Melvin J. Panizza Collection, Stockton, CA.

25. Bert Eljera, "Compulsive Gamblers in an Unlucky Grip," *The Record*, 22 October 1995, p. A-1, col. 2.

26. Jim Sams, "Cards 'N' Crime-Stockton Can Learn from San Jose," *The Record*, 3 December 1995, p. A-1, col. 2.

27. Jim Sams, "Casinos' Voter Support Is Folding," *The Record*, 11 February 1996, p. A-1, col. 2.

28. Aurelio Rojas and Thaai Walker, "Gaming's Violent Price," *San Francisco Chronicle*, 15 February 1996, final edition.

World Wildlife Museum: Educational Opportunity or Tax Write-off

1. Paula Sheil, "Jumbo Jigsaw: World Wildlife Museum Gains a Heavyweight Attraction," *The Record*, 14 June 1998, p. E-1, col. 1.

2. Michael Fitzgerald, "City Officials Still Aloof to Animal Museum," *Stockton Record*, 18 September 1992, p. B-1, col. 1.

3. Michael Fitzgerald, "Stockton Loses Shot at Big Time," *Stockton Record*, 19 March 1993, p. A-1, col. 1.

4. Ibid.

5. Ibid.

6. Editorial, *Stockton Record*, 16 August 1993, p. A-4, col. 1.

7. See note 2 above.

8. Dana Nichols, "Mayor, Museum Backers Clash," *The Record*, 5 December 1994, p. B-1, col. 1.

9. *Stockton City Council Meeting*, prod. and dir. Continental Cablevision, 5 December 1994, videocassette from the Melvin J. Panizza Collection, Stockton, CA.

10. Editorial, *The Record*, 21 January 1996, p. A-12, col. 1.

11. Jim Sams, "High Noon for Dueling Waterfront Proposals," *The Record*, 21 January 1996, p. B-1, col. 2.

12. Amy Starnes, "World Wildlife Museum Packs It In," *The Record*, 11 August 1999, p. A-1, col. 2.

13. Ibid.

14. Amy Starnes, "Wildlife Museum Founder Jack Perry Dies," *The Record*, 30 June 2000, p. B-12, col. 1.

15. Amy Starnes, "Museum Collection Moving," *The Record*, 13 December 1999, p. C-1, col. 1.

16. Michael Fitzgerald, "Wildlife Museum Odyssey a Tale of Missed Opportunities," *The Record*, 19 September 1999, p. B-1, col. 1.

Concealed Weapons: Gun Control or Armed Citizenry
1. Dana Nichols, "Council in Gun-Control Showdown," *The Record*, 5 September 1994, p. B-1, col. 1.
2. Richard C. Paddock, "Proposal to Let Residents Carry Guns Divides City," *Los Angeles Times*, 14 November 1994, final edition.
3. Dana Nichols, "A Plan to Conceal Guns," *The Record*, 19 October 1994, p. A-1, col. 2.
4. Editorial, *The Record*, 21 October 1994, p. A-8, col. 1.
5. Editorial, *The Record*, 13 November 1994, p. A-12, col. 1.
6. Dianne Barth, "Proposal Scaring Tourists, Business, Opponents Say," *The Record*, 15 November 1994, p. A-1, col. 2.
7. *Stockton City Council Meeting*, prod. and dir. Continental Cablevision, 21 November 1994, videocassette available from the Melvin J. Panizza Collection, Stockton, CA.
8. Editorial, *The Record*, 23 November 1994, p. A-10, col. 1.

Final Two Years: Getting More Done
Graffiti, Blight, Code Enforcement
1. Joan Darrah, letter to Municipal Court Judge Bernard Garber, 30 July 1993.
2. Editorial, *The Record*, 5 June 1995, p. A-4, col. 1.
3. Ann Johnston, "Stockton's Cleaning Up Its Graffiti Act," *The Record*, 25 September 1995, p. D-2, col. 1.
4. Jim Sams, "Stockton Boosts Its Fight Vs. Blight," *The Record*, 8 October 1997, p. B-1, col. 2.
5. Amy Starnes, "Signs of Shame Targeting Blight," *The Record*, 14 July 1998, p. A-1, col. 2.

Senator Feinstein and Senator Boxer: Role Models and Key Players in Stockton's Battle with FEMA
1. "Feinstein's City Hall Address-'Let's Rebuild S.F. Spirit,'" *San Francisco Chronicle*, 30 November 1978, final edition.
2. Terry Kroeger, "Don't Let the Feds Destroy Stockton," *The Record*, 19 March 1995, p. A-12, col. 1.
3. Editorial, *The Record*, 5 April 1995, p. A-10, col. 2.
4. Editorial, *The Record*, 19 April 1995, p. A-12, col. 1.
5. Ann Schuyler, "Feinstein Supports a Delay in Maps," *The Record*, 5 August 1995, p. B-1, col. 5.
6. Joan Darrah, "Barbara Boxer a Proven Friend of Stockton," *The Record*, 11 October 1998, p. B-7, col. 1.

Redesigning Stockton's Waterfront: The Legacy
1. Much of the historical information in the next few pages is based on Olive Davis, *Stockton: Sunrise Port on the San Joaquin* (Sun Valley, CA: Ameri-

can Historical Press, 1998). Additional information was also provided in telephone conversations Alice Crozier had with Olive Davis (7/29/99), Lee Hieber, Director, Port of Stockton (7/29/99) and Tod Ruhstaller, Director, The Haggin Museum (7/30/99).

2. Walter A. Payne, ed., *Benjamin Holt: The Story of the Caterpillar Tractor* (Stockton, CA: University of the Pacific, 1982).

3. Dana Nichols, "Waterfront Expert Shares Ideas," *The Record*, 12 December 1994, p. A-1, col. 2.

4. Editorial, *The Record*, 25 January 1995, p. A-10, col. 1.

5. Michael Fitzgerald, "Don't Leave Waterfront an Island," *The Record*, 27 January 1995, p. B-1, col. 1.

6. Richard Marsh, "Of Public Art, Trolley Wannabes, Council Action," *The Record*, 2 August 1999, p. B-5, col. 1.

VII Getting Out of Politics

Running for Congress: What the Recruiters Don't Tell You

1. Ellen Malcolm, "Women Running for Congress," speech presented at UC Davis, Davis, CA, 10 July 1993.

2. Andrew Pollack, "Pombo Makes Right Office Move, Spares Taxpayers," *Stockton Record*, 16 February 1993, p. B-1, col. 1.

3. Dana Nichols, "Pombo Put on Spot by Student," *Stockton Record*, 20 March 1993, p. B-1, col. 1.

4. Richard W. Pombo, "Holiday Greetings," *Stockton Record*, 2 July 1993, p. G-13, col. 2.

5. David Judson, "Pombo Proving He's His Own Man," *Stockton Record*, 29 August 1993, p. B-1, col. 4.

6. Editorial, *The Record*, 8 December 1995, p. A-14, col. 1.

7. Richard Pombo and Joseph Farah, *This Land is Our Land: How to End the War on Private Property,* (New York: St. Martin's Press, 1996).

8. Dianne Barth, "Critics View Pombo's Book as Pulp Affliction," *The Record*, 25 September 1996, p. B-1, col. 2.

9. Jim Sams, "Stockton Flood-Map Delay Dies in Congress," *The Record*, 21 November 1995, p. A-1, col. 5.

10. Karin Johanson, letter to the author, 29 November 1995.

11. Nancy Price, "Democrats Luring Darrah to Challenge Pombo," *The Record*, 10 December 1995, p. A-1, col. 2.

12. Editorial, *The Record*, 30 September 1996, p. A-6, col. 1.

Index

About the Authors

Joan Darrah was elected mayor of the city of Stockton, California, in February 1990 and re-elected in 1992 to a four-year term. Previously she had been a high school English teacher and counselor and a leader in volunteer organizations, including the United Way of San Joaquin County and the Board of Regents of the University of the Pacific. She now serves on the board of Planned Parenthood Mar Monte. She and her husband Jim live in Stockton.

Alice Crozier and Joan Darrah were classmates at Radcliffe. A specialist in American literature and the author of *The Novels of Harriet Beecher Stowe* (Oxford University Press), Crozier is now Professor of English Emerita from Rutgers University in New Brunswick, New Jersey. She has had a life-long interest in American politics. Crozier currently lives in Hoboken, New Jersey.